THE GREATEST SKI RESORTS IN AMERICA

Robert E. Weber

GuideBook Publishing Co.
Dallas

Cover Photo: Top of The Plunge, Telluride, Colorado

Library of Congress Cataloging-in-Publication Data

Weber, Robert E.
   The Greatest Ski Resorts in America

Bibliography: p.
Includes index

Copyright © 1988 by Robert E. Weber

All rights reserved. No portion of this book may be reproduced, by any process or technique, without the express written consent of the publisher.

ISBN: 0-929498-00-3

First published in 1988 by GuideBook Publishing Co.

GuideBook Publishing Co.
7606 McKamy Blvd. Dallas, Texas 75248

Printed in the United States of America

The paper used in this book complies with the Permanent Paper Standard issued by the National Information Standards Organization (Z39.48-1984).

10 9 8 7 6 5 4 3 2 1

This book is dedicated to my father,
Joseph A. Weber

Trail Maps

ASPEN MOUNTAIN	1
ASPEN HIGHLANDS	1
BUTTERMILK MOUNTAIN	2
BRECKENRIDGE	2
COPPER MOUNTAIN	3
CRESTED BUTTE	3
JACKSON HOLE	4
KEYSTONE MOUNTAIN	4
NORTH PEAK	5
ARAPAHOE BASIN	5
KILLINGTON	6
PARK CITY	6
SNOWBIRD	7
SNOWMASS	7
SQUAW VALLEY	8
STEAMBOAT	8
SUN VALLEY	9
TAOS SKI VALLEY	9
TELLURIDE	10
VAIL (FRONT FACE)	10
VAIL (BACK BOWLS)	11

Acknowledgments

I am grateful for the help afforded me by the following persons:

Diana Arington, Ski Hostess; Heavenly: Harry Baxter, Director of Marketing; Jackson Hole Ski Corporation: Ronald J. Berenson, Manager/Public Relations and Promotions; American International Group, Inc: Shannon Besoyan, Public Relations; Sun Valley Company: Susan C. Bonomo, Sales Manager; Aspen Resort Association: Ed Bowers, Director of Public Relations; Copper Mountain Resort: Bill Brehmer, Vice President Marketing; Aspen Highlands: Alan Bush, Ski Instructor; Aspen Highlands: Joseph S. Carton, Director of Resort Sales; Mount Mansfield Resort: Jean Paul Cazedessus, Ski Instructor; Taos Ski Valley: Greg Cisco, Property Management Administrator; Jackson Hole Realty: Beverly Craddock, Communications Director; Telluride Ski Resort, Inc.: Kathy DeWolfe, Public Relations Coordinator; Aspen Skiing Company: Jim Felton, Public Relations Specialist; Breckenridge Ski Area: Pamela Frenette, Advertising Manager; Crested Butte Mountain Resort: Robert L. Gillen, Director Communications; Crested Butte Mountain Resort: Rod Hanna, Director of Public Relations and Advertising, Steamboat Ski Corporation: Terri Hart, Director of Public Relations; Snowmass: Dick Hulla, Ski Patrolman; Sun Valley Company: Kerry R. Langstaff, Promotions/Publicity Coordinator; Squaw Valley USA: William H. Lewkowitz, Sales; Jackson Hole Ski Corporation: Todd R. Lund, District Sales Manager; Big Sky of Montana Resort: Mary M. Madden, Executive Vice President; Taos Ski Valley, Inc.: Annette Martin, Hostess; Snowbird Ski and Summer Resort: Carolyn Maxson, Ski Guide, Crested Butte Mountain Resort: Andrea McQuade, News Bureau Writer; Killington Ltd.: Mark Menlove, Communications Director; Park City Ski Corp.: Mary Beth Moeller, Marketing Sales Representative; Steamboat Ski Corporation: Tim Newhardt, Public Relations; Heavenly: John Okalovich, Director of Ski School; Killington Ltd.: Pat Peeples, Director of Public Relations, Vail Associates, Inc.: Erven Rockwood, Host; Snowbird Ski and Summer Resort: Lillian Ross, Director of Communications; Keystone Resort: Angus Ruck, Ski Guide; Ptarmigan Inn, Steamboat: Bill Schreiber, Host; Jackson Hole Ski Corporation: Chris Stagg, Director of Marketing; Taos Ski Valley: Carroll Tyler, Realtor; Vail/Beaver Creek Resort Real Estate: Jeff Wheeler, Communications Manager; Snowbird Ski and Summer Resort: Jack Wolf, Public Relations, Kirkwood Associates, Inc.

Preface

The Greatest Ski Resorts in America was originally to be entitled The **Twenty** Greatest Ski Resorts in America. During the winter of 1987-1988, I personally reviewed over forty resort trail maps and literature. From this study, and calling upon my thirty years of skiing experience, the list was culled to twenty-three resorts for actual visitation. All restaurants featured were personally visited and all accommodations featured were toured. As a result of these visitations, it became apparent there were not twenty resorts capable of meeting the previously established criteria of "great."

Thus, the seventeen greatest ski resorts in America are featured. Each resort will test skiers' ability, whether novice or expert. All ability levels can ski at these resorts for a week without becoming bored or failing to be challenged. All of the resorts will give their visitors an adequate choice of accommodations, and skiers will find enough restaurants so they will not always have to eat in the same ones. On days when skiing is not desired, or if some members of a party do not ski, there are adequate non-skiing events and activities available to keep everyone occupied.

Many times when I previously have visited resorts, I returned home thinking next time I would do things differently; usually, I would have chosen different accommodations or eaten in a particular restaurant more than once, if only I had discovered it before the last day of the trip. It always took too long to understand a resort's lift system, and certainly getting around the mountain would have been easier and faster if I had been more familiar with the terrain. Bearing this in mind, I have attempted to identify when and where crowds occur and how to avoid them. I have taken the total number of skiable acres at each resort and divided it by that resort's maximum uphill lift capacity. The resultant number (the higher the number, the less the crowding) can be used by the reader to gauge the potential for lift lines at any of the resorts featured.

Discerning the quality and amenities of accommodations from a brochure is difficult, at best. Although all brochures list amenities, none describe the housekeeping, nor the physical condition of the property. In fact, photographs illustrating accommodations occasionally can be misleading. This book's detailed descriptions will make it easier for skiers to choose suitable lodging than by simply relying on literature or a telephone call to the resorts 800 number.

Although resorts use similar descriptions and symbols to identify trails' relative difficulties, they do not correlate them with competitors' signage. These valuable comparisons are provided in this review.

Robert E. Weber

Author's Note

Throughout this book I have used the terms "beginner," "intermediate," and "expert" to describe the relative difficulty of skiable terrain. This terminology is considered archaic by many ski resorts that prefer the terms "easiest," "more difficult," and "most difficult." My use of the terms was a conscious decision because I believe most skiers actually refer to runs and trails as "beginner, intermediate, expert." The use of these terms in no way implies approval by the resorts featured in this review, nor should the terms be taken literally by the reader.

Also, I have attempted to identify when and where crowds occur and how to avoid them. I have divided the total number of skiable acres at each resort by the resort's maximum uphill lift capacity. The resultant number (the higher the number, the less the crowding) can be used by the reader to gauge the potential for lift lines at any of the resorts featured (see table 1). There are numerous situations where this system does not take into account actual conditions that may exist at the resort, and the reader is cautioned only to use the relative crowding ratio as a guide. For example, the system does not take into consideration lifts that are frequented by disproportionate numbers of skiers. Obviously, there will always be more crowding at lifts serving intermediate terrain than at lifts serving expert terrain. It is, therefore, possible that one or more expert lifts may have vacant seats while the intermediate lifts are experiencing delays.

There is also the reality that all ski resorts do not comparably record their skiable terrain. For example, Steamboat counts all the terrain within its Forest Service permit because it justifiably believes that the tree skiing at Steamboat is one of its strongest assets. However, other resorts with equally good tree skiing may not count such terrain in their total skiable acreage.

All featured resorts are presented in alphabetical order.

Introduction

As an avid skier and past president of one of the largest ski clubs in the United States, I have been called upon many times over the years to give advice to friends and small private groups on the best American ski resorts. I have often been asked about lift ticket prices, lodging facilities' convenience to slopes, the best places to eat, child care, and ski instruction, and even activities non-skiers and teenagers could participate in off the slopes.

Because of my active role publishing ski club and ski shop newsletters, and because of my role as a freelance travel writer, I have for many years had a wealth of information on American ski resorts at my fingertips. But, until now, I have not seen a guidebook on American destination ski resorts which benefits the *general* public, both skiers and non-skiers alike. But now comes the first edition of *The Greatest Ski Resorts in America* by Robert E. Weber.

As a guidebook of American destination ski resorts, I am certain that Weber's book will not only enable families and individuals who ski to make the best winter vacation selections, but it will enable travel agents, ski writers, ski clubs, and other organizations to learn more about ski resort life, crowding variants, restaurants, shopping and nightlife, as well as snow conditions and average temperatures during various months of the ski season. Firsthand knowledge of child care facilities and ski lessons, special non-skiing activities, and medical facilities is also included in Weber's book. Detailed trail maps of each resort featured will enable skiers to learn more about each mountain's skiable terrain *prior* to a vacation, not *during* a trip when time is of essence.

The Greatest Ski Resorts in America promises to give readers a realistic and authoritative preview of seventeen American destination resorts and will serve as a tool for learning about the ins and outs of airline carriers to a particular resort, car rentals, child care, lift ticket and ski lesson prices, equipment rentals and ski tuning tips *before* a trip, not mid-week or on the last day before heading home.

Weber's book opens doors to condominiums and hotels with details that will help travel agents and the general public alike select the very best accommodations and amenities for the very best price. This book allows readers into some of each resort's very best restaurants enticing palates to mouth watering longings for some of the best food to be found in American ski resorts. Finally, *The Greatest Ski Resorts in America* has been designed to be a handy reference guide to special events and activities and includes many phone numbers which will enable resort visitors to make necessary advance restaurant and/or day care reservations, and to make prior arrangements for such things as helicopter or cross-country skiing, wilderness adventures, a hot air balloon ride, or a dinner sleigh ride depending on a person's whim a the moment.

As a writer and sometimes travel consultant, I implore skiers and non-skiers alike to examine the pages about to unfold. *The Greatest Ski Resorts in America* promises to open and to examine American destination ski resort life in a unique and fresh manner. Its most current prices (available up to press time) will save readers' valuable time when planning that remarkable winter vacation.

Margaret Darphin Mall, Editor

Contents

Trail Maps — v
Acknowledgments — vii
Preface — ix
Author's Note — xi
Introduction — xiii

The Greatest Ski Resorts in America

ASPEN — 13

ASPEN HIGHLANDS — 27

BRECKENRIDGE SKI AREA — 35

COPPER MOUNTAIN RESORT — 47

CRESTED BUTTE MOUNTAIN RESORT — 57

JACKSON HOLE — 69

KEYSTONE RESORT — 81

KILLINGTON, LTD. — 91

PARK CITY SKI AREA — 99

SNOWBIRD SKI & SUMMER RESORT — 111

SNOWMASS — 121

SQUAW VALLEY U.S.A. — 133

STEAMBOAT — 145

SUN VALLEY — 159

TAOS SKI VALLEY — 169

TELLURIDE SKI RESORT, INC. — 181

VAIL — 191

Table — 205
Index — 207

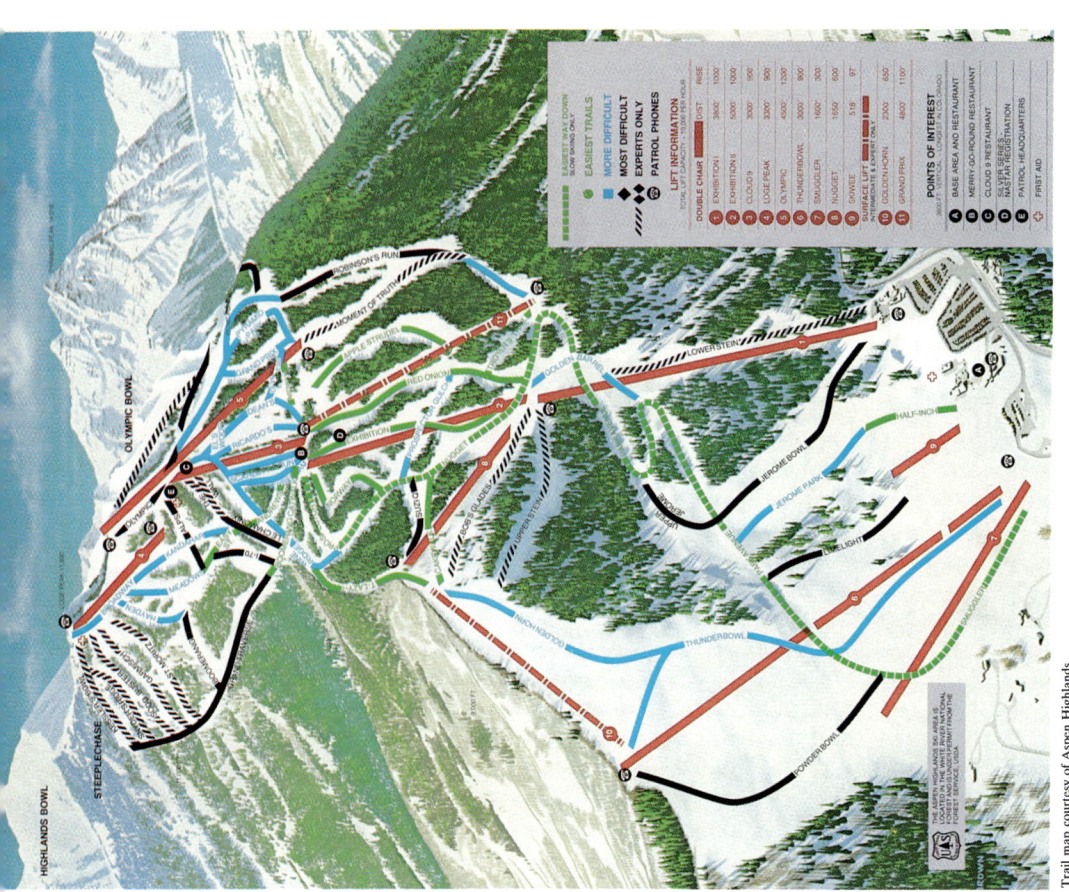

Trail map courtesy of Aspen Highlands

This is not the official 1987-88 trail map for Aspen Mountain. Please pick up an official trail map when you arrive at the area.
© 1987, Aspen Skiing Company

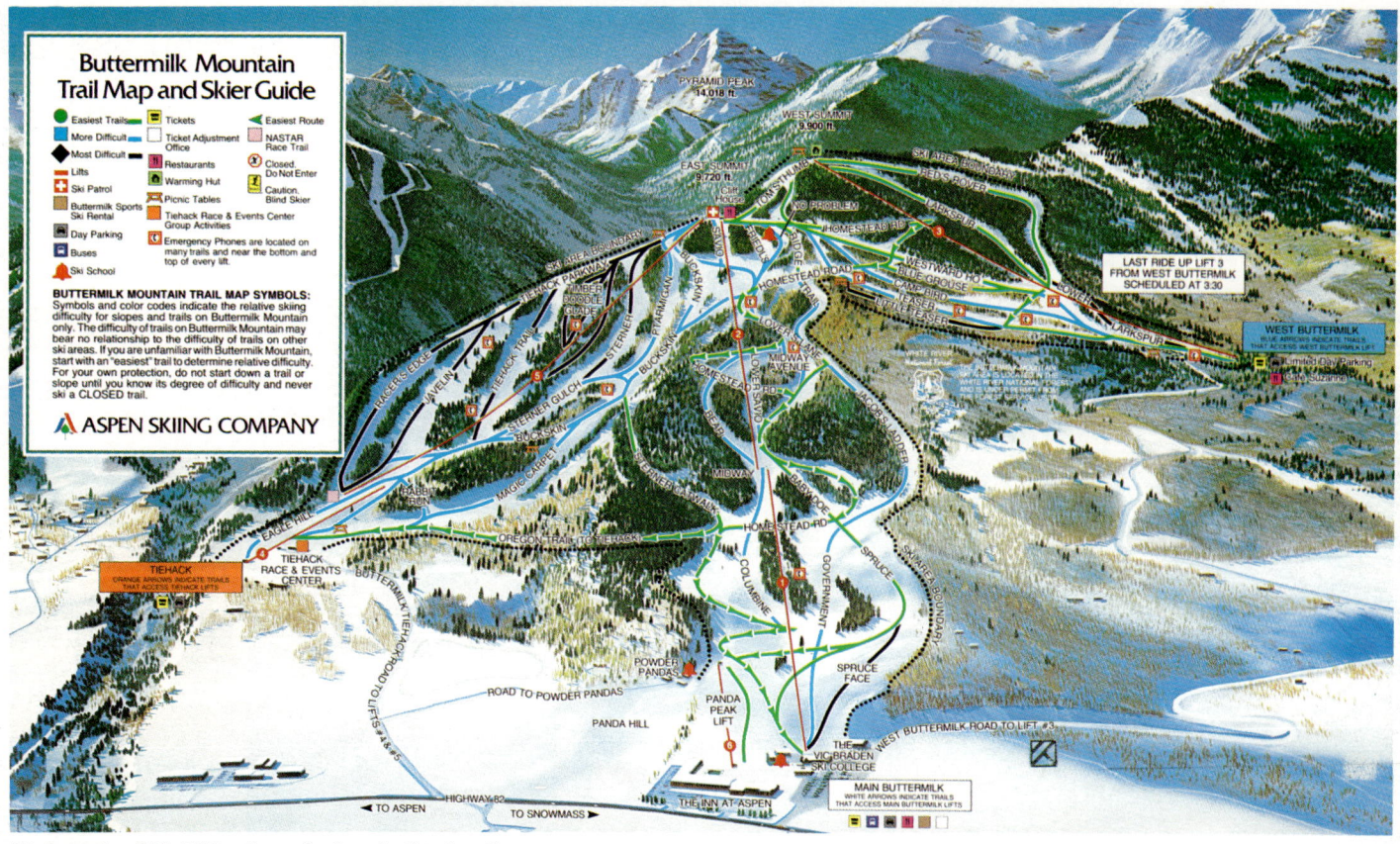

Buttermilk Mountain Trail Map and Skier Guide

- 🟢 Easiest Trails
- 🟦 More Difficult
- ⬛ Most Difficult
- 🟩 Lifts
- ✚ Ski Patrol
- Buttermilk Sports Ski Rental
- Day Parking
- Buses
- Ski School
- Tickets
- Ticket Adjustment Office
- Restaurants
- Warming Hut
- Picnic Tables
- Tiehack Race & Events Center Group Activities
- Emergency Phones are located on many trails and near the bottom and top of every lift.
- Easiest Route
- NASTAR Race Trail
- Closed, Do Not Enter
- Caution, Blind Skier

BUTTERMILK MOUNTAIN TRAIL MAP SYMBOLS: Symbols and color codes indicate the relative skiing difficulty for slopes and trails on Buttermilk Mountain only. The difficulty of trails on Buttermilk Mountain may bear no relationship to the difficulty of trails on other ski areas. If you are unfamiliar with Buttermilk Mountain, start with an "easiest" trail to determine relative difficulty. For your own protection, do not start down a trail or slope until you know its degree of difficulty and never ski a CLOSED trail.

ASPEN SKIING COMPANY

This is not the official 1987-88 trail map for Buttermilk Mountain. Please pick up an official trail map when you arrive at the area.

© 1987, Aspen Skiing Company

The trail map pictured is not to be used as a guide to the Breckenridge Ski Area. Use the trail maps provided by the resort at the ticket windows.

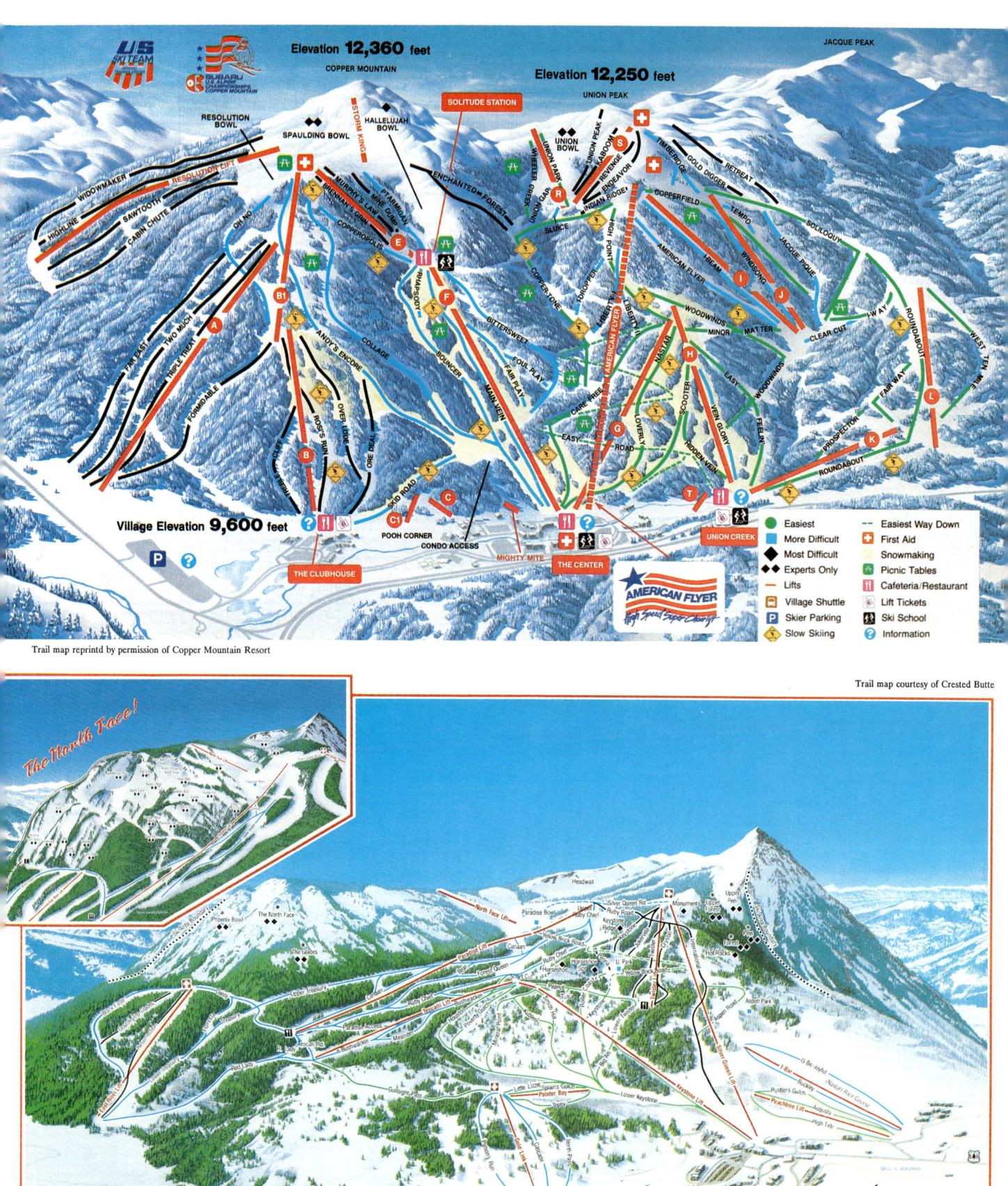

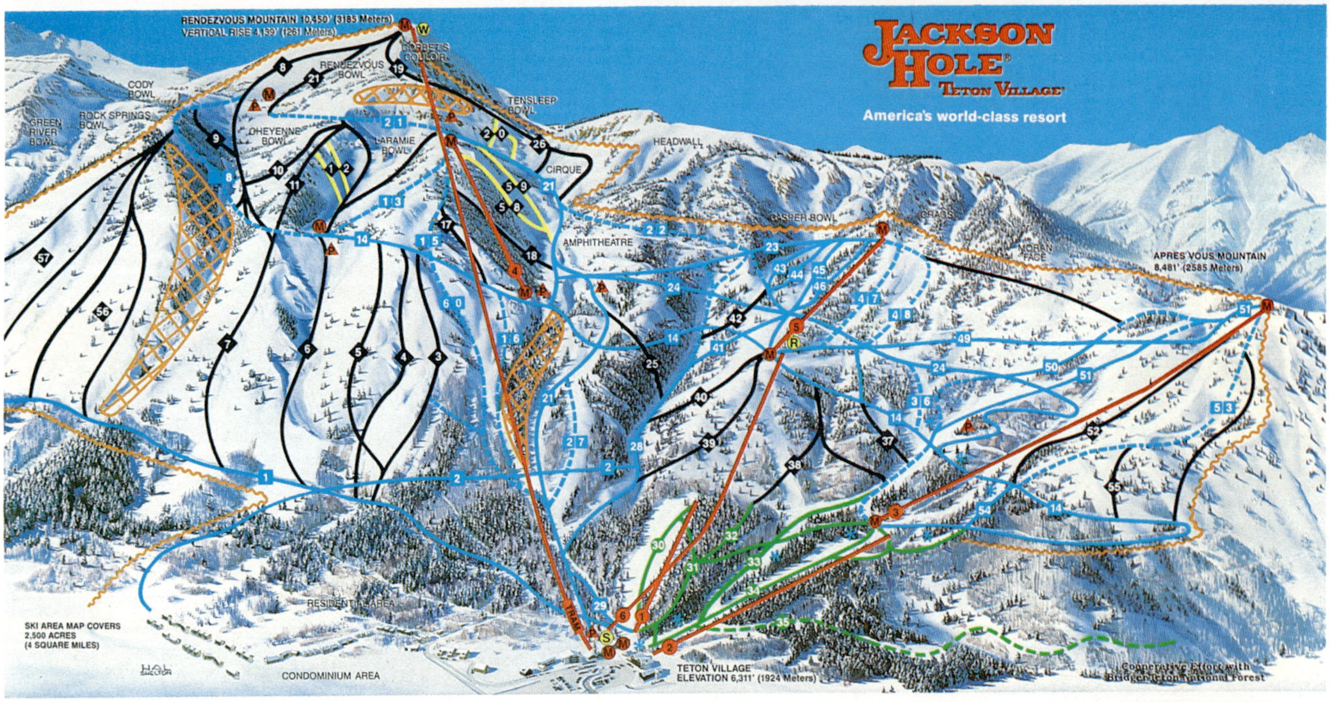

MAP KEY

- M — MOUNTAIN MAPS
- P — PATROL PHONE
- LIFTS
- R — MOUNTAIN RESTAURANT
- W — WARMING HUT (FOOD)
- S — SKI SCHOOL MEETING PLACE
- * — SNOWMAKING
- PATROLLED AREA BOUNDARY—DO NOT CROSS
- CLOSED AREAS SEVERE AVALANCHE HAZARD AREA
- CAUTION

TRAIL DIFFICULTY SYMBOLS

- EASIEST
- MODERATELY DIFFICULT
- MORE DIFFICULT VARIED TERRAIN PLUS SNOW CONDITIONS FOR THE BETTER THAN AVERAGE SKIER
- MOST DIFFICULT—EXPERT
- MOST DIFFICULT—EXPERT USE EXTRA CAUTION

TRAIL NAMES

1. Union Pass Traverse	21. Gros Ventre	41. Blacktail
2. Way Home	22. Nez Perce Traverse	42. Surprise
3. North Colter Ridge	23. Amphitheatre Traverse	43. Camp Ground
4. Buffalo Bowl	24. Solitude Traverse	44. Timbered Island
5. South Colter Ridge	25. Avalanche	45. Easy Does It
6. Rawlins Bowl	26. Downhill	46. Lift Line
7. Lower Sublette Ridge	27. Slalom	47. Sleeping Indian
8. Rendezvous Trail	28. Sundance Gully	48. Wide Open
9. Bivouac	29. Eagle's Rest Cutoff	49. Togwotee Pass Traverse
10. Bird In The Hand	30. Eagle's Rest	50. Moran
11. Pepi's Run	31. Pooh Bear	51. Upper Werner
12. Alta Chutes	32. Antelope Flats	52. Upper Teewinot
13. Grand	33. Lower Werner	53. St. Johns
14. South Pass Traverse	34. Lower Teewinot	54. Teewinot Gully
15. Gannett	35. Cross Country Ski Trail	55. Secret Slope
16. Lower Tram Line	36. Solitude Cutoff	56. North Hoback
17. Riverton Bowl	37. Ashley Ridge	57. South Hoback
18. Thunder	38. Beaver Tooth	58. Tower Three Chute
19. East Ridge Traverse	39. Jackson Face	59. Paint Brush
20. Expert Chutes	40. Nez Perce	60. Lander Bowl

LIFTS

AERIAL TRAM — 12 Minutes — 2.4 Miles Long — 4,139' Vertical Rise

1. **EAGLE'S REST DOUBLE CHAIR** — 5 Minutes — 2,260' Long — 330' Vertical Rise
2. **TEEWINOT DOUBLE CHAIR** — 7 Minutes — 3,060' Long — 425' Vertical Rise
3. **APRES VOUS DOUBLE CHAIR** — 10 Minutes — 5,000' Long — 1,745' Vertical Rise
4. **THUNDER DOUBLE CHAIR** — 8 Minutes — 3,770' Long — 1,466' Vertical Rise
5. **CASPER BOWL TRIPLE CHAIR** — 8 Minutes — 3,450' Long — 1,046' Vertical Rise
6. **CRYSTAL SPRINGS DOUBLE CHAIR** — 9 Minutes — 4,113' Long — 1,196' Vertical Rise

IMPORTANT NOTICE

This trail map is conceptual in nature and generally represents the location and difficulty of ski trails. The classification of ski runs is based on good weather and snow conditions. During periods of low visibility or other inclement weather and snow conditions, the degree of difficulty of the ski runs may change. For specific trail conditions, ask ski patrol or ski host.

Be aware of changing conditions. Natural and man-made obstacles exist. Grooming activities are routinely in progress on slopes and trails. ***Use caution, ski in control and ski only on designated slopes or trails.***

Skiing closed areas is a misdemeanor and subject to a fine of up to $100.00.

FOR SKI PATROL ASSISTANCE, DIAL 150 ON ANY SKI PATROL TELEPHONE OR CONTACT NEAREST LIFT OPERATOR.

PRINTED IN USA

Trail map reprinted by permission of Jackson Hole

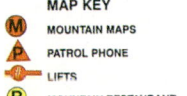

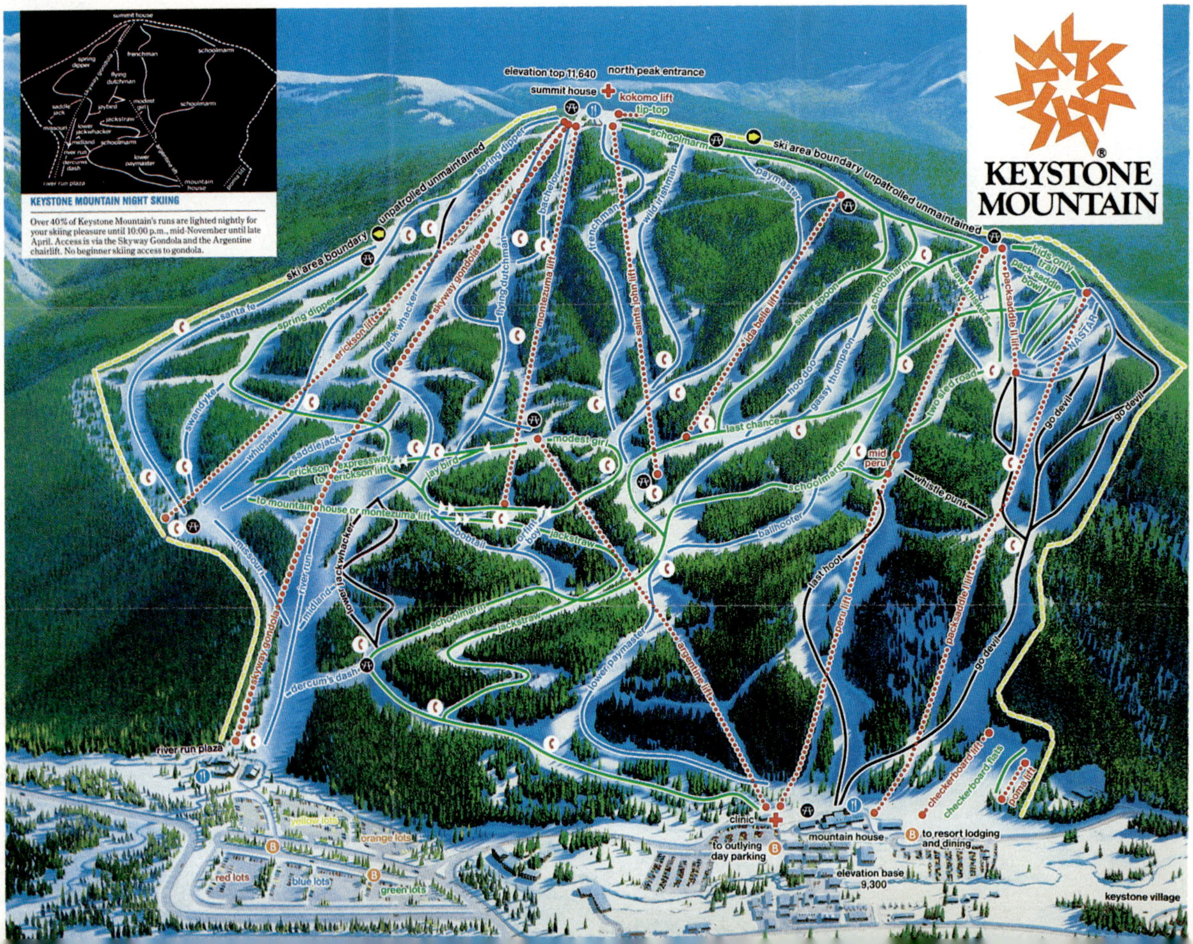

Trail map reprinted by permission of Keystone

Trail map reprinted by permission of Killington

Trail map reprinted by permission of Park City Ski Corp.

Snowbird Trail Map

LIFTS:	VERTICAL RISE	TRAVEL TIME	TRAVEL LENGTH	*Skiers per hour
AERIAL TRAMWAY	2,900 ft. / 883.9 m.	8 min.	8,395 ft. / 2558.8 m.	125 per cabin
PERUVIAN	1,000 ft. / 304.8 m.	6 min.	2,943 ft. / 897.0 m.	1,200*
WILBERE RIDGE	668 ft. / 207.7 m.	4.5 min.	2,154 ft. / 656.5 m.	1,200*
GAD I	1,827 ft. / 557.0 m.	13 min.	6,704 ft. / 2062.8 m.	1,200*
GAD II	1,239 ft. / 377.6 m.	9 min.	4,397 ft. / 1340.2 m.	1,200*
MID-GAD	1,315 ft. / 401.0 m.	9 min.	4,310 ft. / 1314.0 m.	1,100*
LITTLE CLOUD	1,304 ft. / 398.0 m.	7 min.	3,515 ft. / 1072.0 m.	1,200*
CHICKADEE	142 ft. / 43.3 m.	3 min.	830 ft. / 252.9 m.	710*

TOTAL LIFT CAPACITY: 8810 skiers per hour

1. Chip's Run•
2. Primrose Path
3. Silver Fox
4. Dalton's Draw
5. Blackjack
6. Chickadee•
7. Little Cloud
8. Regulator Johnson & Regulator Traverse
9. Wilbere Bowl
10. Wilbere Chute
11. Mach Schnell
12. Rothman Way
13. Harper's Ferry East
14. Harper's Ferry
15. Wilbere Ridge •
16. Wilbere Cutoff
17. Bassackwards
18. Election•
19. S.T.H.
20. Black Forest
21. Organ Grinder
22. Lunch Run
23. Big Emma•
24. Bananas
25. Gadzooks
26. Tiger Tail
27. Carbonate
28. Lower Bassackwards•
29. West Second South•
30. Miners Road
31. Bass Highway • (Easiest route to Tram)
32. Chip's Face
33. Great Scott
34. Upper Cirque
35. Cirque Traverse
36. Gad Chutes
37. Chip's Bypass
38. Mark Malu Fork
39. Adager

SKI SCHOOL MEETING AREAS
A—Chickadee — All children, adult beginners
B—Big Emma — All adults, above beginner level
C—Children's Center — Level "C", Cliff Lodge

• DENOTES SLOW SKIING AREAS. Fast or reckless skiing is not permitted at Snowbird.

ATTENTION SKIERS: EMERGENCY PHONE
The various difficulty ratings are relative to the Snowbird area. During periods of low visibility or other inclement weather and snow conditions the degree of difficulty of the area may change. If you are unfamiliar with the area, begin with those runs marked EASIEST and progress to MORE DIFFICULT or MOST DIFFICULT as your ability allows. CAUTION: Check with the Ski Patrol for current conditions.

FOR YOUR SAFETY
Skiing is a mountaineering sport which has inherent risks. While efforts have been made to provide for your skiing safety, there are still hazards which require your alertness and vigilance. Good physical condition, proper clothing, appropriate equipment and a knowledge of the principles of skiing will dramatically reduce your chances of having an accident. Please enjoy skiing Snowbird while exercising common sense and caution. This brochure is not intended for use as a skier's guide.

Trail map reprinted by permission of Snowbird

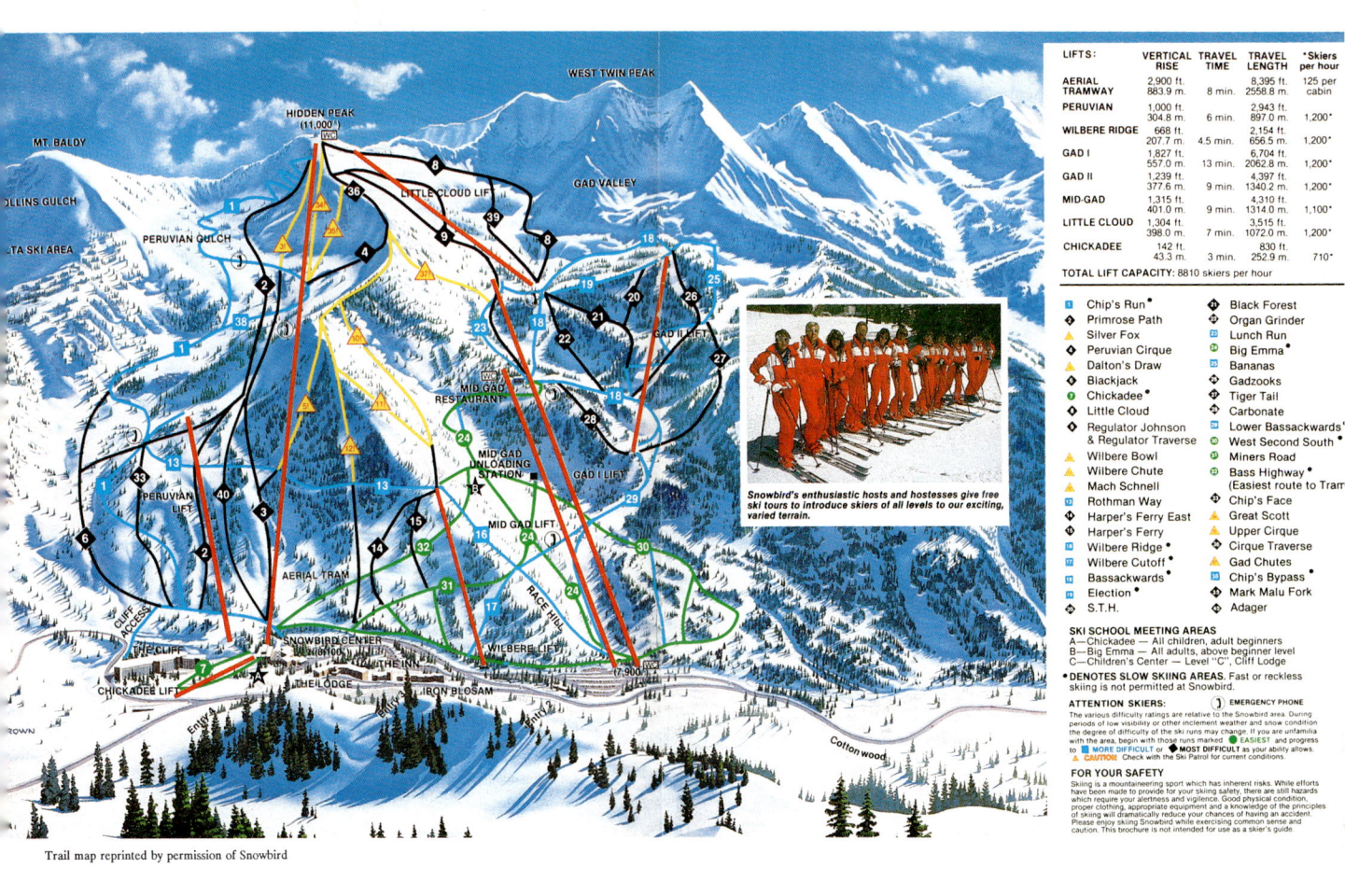

Snowmass Ski Area Trail Map and Skier Guide

Legend:
- ● Easiest Trails
- ◆ More Difficult
- ◆ Most Difficult
- ◆◆ Expert Only
- Quad SuperChair
- Lifts
- Ski Patrol
- Clinic
- Ski School
- Route Down
- Tickets
- Ticket Adjustment Office
- Warming Hut
- Group Activities
- Restaurants
- Buses
- NASTAR
- Spider Sabich Race Center
- Marlboro Ski Challenge
- Danger
- Closed. Do Not Enter
- Caution. Blind Skier
- Emergency Phones are located on many trails and near the bottom and top of every lift.

SNOWMASS SKI AREA TRAIL MAP SYMBOLS:
Symbols and color-codes indicate the relative skiing difficulty for slopes and trails on Snowmass Ski Area only. The difficulty of trails at the Snowmass Ski Area may bear no relationship to the difficulty of trails on other ski areas. If you are unfamiliar with Snowmass Ski Area, start with an "easiest" trail to determine relative difficulty. For your own protection, do not start down a trail or slope until you know its degree of difficulty and never ski a CLOSED trail.

ASPEN SKIING COMPANY

This is not the official 1987-88 trail map for Snowmass Ski Area. Please pick up an official trail map when you arrive at the area.

© 1987, Aspen Skiing Company

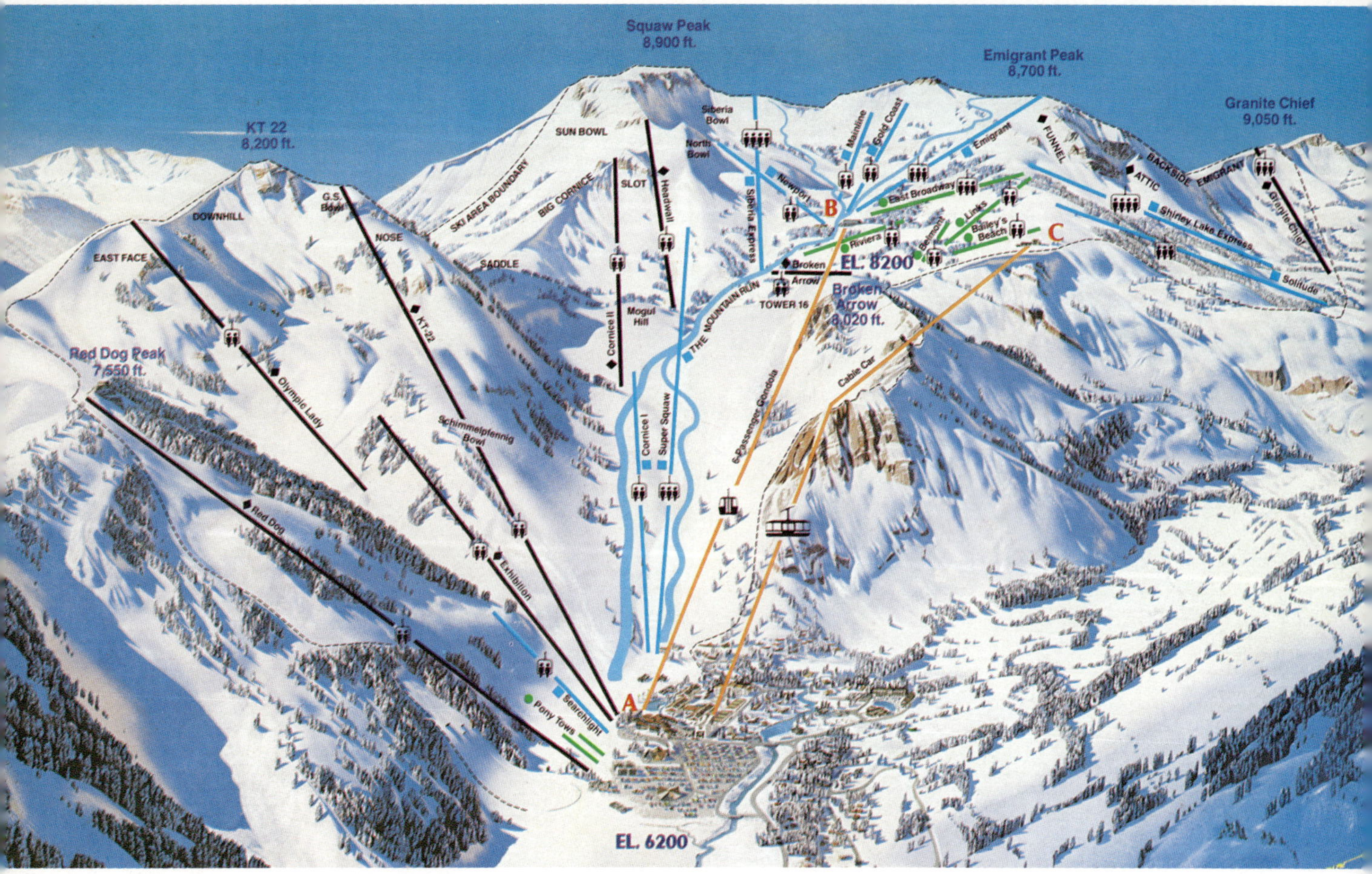

Trail map reprinted by permission of Squaw Valley USA

Trail map reprinted by permission of Steamboat

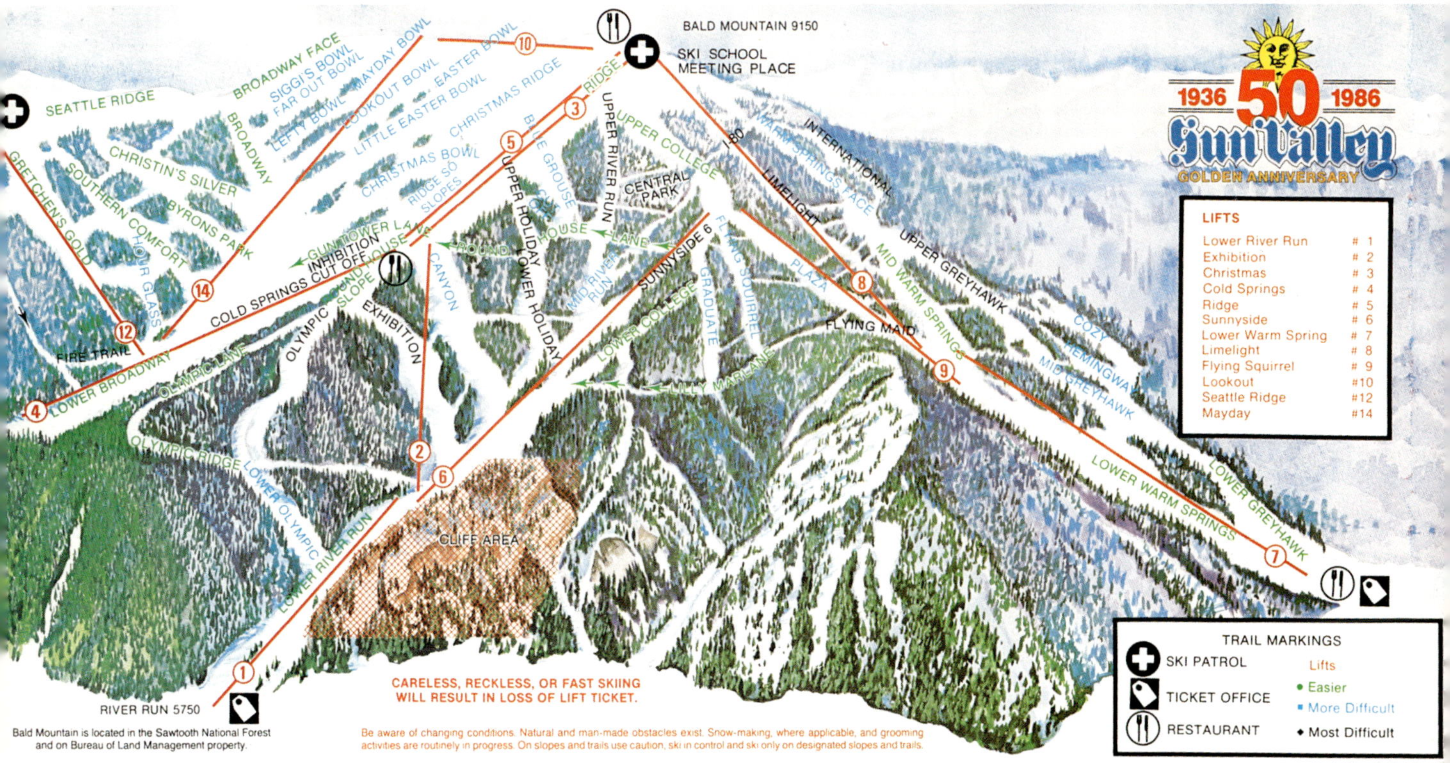

Trail map reprinted by permission of Sun Valley Company

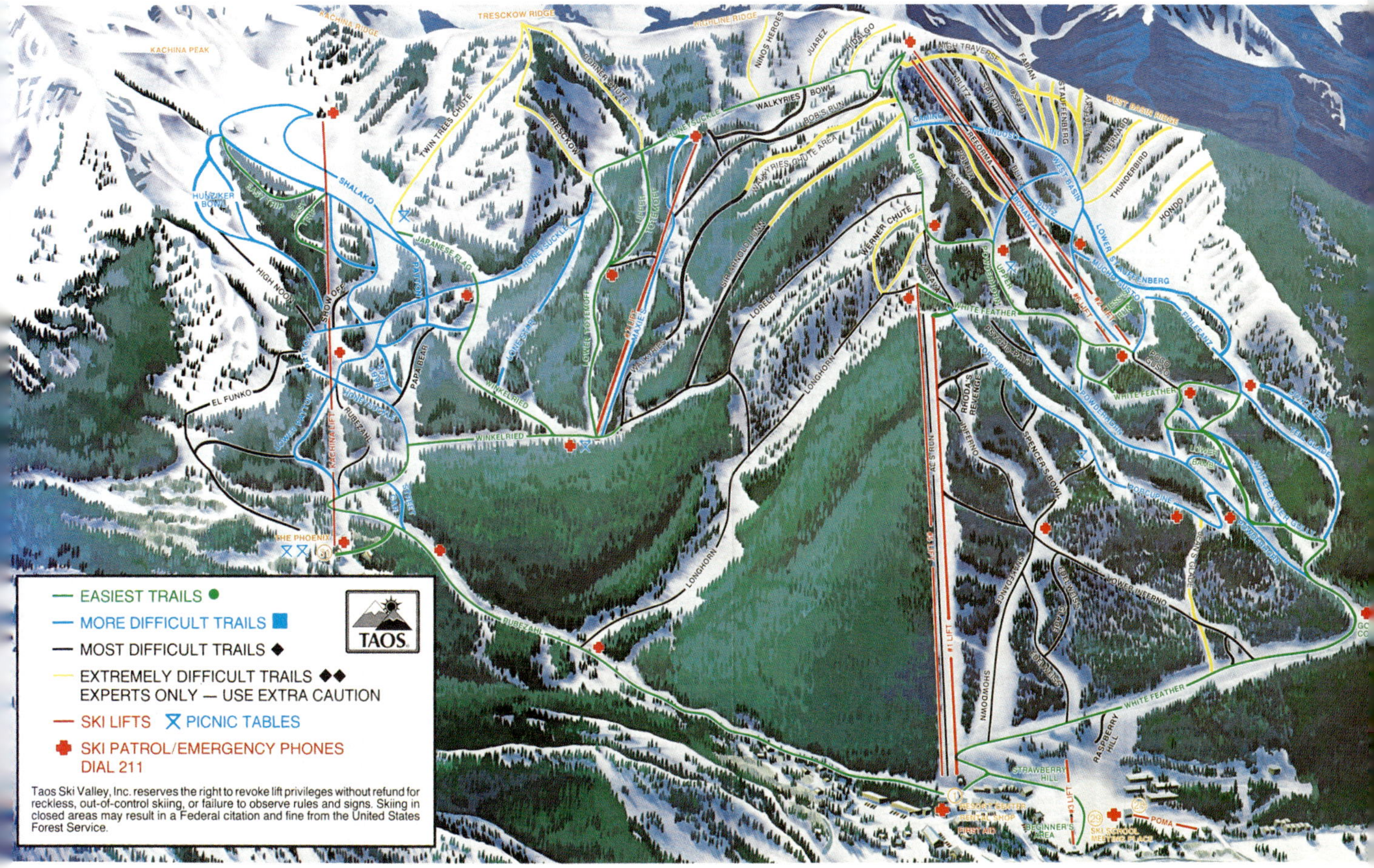

Trail map reprinted by permission of Taos Ski Valley

TELLURIDE FACE
Elevation: 11,890'

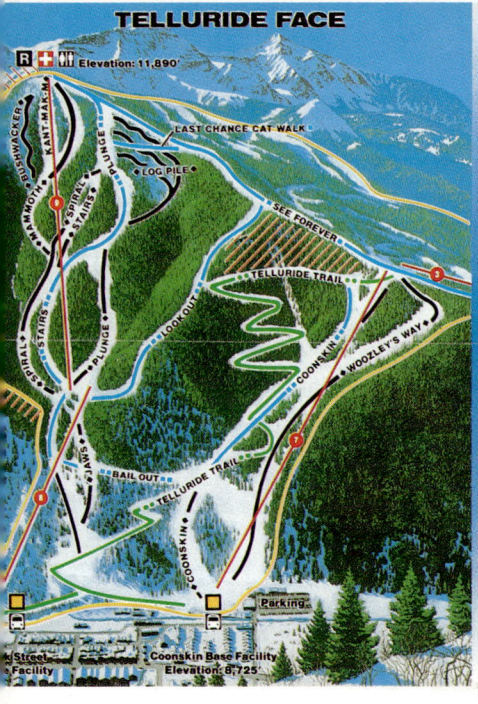

GORRONO BASIN
Elevation: 11,890' / 12,247'

SUNSHINE PEAK

TRAIL DIFFICULTY SYMBOLS

Symbol	Difficulty	Trail Name Marker
● (green)	EASIEST	Beginner
●● (green)	EASIEST	Advanced Beginner
■ (blue)	MORE DIFFICULT	Intermediate
■■ (blue)	MORE DIFFICULT	Advanced Intermediate
◆ (black)	MOST DIFFICULT	Expert
◆◆ (black)	MOST DIFFICULT	Experts Only

SKI AREA BOUNDARY
/////// CLOSED AREAS

Trail map reprinted by permission of Telluride Ski Resort, Inc.

THE SKI SAFETY ACT OF 1979

The Ski Safety Act of 1979 became law in Colorado on July 1, 1979. Copies of this act, dealing with your duties and responsibilities as a skier, are available from our information at ticket offices and patrol headquarters. It is your obligation and responsibility to obey the provisions of this act.

SKIING IN CLOSED AREAS AND OUT OF CONTROL SKIING ARE ILLEGAL. VIOLATORS ARE SUBJECT TO ARREST, PROSECUTION AND REVOCATION OF SKIING PRIVILEGES.

Off-trail areas within the ski area boundary are not patrolled on a regular basis. Ski with caution. Do not ski alone.

Ski Area Boundary
The Telluride Ski Resort has no duty to any skier skiing beyond the ski area boundaries. Should skiers choose to leave the ski area, they do so at their own risk and assume the burden of responsibility for their actions. Avalanche danger and other hazards exist. You are solely responsible for your safety and welfare.

In Case of Accidents
1. Place crossed skis upright in snow above the scene of the accident.
2. Note the exact location of the accident and the nature of the injury.

TRAIL MAP SYMBOLS

- Ski Patrol
- N NASTAR
- R Restaurant
- Restrooms
- Free Bus Stop
- Nordic
- Base Area Services: Ticket Office, Rental Sports Shop, Ski School, Restrooms, Storage, Lost and Found

Operating Hours
9:00 a.m.–4:00 p.m. Lifts 1, 3, 4, and 7
9:00 a.m.–3:30 p.m. Lifts 5, 6, 8, 9 and 10
10:00 a.m.–3:00 p.m. Lift 2

All trails close at 4:30 p.m.

This is not the official 1987-88 trail map for Vail Mountain. Please pick up an official trail map when you arrive at the area.
© 1987, Vail Associates, Inc.

Vail

MAP KEY

- The Vail Express Lifts
- Downloading Lift
- Experts Only
- Most Difficult ◆
- More Difficult ■
- Easiest ●
- Slow-Skiing Run
- Chairlift
- Area Boundary (do not cross)
- Road or Catwalk (may include flat terrain)
- Slow-Skiing Area

- Ski Patrol
- Ticket Office
- Ski School
- Picnic Area
- Bus Stop (every 10 min)
- Warming Room
- Restaurant and Lockers
- Ski Storage

Access to Cross-Country Area — Ask the Vail/Beaver Creek Ski School for details on equipment and use.

Skiway — Access to homesites and lodging beyond ski area boundary. No lift service.

VAIL LIFT RIDE TIMES

Ride times are based on ideal conditions with no stops.

Lift	Lift Name	Ride Time (minutes)	Lift	Lift Name	Ride Time (min)
1	Giant Steps	7	11	Northwoods Express	
2	Avanti	13	12	Gopher Hill	
3	Hunky Dory	7	14	Sourdough Special	
4	Mountain Top Express	4.5	15	Little Eagle	
5	High Noon	11	16	Vista Bahn	
6	Golden Peak	N, 10, 5, 3	17	Upper Mid-Vail	
7	Game Creek Express	4.5	20	Cascade Village Express	
8	Bwana	9.5	ENP	Eagle's Nest Poma	
9	Minnie's	12	LHG	LionsHead Gondola	
10	Highline				

VAIL CHILDREN'S ADVENTURE

Children's Ski School Only
- C1 Fort Whippersnapper
- C2 Gitchigumee Gulch
- C3 Race Area
- C4 Video Filming Area

Children's Adventures for All
- C1 Silver Mine
- C6 Chinatown Picnic Area
- C2 Mountain Lion's Den
- C7 Snow Park
- C3 Indian Burial Ground
- C8 Nursery at Golden Peak
- C4 Slow Skiing Trail (for adults too)
- C9 Snow Park
- Slow Skiing Trail

For details on the Ski S...

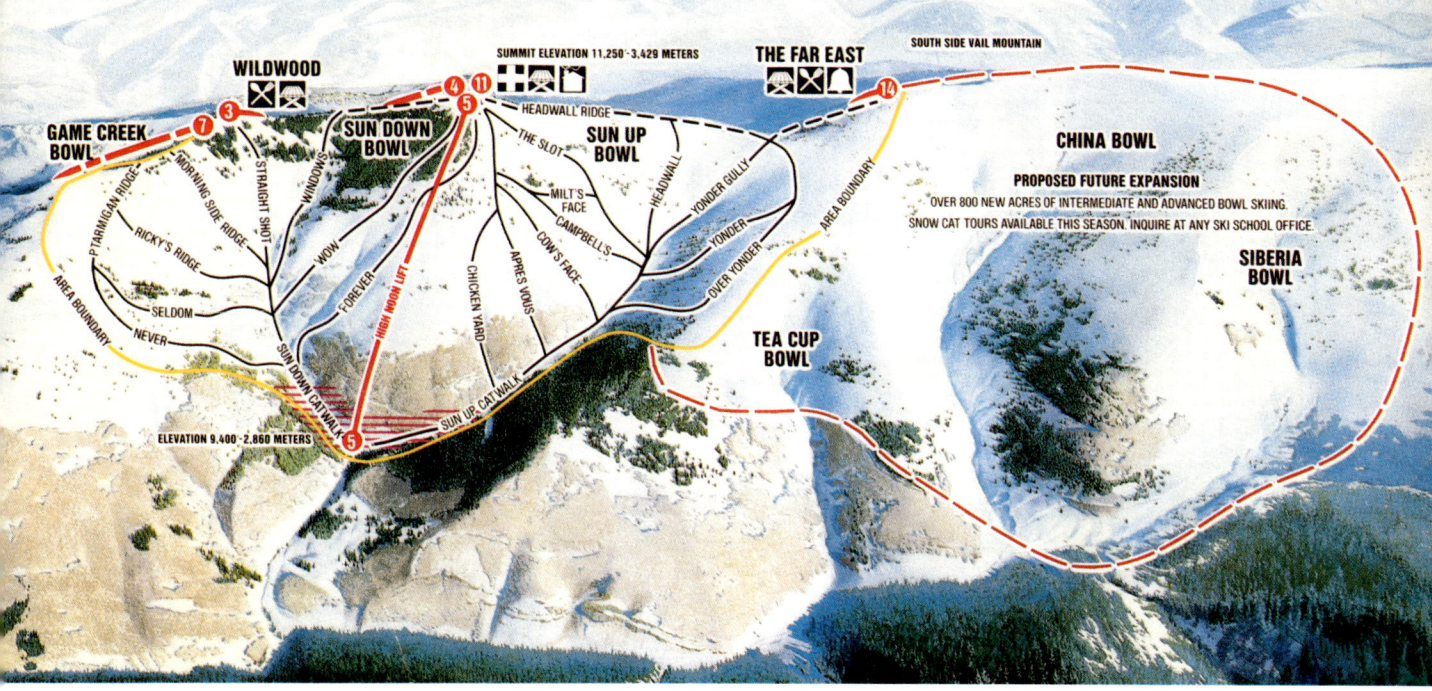

This is not the official 1987-88 trail map for Vail Mountain. Please pick up an official trail map when you arrive at the area. © 1987, Vail Associates, Inc.

ASPEN

P.O. Box 1248
Aspen, CO. 81612

(800) 262-7736 Reservations
(303) 925-1220 Information
(303) 925-1221 Snow Report

Transportation

Aspen is one of the most accessible of the world's major ski resorts. Driving to Aspen from the East is as simple as hopping on Interstate 70 and turning left on Colorado State Highway 82. The distance from Denver is 200 miles, and although weather can be a factor, the completion of the Eisenhower Memorial Tunnel several years ago relieved most of the apprehension associated with this drive.

Skiers from the North and from the South can easily drive to Aspen by taking Interstate 25 to Denver and getting onto Interstate 70. Visitors from the West can also pick up Interstate 70 in Utah.

It is also convenient to travel to Aspen by air. United Express and Continental Express offer quick and convenient service from Denver's Stapleton International Airport to Aspen's Sardy Field. Sardy is an FAA controlled airport and instrument landings are possible. Thus, it is necessary to bus passengers from Denver only during the worst storms.

Denver recently has made great strides in cleaning up Stapleton's image as an inefficient airport with mass delays and inconvenient airline transfers. A new wing served primarily by United Airlines was completed in 1987, and renovation of Continental's annex was well along as this book was going to press. A separate extension built to accommodate airline shuttle services is comfortable and clean. Although this extension is located at the far end of the terminal, in-bound Denver flights are met at arrival gates by hosts or hostesses who quickly assist transferring resort-bound passengers onto buses which take skiers directly to the shuttle wing. Baggage is efficiently handled and usually is on the same flight as the passenger. Even if the scheduled air shuttle flight is missed, the skiers can usually take another of the many daily Denver-Aspen flights.

During the 1987-88 ski season, several direct flights from Denver to Aspen were available. Check with your travel agent or call Aspen to confirm flight schedules for subsequent seasons. During 1987-88, direct flights to Aspen originated from Chicago, Dallas, Los Angeles, Long Beach, and San Francisco. These flights were offered during the peak season commencing December 17 and continuing through March 28. It is anticipated that a similar schedule will be maintained each year.

The town of Aspen is located only a two and a half miles from Sardy Field and is accessible by taxi (High Mountain), limousine, and courtesy van.

Most major car rental agencies are located at Sardy Field. They provide *skierized* cars equipped with snow tires and ski racks. For a slightly higher price, many rental agencies will provide four-wheel drive vehicles. Travelers are cautioned to reserve these vehicles far in advance of arrival because demand for them is great.

Having a car at Aspen is not necessary and may not even be desirable because the local transportation system is so good. Free shuttle buses run daily between Aspen, Aspen Mountain, Aspen Highlands, Snowmass, and Buttermilk.

Mountain Statistics

Aspen has two separate mountains, each distinct and unique. Aspen Mountain, known as Ajax to many of the locals, is situated in the center of town and is designated for intermediate and expert skiers only. Buttermilk Mountain is located a short distance to the west.

Aspen Mountain

Aspen Mountain is different from other mountains featured in this guide book. It is one of only two mountains that does not have beginner slopes (the other is Sun Valley)! It may also be the only mountain where the majority of the trails are short. Ajax appears to have "blown" its top, because much of the skiable terrain is directed from its outer edges into its center crater. Most of the skiing on the upper third of the mountain is intermediate in nature and not particularly exciting.

However, expert skiers will find Aspen Mountain truly exhilarating. The expert runs on Ajax are steep, frequently gladed, covered with enormous bumps, and definitely not for advanced skiers who fancy themselves experts. The main attractions to this mountain are its legend for being located in one of the oldest ski resorts in America, and its breathtaking view from the top. From the mountain's summit, visitors can view the town of Aspen lying at its base and Starwood, a wealthy show business neighborhood, located on the other side of town.

During the 1986-87 season, Aspen Skiing Company replaced some of its old lift system with a new six passenger gondola which enables skiers to reach the mountain's summit in thirteen minutes, while protecting skiers from the winter elements. A new quad SuperChair™ was also added to access the new double black diamond runs that formerly were out of bounds.

Some of Aspen Mountain's most awesome runs are situated in the middle third of the mountain. As previously mentioned, these short runs terminate on an intermediate run named Spar Gulch. In order to re-ski the mountain, it is necessary to traverse almost all the way to the bottom of the hill and take the lift up again. This translates to less ski time and more lift time. The runs included in this situation are primarily Bear Paw, Short Snort, Zaugg Dump, Perry's Prowl, Last Dollar, the Face of Bell and the Shoulder of Bell.

Until the 1981-82 season, Aspen Mountain had no artificial snowmaking capabilities. During lean snow years, the lower third of the mountain was virtually unskiable. Now, however, snow-making equipment has been added, and the lack of natural snow should not inhibit anyone from enjoying the lower third.

Located in the White River National Forest, Aspen Mountain consists of 625 acres (253 ha) skiable acres and has over twenty-three miles (37 km) of trails. Of these trails 35% are rated more difficult, 35% are most difficult, and 30% are expert. "More difficult" relates to the blue square sign used at most resorts to denote intermediate, while the black diamond denotes "most difficult," which most resorts usually refer to as "expert." Aspen Mountain illustrates its "expert" terrain with two black diamonds.

The base elevation of Aspen is 7,945 feet (2,422 meters) and its summit is 11,212 feet (3,417 meters). This provides the skier with 3,267 vertical feet (996 meters) of skiing.

This terrain is serviced by:

1 Gondola (Silver Queen)
1 Quad SuperChair
2 Fixed Grip Quads
4 Double Chairs

Aspen's uphill lift capacity is 10,775 skiers per hour. The number of skiable acres divided by the maximum number of skiers transported per hour is .058. Compared to the other resorts featured, Aspen Mountain is no more crowded than most other mountains.

Aspen receives an annual snowfall of about 300 inches (762 cm) at its summit and 155 inches (394 cm) at its base. Its average monthly snowfall is:

Nov.   34" (86 cm)
Dec.   52" (132 cm)
Jan.   40" (102 cm)
Feb.   51" (130 cm)
Mar.   66" (168 cm)

Ajax has the snowmaking capacity to cover 210 acres (85 ha) which is somewhat limiting, especially during the beginning of ski season. Most of the snowmaking capabilities are located on the lower portion of the mountain near the base lift where traffic tends to rapidly ski off the base. Aspen Mountain's snowmaking equipment assures skiers that there will be enough coverage for them to enjoy the slopes during the entire period of operation.

During the season, weather permitting, it is possible to ski the back bowls of Aspen Mountain. These are powder runs suitable for both intermediate and expert skiers. Reservations are necessary prior to skiing the backside, because access to the terrain is via snowcat. Telephone (303) 925-4444 for reservations.

Buttermilk Mountain

Located on Colorado Highway 82 two miles from Aspen Mountain, Buttermilk is almost midway between Aspen and Snowmass. For beginning skiers, there is probably not a finer mountain in Colorado on which to learn to ski. Buttermilk's gentle ski terrain is meticulously maintained throughout the winter season.

Buttermilk Mountain consists of 402 skiable acres (162 ha) and has over 20 miles (32 km) of trails. It is a small mountain by Colorado standards, but is completely adequate for beginners and intermediate skiers. This is especially true when one considers the expansive terrain available at Snowmass and Aspen Mountain proper. Of the skiable trails available, 35% are considered easiest, 39% are more difficult, and 26% are most difficult.

The base elevation of Buttermilk is 7,870 feet (2,399 meters) and its summit is 9,900 feet (3,018 meters). This provides the skier with 2,030 vertical feet (619 meters) of skiing.

Buttermilk Mountain is serviced by six double chairlifts capable of transporting 6,297 skiers per hour. The number of skiable acres divided by the number of skiers transported per hour is .063. This figure suggests a little more potential crowding than at Snowmass, but less than at other major resorts such as Keystone and Aspen Highlands.

Buttermilk's longest run is Tom's Thumb to Homestead Road to Spruce. It is 3 miles (4.8 km) long and rated easiest (beginner) its entire length.

Buttermilk receives an annual snowfall of about 300 inches (762 cm) at its summit and 155 inches (394 cm) at its base. Its average monthly snowfall is:

Nov. 33" (84 cm)
Dec. 36" (91 cm)
Jan. 35" (89 cm)
Feb. 45" (114 cm)
Mar. 6" (142 cm)

The average monthly temperatures during the season are:

Nov. 31° 0°C
Dec. 22° -5°C
Jan. 20° -6°C
Feb. 23° -5°C
Mar. 29° -2°C

LIFT TICKET PRICES (1988-89)

Aspen Skiing Company offers many different lift ticket rates for individuals, and for groups over 65, the physically challenged, and combination lift ticket/ski lesson packages.

Single day rates:

$35 Adult, Aspen Mountain
$33 Adult, Buttermilk Mountain
$17 Child, 12 and under

Adult rates 3 and 4 mountain:

$186 6 of 7 Days; 3 Mountain
$192 6 of 7 Days; 4 Mountain
$155 5 of 6 Days; 3 Mountain
$124 4 of 5 Days; 3 Mountain
$128 4 of 5 Days; 4 Mountain
$ 96 3 of 4 Days; 3 Mountain

Rates for children aged twelve and under during the 1988-89 season are:

$102 6 of 7 Days
$ 85 5 of 6 Days
$ 68 4 of 5 Days
$ 51 3 of 4 Days

Hours of Operation

9:00 A.M. to 3:30 P.M., Aspen Mountain
9:00 A.M. to 4:00 P.M., Buttermilk Mountain

Lift Ticket Purchase Locations

Lift tickets are sold at the base of the Silver Queen Gondola, the Little Nell Quad Chairlift, and the 1-A Chairlift at Aspen Mountain. Buttermilk Mountain lift tickets may be purchased at the base of the Main Buttermilk Lift, located just behind the Inn at Aspen. Lift tickets may also be purchased at the base of Lift # 3 at West Buttermilk, and at the edge of the parking lot by the Race and Events Center.

Regardless of where tickets are purchased, they will be honored at Aspen Mountain, Buttermilk, and Snowmass. The special four-mountain rate also includes Aspen Highlands.

Crowd Control

In 1987, Aspen Skiing Company spent millions of dollars improving Aspen Mountain. The addition of the Silver Queen Gondola and the Quad SuperChair™ significantly changed the demographics of the mountain. Although the additions were designed to improve the mountain's uphill services, they had the unplanned effect of increasing the number of persons who ski Ajax. Formerly, many people skied Snowmass in order to avoid the crowds on Aspen Mountain. However, with the improved lifts, many skiers apparently decided to return to Aspen Mountain. The result has been that the mountain is now as crowded as it ever has been.

One of the ways skiers have discovered to avoid crowded lift lines is to hire an instructor for the day. By doing this, they can break into lift lines, a viable alternative to waiting in line if one is not opposed to spending $250 per day for an instructor. Most people who choose this option also treat the instructor to lunch.

The most common way down Ajax mountain at the end of the day is via Spar Gulch to Little Nell. This is a narrow ravine which becomes very crowded with skiers of all ability levels. In the evening particularly, use caution and ski slowly when returning to the base. As an alternative to negotiating traffic on Spar Gulch, take Ruthie's Run to Dago Cut Road or to Magnifico. By doing so, you will exit the mountain a little further north of Little Nell, but you will avoid the congestion. If this is not acceptable, exit onto Tower Ten Road. This catwalk, located very near the bottom and bisecting Franklin Dump, will return the skier to Little Nell.

Ski School

The Aspen Skiing Company employs over four hundred certified ski instructors. However, most of these instructors teach at Buttermilk and Snowmass. Because there are no beginner runs nor easy intermediate runs on Aspen Mountain, ski classes are limited to advanced intermediates and experts. The 1988-89 rates may be found in the section of this book dealing with Snowmass.

Equipment Rental

There are more than twenty ski rental locations in Aspen. As in all ski resorts, the prices for rental equipment are similar. Rates for skis only are usually between $10 and $12 per day. If boots and poles are required, the rate will usually vary from $12 to $15 per day. An up-charge of 10 to 20% for performance skis is typical, and most (if not all) shops offer performance packages. Aspen ski rental shops will usually discount their rates for equipment if it is to be rented for three or more days. A cash or credit card deposit must be posted at the time the rental agreement is made.

Ski Tuning And Repair

Aspen offers an excellent selection of stores and companies in various locations for ski tuning and repair. Most rental establishments repair skis; in addition, there are companies that only sell new skis and companies that only repair older ones. Almost without exception, the shops do a competent job of repairing or waxing skis. However, there are a few stores which have state-of-the-art ski tuning equipment. All things being equal, skiers should consider having their skis and bindings tuned or repaired where this up-to-date machinery is utilized.

Ski Service Center, located on Mill St., is one of the firms in Aspen that features Montana Crystal Glide ski tuning equipment. Typical rates during the 1987-88 season were:

$ 5 Hot Wax
$15 Flat File
$20 Complete Tune-up
$ 5 Bindings Adjusted
$20+ P-tex

In addition, several Aspen shops including Sport Kaelin contract their ski tuning work with the Ski Service Center.

For a complete explanation of the benefits of state-of-the-art ski tuning, refer to the *Ski Tuning and Repair* section of the review of *Killington* in this book.

Mountain Restaurants

Four mountain restaurants are found on Aspen Mountain. All are cafeterias except the Coyote Grill, which is managed by Pour La France, a notable restaurant in downtown Aspen. The Coyote is located in Ruthie's Restaurant at the top of the A-1 Lift. Although originally built as a lunch and dinner restaurant, the town of Aspen never granted the restaurant a permit to operate at night. It remains, however, the only restaurant with table service on Ajax. The Coyote's food is good, but not great. Certainly with a little effort it could be one of the better mountain eating establishments. Few mountain restaurants, however, afford visitors as spectacular a view as the town of Aspen directly below.

Bonnie's Restaurant, located at Tourelotte Park high on the mountain, is convenient to the Quad SuperChair™. The views from the sizable deck are of Snow Bowl. Bonnie's serves cafeteria-style food which is typically nondescript. The ambience, however, is unique. The restaurant has a pseudo-beach decor with thatched umbrella topped tables outside, and a similar thatched topped bar which is open when weather permits. It is a popular place to stop at the end of the day before embarking down the mountain.

At the top of the Silver Queen Gondola another cafeteria, The Sundeck, serves fare similar to that found in other restaurants on the mountain. In clear weather its outside deck is open and skiers can enjoy spectacular views including the Maroon Bells.

Buttermilk Mountain has four mountain restaurants. The Cliffhouse, a cafeteria-style restaurant located at the top of the #2 Lift, serves Swiss specialties as well as traditional fare.

Another restaurant, Café Suzanne's, is located at the base of West Buttermilk. Also a cafeteria, Suzanne's is smaller and more intimate than other mountain restaurants. Try the excellent crepes.

The Race and Events Center Cafeteria, located at the base of Eagle Hill on Tiehack, is open for public dining and is frequently used by clubs and groups.

Another cafeteria is located at the base of the Main Buttermilk chairlift. On warm, bright days its deck is a favorite place to relax and watch skiers negotiate their way down Government or Spruce Face.

Day Care

Because Aspen is one of the country's oldest established ski resorts, many services have evolved rather than having been planned. Child day care is an example of a service that was needed but not planned. The result is that it is inconvenient for skiers to place their children in day care. There are three services, all of which are located out of town. In order for skiers to place their children in such facilities, they must either drive to the centers or take the free shuttle to and from the service.

Aspen Sprouts is located in the Airport Business Center midway between Aspen and Snowmass, near Buttermilk Mountain. Care for children between the ages of one and five is available Monday through Saturday. Reservations may be booked by telephoning (303) 920-1055.

Little Feet, also located in the Airport Business Center, will accept some walk-in visitors. However, it is primarily a service for working parents in Aspen. Little Feet will accept children aged six weeks through eighteen months. The 1987-88 rate was $40 per day or $25 per half day. Three meals a day are provided. As with all day care centers, diapers and formula should be provided by the parents. Operating hours are from 7:30 A.M. to 5:30 A.M. Telephone for advance reservations: 303/925-1548.

Much more convenient facilities are available for children old enough to be enrolled in either ski school or in The Powder Pandas at Buttermilk Mountain, which operates from 8:30 A.M. through 4:00 P.M. and accepts children aged three to five. Lunch and specialized ski instruction are provided for all ability levels.

Aspen Highlands', Snowpuppies Ski School accepts students aged three through six. Classes begin at 9:30 A.M. and continue until 3:30 P.M. each day.

Snowbunnies Ski School and Nursery at Snowmass has two programs. One program is basically day care for children aged eighteen months through three years. The second program, designed for youngsters three through six, includes skiing.

Recognizing that existing day care facilities are limited, Aspen Skiing Company has announced plans to establish a day care center in the newly remodeled Timbermill Restaurant, located at the west end of the Village Mall in Snowmass. This facility will accommodate children eighteen months through three years. Tentatively, the program is being called The Snow Cubs. For more information, telephone (303) 925-4444.

Baby sitters are available in Aspen by telephoning the Aspen Resort Association at (303) 925-1940 or the Snowmass Resort Association at (303) 923-2000.

Medical Facilities

Injuries which occur on the slopes are treated on an emergency basis by the ski patrol. Broken bones are immobilized and trauma is contained. Once emergency treatment has been rendered and the patient has been stabilized, the injured is transported to the Aspen Valley Hospital for specialized care as needed.

The Aspen Valley Hospital is a full-service hospital with all the equipment and expertise one expects of a large city hospital. Services offered include:

Emergency Department Ambulance
Obstetrics
Coronary and ICU
Physical/Rehabilitative Therapy
Radiology
Cardiac Stress Testing
Mammography
Clinical and Pathology Lab
Outpatient Surgery
Respiratory Therapy
Pharmacy

The hospital staff's credentials are impressive. Many staff members received their training at some of the most prestigious institutions in America such as Johns Hopkins, Columbia, Yale, UCLA, Cornell, NYU, and Harvard.

Cross-Country Skiing

Track skiing is available through the Ute Nordic Center on the Aspen Championship Golf Course, located on Highway 82 near Sardy Field. Lessons and tours are available. A retail shop on the premises has complete lines of clothing and cross-country ski equipment. Rental equipment is also available for the three-pin skier.

The largest cross-country ski company is Ashcroft Ski Touring, located twelve miles west of town along Castle Creek. Ashcroft has thirty kilometers of groomed double tracks offering spectacular views of the Maroon Bells and the White River National Forest. Huts, stocked with firewood and hot drinks, are placed along the trails for skiers' convenience. Ashcroft offers all levels of instruction and provides guides for longer tours which can last up to several days.

Each evening at 4:30, groups enter the trailhead from Ashcroft's parking lot headed for dinner and night skiing at the Pine Creek Cook House. Participants are provided with miners' head lamps to light the way which is not usually necessary if a full moon is out. Non-skiers can visit the Cook House by sleigh. Telephone (303) 925-1971 for additional information or to make reservations for specific trips.

Back-country skiing has received a great deal of bad press in recent years due to deaths caused by avalanches. The early 1987-88 season saw a great deal of avalanche activity. The back-country skier should be aware of potential dangers **before** embarking on such a journey, **always** wear a beeper and know how to use it, **never** travel alone, and use a competent guide familiar with the area to be traversed.

There are few feelings as exhilarating as being away from everybody and in the wild for several days. Many people recognize the joys of this activity and reserve such trips several months ahead.

Advance reservations to use the hut system are essential, in order for skiers to avoid being stranded on the mountain at night without shelter. However, once a reservation is made, it cannot be readily rescheduled. Therefore, many skiers find themselves in the unenviable position of forfeiting their deposits and their cross-country experience if avalanche danger prevents them from leaving at their reserved time. Unfortunately, people have been known to put pressure on guides to go out during marginal conditions and, as a result, deaths due to avalanches have occurred. Please use good judgment and if the conditions are not right, reschedule at the earliest possible date, even if it is not until the following year.

Special Events

The single biggest event each year at Aspen/Snowmass is the Wintersköl celebration, or Festival of Snow. Each January for five days events such as the canine fashion show, beauty pageants, pancake breakfasts, ice sculpting, freestyle contests, recreational ski races, bartenders drink contest, avalanche awareness presentation, live concerts, ice hockey, hot air balloon races, telemark bump contest, sky diving demonstrations are scheduled all day and late into the evenings. There is even a chili shootout on the Snowmass Mall and a terrific fireworks display accompanied by music on a local radio station. As if this were not enough, celebrations generally include one or more races on the Pro Ski Tour, USSA races, Coca-Cola Challenge, NASTAR finals, and Golf on Skis Weathermen's Cup.

Accommodations

Aspen has a greater variety of accommodations to fit visitors' tastes and pocketbooks than perhaps any other ski resort in the country. The Aspen experience offers visitors two completely different choices in local ambience—Aspen's up-beat, small-town chic, or Snowmass' ski in/ski out convenience.

Hotels

Although it is always difficult to pick the best of anything, the Hotel Lenado must rank as one of the finest hotels, not only in Aspen, but at any ski resort. Located at 200 S. Aspen Street, it is convenient to Aspen Mountain and the free shuttle bus which transports guests to Buttermilk, Aspen Highlands, and Snowmass.

The Lenado's architecture makes it unique. In fact, the hotel received the prestigious American Institute of Architects Award in 1984.

Visitors should enter the multi-story lobby and simply "absorb" the space. Large windows overlooking Ajax are framed by angled staircases on either side. Visitors are immediately struck by the towering fireplace, constructed from concrete with rough texture and vertical lines. The masculine aesthetics of the fireplace are gracefully softened by the liberal use of such fine, soft woods as apple, birch, cherry, pine, hickory, ironwood, and willow. Guests are so taken in by the ambience that they hardly notice the dark, black wood floors or the fact there is not a picture to be found anywhere in the hotel. The hotel is the artwork; nothing else is needed to decorate it.

The reading room off the lobby is amply stocked with newspapers, magazines, and books. In another corner is the lounge finished in soft woods. Markam's is an adult bar—quiet, elegant, and comfortable. The breakfast room across from the lobby is sunny and bright and affords visitors a view of the mountains and street scene. In total, the atmosphere is comforting, enabling guests to prepare mentally for tackling the slopes of Ajax. It is quite obvious why this hotel is the recipient of the prestigious Mobil 4-Star Award.

The same care and attention given the lobby and other public rooms is most evident in the guest rooms. Windows are fitted with naturally finished shutters; the beds are constructed locally from native willow. The headboards and footboards are made from thin apple limbs twisted into an architectural form. Each unique bed is covered with a beautiful feather duvet. Wood-burning fireplaces are perfect for casting a warm glow in the room, and built-in Jacuzzi tubs provide a "finishing touch" to guests' relaxing evenings.

Another unique feature which separates The Hotel Lenado from run-of-the-mill hotels is the placement of boot and glove warmers in the lobby. Imagine getting into warm boots and gloves first thing each morning!

During the 1988-89 season, rates will begin at $170 per night and peak at $350 per night for one of the parlor suites.

Sardy House, a gracious turn-of-the-century hotel with only fifteen rooms and five suites, consists of two homes that were combined and rebuilt into a hotel. Each room, some of which are referred to as "carriage houses," not only contains cherry wood Victorian furnishings, but also other distinctive amenities. For example, one carriage house only a few steps from the heated outdoor pool contains a huge feather bed, complete stereo, color TV with HBO, a VCR, Jacuzzi, and heated towel racks.

Upon entering Sardy House, guests would feel as if they were entering someone's living room were it not for the registration table opposite the front door. The Carriage House restaurant, renowned in Aspen, is small; therefore, dinner reservations are necessary. An intimate bar behind the restaurant will remind you of an old English pub. Seating is also limited, but Aspen visitors should certainly make a point of visiting the Sardy Bar. Only the conversation affirms that guests are in a ski resort.

During the 1988-89 regular season rates will vary from a low of $185 per night for Room Five in the Main House which contains a queen bed and an antique bath, to $395 per night for the O.J. Wheeler Suite which contains two bedrooms, whirlpool bath, steam shower, stereo, VCR, and bar.

Those who have visited Aspen in the past are certainly aware of the Hotel Jerome, established in 1889. Renovations made during 1987 have restored the Belle of the Roaring Fork Valley to her former self, no doubt with many improvements original designers never even considered.

Having spent a total of $22 million on its ninety-five rooms, its public areas, and its ballroom, a Victorian "gem" has emerged with a mixture of old and new skillfully woven together. The outdoor, heated swimming pool and spa continually plume steam into the cold Aspen night air while guests and visitors mingle in the spacious public areas. The Silver Queen dining room, elegant and comfortable, provides a welcome respite from the day's activities. A private dining room can be reserved for larger parties.

Jacob's Corner, a tastefully furnished and comfortable restaurant located off the pool promenade, is open for breakfast and lunch. For special functions, the Jerome will make available the Antler Bar. Hotel Jerome remains the in-place for après-ski and before dinner cocktails.

Rooms at the Hotel Jerome during the 1988-89 season will start at $135 and peak at $295 per night.

Those who do not want to spend upwards of $200 per night for lodging should try the recently restored Independence Square Hotel. Situated on the Aspen Mall at 404 South Galena Street, the Independence offers a convenient location with modern, tastefully decorated rooms.

Comprising only twenty-eight rooms, the hotel is a recent renovation incorporating the most-often requested amenities including cable TV, wet bar/refrigerator, queen-size beds, and individual ski lockers. Nightly turn-down service is available by requesting it from the concierge. Although the rooms are small, available space has been put to good use. For example, the queen size beds, modern versions of the old Murphy bed, fold into the wall during the day. Even most of the cabinetwork, such as dressers, is built-in to conserve space. A Jacuzzi on the hotel's roof affords bathers spectacular views of Aspen Mountain and the town of Aspen.

The Independence Square Hotel during the 1988-89 season is advertising rates ranging from $95 to $225 per night.

For skiers whose fancy runs to the more traditional lodging facilities, there are numerous hotels in town that are small, family-owned facilities, such as the Innsbruck Inn located at 233 W. Main Street. Convenient to a shuttle bus stop, it is owned and operated by Karen and Heinz Coordes. The rooms are small and somewhat spartan, but are clean and convenient to everything Aspen has to offer. The room rate at the Innsbruck includes Continental breakfast served in the upstairs lounge. Furnished in a Swiss/Austrian style complete with Bauernsthle seating and potted geraniums, the lounge is typical of Europe's famous bed and breakfast establishments.

The Innsbruck also features a small outdoor, heated pool and whirlpool. A sauna is located in the basement.

Rates at the Innsbruck will begin at $70 per night during the 1988-89 ski season.

Another great value in lodging is found at the downtown Limelite Lodge. Clean, large rooms with queen-size beds and down comforters are the norm. Cable TV, complimentary breakfast, and use of an outdoor heated pool is included in the base price of $58 per night, making the Limelite quite a good value.

Condominiums

One of the most distinctive rental properties in Aspen has to be the Brand Building. Situated in mid-town at Galena and Hopkins where "the action" is, the Brand Building is an extensive renovation of a turn-of-the-century building. It is divided into eight one and two bedroom apartments, each unique unto itself.

The largest apartment, the Silver Queen, consists of 2,000 square feet of living space. It is very contemporary in design and is furnished with large, colorful abstract paintings and white pickled woodwork. The upstairs bathroom features a gas fireplace and marble bath complete with a French shower! Although the kitchen is small, it is adequate and includes all the GE appliances one could desire. Should arriving guests have any special bedding requirements, such as size of the beds, the on-site management will be pleased to accommodate the visitor's needs. During the 1988-89 ski season, this apartment will rent from a low of $565 per night to a high during the Christmas Holidays of $1,575 per night.

The Durant is a very contemporary and masculine apartment. Furnished in stark white, the bedroom is cantilevered over the entry and is accessible by a spiral staircase. An electrically-controlled canopy opens to the roof, affording guests a 360° view of Aspen Mountain and Red Mountain. A hot tub and gas grill are on the roof. The Durant rented between $265 and $700 per night during the 1987-88 ski season.

The Cascade apartment is as feminine in motif as the Durant is masculine. Furnished in a traditional style bordering on Victorian, the Cascade is all ruffles and flowers. During 1987-88, it rented for between $265 and $575 per night.

All apartments at the Brand Building feature both private hot tubs and gas grills on the roof. They also come complete with 36 channels of cable TV and two-line telephones. Each apartment is complemented with objets d'art particularly suited to it.

The basement, completely outfitted as a luxury spa, offers free weights, Universal Gym, steam showers, a shallow therapy pool, and is enhanced by a a motor-driven roof canopy. On the way to the spa, the guest is immediately intrigued by the artwork on the wall. At first, it is difficult to identify the subject. However, upon closer examination, one discerns that the artist was inspired by the existing art of the New Mexico Indians. Starting with an old wall, the artist composed an entire painting to decorate it. When it came time to paint the scene, the artist only painted portions of the picture, thus creating a painting that is a faithful representation of ancient Indian paintings which have partially deteriorated due to age and weather. The artistry offers an excellent commentary on the old 1890 Brand Building.

Located just south of town are the Aspen Club Condominiums. Constructed primarily of gray barnboard, they resemble button mushrooms. Highlighted with native stone, they blend in well with the ubiquitous aspen and birch trees.

Available in two, three, and four bedroom configurations, these family units carpeted in dark green wool and trimmed in mahogany, offer spectacular accommodations. A moss-rock fireplace in the living room adds cordiality to the room, and a second fireplace graces the master bath. A glass dining room table seats eight, and the small, adjacent bar is convenient for serving cocktails.

In the master bedroom, a king-size bed with a handmade patch quilt cover, walk-in closets, and an intercom assure guests that every comfort and amenity has been provided.

The kitchen offers guests the finest appliances, including a Jenn-Air range, convection and radiant double oven, as well as matching washers and dryers.

The Aspen Club, located on the same grounds as the Aspen Club Condominiums, is a 60 thousand square foot, three-level private club. The Club features a small restaurant which serves nutritious health food for diet-conscious guests, a Nautilus room, a free weights room, a room for aerobic exercise equipment, and a full-size gym for volleyball, basketball, and aerobic dancing. There are also six racquetball courts, three indoor and seven outdoor tennis courts, three squash courts, and an indoor lap pool. Dr. Julie Anthony, a founder of the Aspen Club and former sports psychologist to the Philadelphia Flyers, and other well-known fitness experts are often on hand to give seminars on health, fitness, and stress management to sports enthusiasts.

The three bedroom Aspen Club Condominiums will rent during the 1988-89 season for between $318 and $578 per night.

Visitors should not confuse the Aspen Club Condominiums with the Aspen Club Lodge. The Lodge is directly to the left of Aspen Mountain's base facility. The renovation which took place in 1985 has placed the Aspen Club Lodge on the list of nice, convenient lodges with reasonable nightly rates. An improved dining and bar area is very accessible to guests. Lodge guests are offered full access to the Aspen Club and are provided free shuttle service between the two facilities.

Many other lodging accommodations are available in Aspen. To receive a complete price list, write to the Aspen Resort Association, 303 East Main Street, Aspen, Colorado 81611, or telephone (303) 925-1940 and ask for "Aspen Resort Association Rates and Accommodations."

Restaurants

It is fair to say that Aspen's restaurants are as diverse as its lodging. There is truly something for everyone.

One of the most unique eateries anywhere has to be Boogie's. Located in downtown Aspen, Boogie's is a two-storied structure, the first floor being a chic and trendy retail clothing shop similar to an Esprit Warehouse. Elvis Presley's red Corvette dominates the decor of this floor. The upstairs restaurant, modeled after a 1950's diner, serves short-order food that is very good. Even if one does not eat here, its exciting and enjoyable atmosphere provides an environment that both teenagers and their parents find appealing. Waitresses dressed in period costumes of very short skirts, tri-cornered aprons, and caps add drama to the setting.

One of Aspen's most elegant dining rooms, the Silver Queen, is located in the Hotel Jerome on East Main Street. Soft piano music, a romantic fireplace, and superb wine selections are certain to help guests unwind. Featuring nouvelle cuisine with traditional service, the Silver Queen is designed with the diner's comfort in mind. The large floral arrangement which dominates the dining room and expensively embroidered banquettes attest to the extent owners have gone to create an ambience complementary to excellent dining.

The menu features a wide selection of appetizers including Sevruga caviar. The house spinach salad with raspberry vinaigrette and duck breast is highly recommended. All entrées are cooked to order, using only the best and freshest ingredients. The Dover sole, always a difficult dish to prepare, is truly wonderful. Although expensive, the Silver Queen's meals are worth the expense, thanks to an excellent chef.

Most people would agree that the best Oriental restaurant in Aspen is Asia, located on Main street. The only truly Oriental aspects of its ambience are the waiters, waitresses, and its red walls. Otherwise, it is a typical Aspen establishment created by joining two houses together. The restaurant features an extremely long 100 year old bar, which was originally located in Liverpool and brought to Aspen especially for Asia. The extensive bill of fare rivals that of any Chinese restaurant found anywhere, and the prices are most reasonable.

Other good restaurants include: The Ute City Banque, formally a real bank. The vault is open for inspection. Featuring an eclectic menu, the Ute City Banque typically serves dishes such as Mayan swordfish, fettucini with grilled duck, rack of lamb, and veal Val D'Ostana (sig).

The Cantina, decorated in bright Mexican colors, is a great après-ski gathering location. Only the exceptionally brave should try the 27 oz. Margarita served in a glass as large as a fish bowl.

The Parlor Car, actually a real parlor car at the base of the mountain, serves excellent meals in its unique environment. An expensive, but truly worthwhile dining experience can be had here.

The Mother Lode, an Italian restaurant and an Aspen landmark, is moderately priced and offers a superb menu selection of really good Italian cuisine.

The Golden Horn is known for its veal. Although a bit expensive, this Swiss/Austrian style restaurant is a must for Aspen visitors.

The Aspen Mine Co. is a great place to take the children. Diners get the real feeling of being in a mine at the turn of the century. Try the ribs in this moderately priced eatery.

The Crystal Palace, a dinner theatre, has long been a favorite of Aspenites. The waiters and waitresses serve guests and then provide musical entertainment after dinner. Only one seating is available at 8:00 P.M. each evening. Reservations are required.

Activities

Although Aspen's reputation as one of America's great ski areas is well deserved, it is also one of the greatest all-around winter resorts where numerous non-skiing activities are available.

The T-Lazy-7 Ranch has hundreds of snowmobiles available at reasonable rental rates. Located on Maroon Creek Road just past Aspen Highlands Ski Resort, the T-Lazy-7 is convenient to all accommodations, and its road is always clear. Rent a snowmobile and take the one and a half-hour tour to the Maroon Bells and around Maroon Lake. If snowmobiling is a new experience, the T-Lazy-7 staff will be happy to provide instructions. If one can drive a lawnmower, one can easily maneuver a snowmobile.

Take a sleigh ride through Aspen or through the surrounding countryside. Hansom cabs await customers at the Hyman Avenue Mall.

Tailwinds Aviation offers Aspen visitors scenic flights lasting just under one hour. The management will even organize special flights for photographers. The cost during the 1987-88 season was $35 per person, with a minimum requirement of two passengers.

For a more leisurely look at the mountains, try Unicorn Balloon Company. The hot-air balloons depart daily, weather permitting, from Snowmass and from an area near Aspen. The gondola accommodates up to eight persons, and each flier receives a certificate, a cloisonné pin, and a flight log. Trip durations will vary, as will destinations. Plan on three hours to complete each balloon ride. Reservations can be made by telephoning (303) 925-5752.

Aspen offers more than twenty art galleries. The Aspen Fine Art Dealers' Association publishes a brochure and map showing each member's location. These brochures are available in most hotel lobbies or from the Aspen Resort Association.

Indoor ice skating is available at the Ice Garden located at Hyman and Second Street.

Services

A full complement of sporting goods stores, apparel stores, pharmacies, grocery stores, liquor stores, furniture, bath shops, and specialty stores are all within Aspen proper. In addition, there are antique shops, massage services, bakeries, hair salons, book stores, florists, an historical society, movies, the Aspen Little Theatre, banks, churches, dry cleaning, optical services, and baby sitting.

ASPEN HIGHLANDS

Post Office Box T
Aspen, Colorado 81612

(800) 262-7736 Reservations
(303) 925-5300 Information
(303) 925-5300 Snow Report

Transportation

Aspen is one of the easiest major ski resorts in the world to reach. Driving to Aspen from the East is as simple as hopping onto Interstate 70 and turning left on Colorado Highway 82. The distance from Denver is 200 miles and although weather can be a factor, the completion of the Eisenhower Memorial Tunnel several years ago relieved most of the apprehension associated with this drive.

Skiers from the North and from the South can easily drive to Aspen by taking I-25 to Denver and exiting onto I-70. Visitors from the West can pick up I-70 in Utah.

It is also convenient to travel to Aspen by air. United Airlines and Continental Airlines offer quick and convenient service from Denver's Stapleton Airport to Aspen's Sardy Field. Sardy is an FAA controlled airport and instrument landings are possible. Thus, it is necessary to bus passengers from Denver only during the worst storms.

Denver recently has made great strides in cleaning up Stapleton's image as an inefficient airport with mass delays and inconvenient airline transfers. A new wing served primarily by United Airlines was completed in 1987, and renovation of Continental's annex was well along as this book was going to press. A separate extension built to accommodate airline shuttle services is comfortable and clean. Although this extension is located at the far end of the terminal, in-bound Denver flights are met at arrival gates by hosts or hostesses who quickly assist transferring resort-bound passengers onto buses which take skiers directly to the shuttle wing. Baggage is efficiently handled and usually is on the same flight as the passenger. Even if the scheduled air shuttle flight is missed, the skiers can usually take another of the many daily Denver-Aspen flights.

During the 1987-88 ski season, several direct flights from Denver to Aspen were available. Check with your travel agent or call Aspen to confirm flight schedules for subsequent seasons. During 1987-88, direct flights were offered from Chicago, Dallas, Los Angeles, Long Beach, and San Francisco. These flights were offered during the peak season commencing December 17 and continuing through March 28. It is anticipated that a similar schedule will be maintained each year.

The town of Aspen is located only a few miles from Sardy Field and is accessible by taxi (High Mountain), limousine, and courtesy van.

Most major car rental agencies are located at Sardy Field. They provide *skierized* cars equipped with snow tires and ski racks. For a slightly higher price, many rental agencies will provide four-wheel drive vehicles. Travelers are cautioned to reserve these vehicles far in advance of arrival because demand for them is great.

Having a car at Aspen is not necessary and may not even be desirable because the local transportation system is so good. Free shuttle buses run daily between Aspen, Aspen Mountain, Aspen Highlands, Snowmass, and Buttermilk.

Buses that go to Aspen Highlands are not the same buses that shuttle between Aspen Mountain, Buttermilk, and Snowmass. The Highlands has its own shuttle system which departs daily from Aspen's Ruby Park every 15 minutes from 8:15 A.M. to 11:00 A.M. These buses stop along Main Street en route. The return to Aspen in the evening commences at 3:00 P.M. and continues until 5:15 P.M. Transportation to and from Snowmass is provided every Tuesday and Thursday.

MOUNTAIN STATISTICS

Aspen Highlands is a large mountain nestled between Aspen Mountain on its east side and Buttermilk on its west side. As old as Aspen Highlands is, it has always been overshadowed and outspent by Aspen Skiing Company. Consequently, Aspen Highlands has evolved into a totally different area. There is little of the glitz, glamour, or ambience of Aspen Mountain or Snowmass here. Rather, this area is reminiscent of a past when skiing was a little more primitive and skiers were a little more in touch with nature. To ski Aspen Highlands is similar to skiing at Stowe, Vermont. While the physical facilities are somewhat dated, the runs and trails on this mountain have the patina of time etched into them. This is the mountain where the locals ski because it is rarely as crowded as the other three ski areas, and the prices are slightly lower.

Aspen Highlands Mountain is different from other mountains in the area in that its beginner, intermediate, and expert trails run all over the mountain: they are not confined to one or two specific areas. However, the concentration of expert runs is at mountaintop. This is a mountain that one rarely skis all the way down until the end of the day. The center section, primarily beginner and intermediate terrain, is serviced by four chairlifts.

Located in the White River National Forest, Aspen Highlands consists of 500 skiable acres (202 ha) and has over 21 miles (33 km) of skiable terrain. Of these trails, 23% are rated beginner, 48% are rated intermediate, while 29% are rated expert. Of the expert terrain, 14% are double black diamonds. Intermediate terrain is referred to on the trail map as "more difficult" and is identified on the mountain by a blue square. The black diamond shape denotes "expert." In recent years, most resorts have also added the category of double black diamond. This designation identifies runs that are either extremely steep, gladed, moguled, or all of the above. Skiers attempting to ski a double black diamond run should possess enough skill to turn their skis within the length of the skis and to ski in any conditions from deep powder to crud. "Crud" is deep snow that has been skied on for several days without grooming and which has melted during the day and refrozen during the evening.

The base elevation of Aspen Highlands is 8,000 feet (2,439 meters) and its summit is 11,800 feet (3,597 meters). This provides the skier with 3,800 vertical feet (1,158 meters) of skiing. Aspen Highlands offers the most vertical feet of skiing in Colorado.

Aspen Highlands is served by:

9 Double Chairlifts
2 Poma Lifts

The uphill lift capacity at Aspen Highlands is 10,000 skiers per hour. The number of skiable acres divided by the maximum number of skiers transported per hour is .050. When all lifts at the Highlands are full, the mountain is very crowded. Fortunately, this situation does not occur often. The most crowded time of the year, of course, is the period between Christmas and New Year's. It also tends to become crowded during the universities' spring break.

Aspen Highlands receives an annual snowfall of about 300 inches (762 cm). Its average monthly snowfall is:

Nov.	15"	(38 cm)
Dec.	51"	(130 cm)
Jan.	43"	(109 cm)
Feb.	43"	(109 cm)
Mar.	59"	(150 cm)
Apl.	25"	(64 cm)

The average daily temperatures in the town of Aspen during the season are:

Nov.	31°	0°C
Dec.	22°	-5°C
Jan.	20°	-6°C
Feb.	23°	-5°C
Mar.	29°	-2°C
Apl.	39°	4°C

Snowmaking capabilities at Aspen Highlands are limited to 40 acres (16 ha). Most of the snowmaking is on the beginner runs and at the bases of the most popular lifts. Snowmaking throughout the Aspen area is limited due to restrictions on the use of water. Fortunately, the area is blessed with abundant natural snowfall and the only time man-made snow is needed is early in the season.

The longest beginner run at the Highlands is Nugget to Park Avenue. It is approximately two miles (3.2 km). Most of this run is a catwalk, and it is the most popular way down the mountain in the evening. The longest intermediate run is Golden Horn to Thunderbowl, approximately two miles (3.2 km). Golden Horn and Thunderbowl are terrific cruising runs. Always groomed and wide open, they rival the Big Burn at Snowmass. These are the runs one takes to work on technique or just to get the feeling back into his legs after a summer's lay off from skiing.

The longest expert run is Moment of Truth. It is nearly one mile (1.6 km) long and is a double black diamond.

The natural terrain of the mountain lends itself to many double and triple fall lines. Very few of the trails go straight down the face of the mountain, but tend to be alongside the mountain's ridge, particularly near the top. The expert skiing terrain at Highlands is among the best in the country. The newly opened Steeplechase on the east upper part of the mountain is steep and gladed. Try this area after a big snowfall and learn why everyone raves about tree skiing. On the other side of Aspen Highlands Mountain is Olympic Bowl–not so much a bowl as open, steep runs. Some of the runs in "Oly" bowl are gladed, but not enough to intimidate competent skiers. Many of the runs in Oly are intermediate and are among the best on the mountain. These include Olympic Glades, Pyramid Park, and Grand Prix. For intermediates who love to ski bumps there is Scarlett's Run. Formally known as Flora Dora, this run is short and adds new meaning to the term, "ski the bumps." This is the site of the annual bump ski contest which is a real challenge. Begining skiers will feel at home on Apple Strudel and Red Onion. More advanced skiers should avoid these runs because they are frequently crowded with classes.

Any skiers who have a fear of heights are advised to avoid taking the Loges Peak lift. Just before skiers exit this chairlift, it passes over a ravine that is 800 feet (244 meters) deep! Naturally, it's not as frightening on a snowy day as it is on a bright sunlit day.

Expert skiers who are not sure of their ability to ski double black diamonds should consider skiing The Wall. This is a short steep run and somewhat typical of most double black diamonds. If skiers can negotiate The Wall without trouble and enjoy the experience, they will no doubt enjoy the other double blacks here and at other resorts, as well. It is also a good idea to try the run when there is good snow because one rarely is injured by falling into soft, deep snow.

Lift Ticket Prices *(1987-88)*

$ 22 Adults Half Day (A.M. or P.M.)
$ 30 All Day
$ 50 2 of 3 Consecutive Days
$ 66 3 of 7 Consecutive Days
$100 5 of 7 Consecutive Days

Lift ticket prices for children twelve and under and for adults sixty-five and over:

$16 All Day
$32 2 of 3 Consecutive Days
$42 3 of 7 Consecutive Days
$60 5 of 7 Consecutive Days
Free 70 years and older

In addition to offering its own lift ticket prices, Aspen Highlands cooperates with Aspen Skiing Company and is included in the four-mountain coupon book program. Under this plan there are two seasons: Value and Regular. Four-mountain coupon book prices during the 1987-88 season were priced as follows:

$174 6 of 7 Day Value Season
$186 6 of 7 Day Regular Season
$128 4 0f 5 Day All Seasons

Families who want to ski only the Highlands will appreciate the fixed family plan rate. Two skiing parents and all their children 18 and under can ski for one price. Total cost for:

1 day	$ 72
2 days	$132
3 days	$174
4 days	$260

The family plan makes skiing affordable for most families. For example, a skiing family of five skiing for four days would have an individual lift ticket price of only $10.40.

Hours of Operation

9:00 A.M. to 4:00 P.M.

Lift Ticket Purchase Locations

Lift tickets are available at the base area just off the parking lot. In addition, four area passes may be purchased at any Aspen Mountain, Buttermilk, or Snowmass ticket window.

Crowd Control

During busy days, most crowds seem to congregate at the Cloud 9 and the Exhibition II lifts. To avoid lift lines and still enjoy the same runs, try the Grand Prix poma lift. It runs parallel to the Exhibition lift. The Loges Peak lift is not usually as crowed as some of the other lifts, and it is convenient to ski the intermediate and expert runs near the top of the mountain from here. The Thunderbowl lift also is frequently not crowded, and skiing is great in this area. However, it is low on the mountain so snow conditions are usually not as good as they are farther uphill.

In the late afternoon, the most crowded runs are Park Avenue and Golden Barrel. Avoid these high traffic areas by returning to the base via Golden Horn, Thunderbowl, or Upper Jerome Bowl. If snow conditions are good, the expert skier should return by skiing Lowerstein–it's a great way to finish the day!

Ski School

The Aspen Highlands Ski School employs sixty full-time instructors and another fifteen during peak periods. It teaches a modified American Teaching System (ATS), formerly known as the American Teaching Method (ATM). Instructors also teach Graduated Length Method (GLM). The GLM system has fallen into disrepute of late and is no longer offered at most resorts. However, the instructors at Highlands believe there is a place for it in their teaching programs, so they employ GLM for a brief time with rank beginners.

Ski classes meet daily at the base facility, close to the bell. Classes run from 10:15 A.M. through 3:30 P.M. daily. However, classes of fewer than four students end at 1:00 P.M.

Group lesson rates follow:

$ 23......Half Day
$ 32......One Day
$ 50......Two Days
$ 75......Three Days
$110......Five Days

A special "Learn To Ski" Package is available and includes lessons, lift tickets, and rental equipment.

$170......Three Days, Adult
$147......Three Days, Child
$210......Five Days, Adult
$187......Five Days, Child

Private lessons are $50 per person per hour in groups of one to three and $60 per person in groups of four to six. Private instructors charges $220 per person all day for groups of one to three students and $250 per person for groups of four to six.

Aspen Highlands also conducts special classes designed for skiers who want to learn a particular skill, such as telemark, snowboard, and mono-ski. Additionally, it organizes clinics for racing, for powder hounds, and a special clinic just for ladies which includes a picnic lunch and video critique.

Equipment Rental

Two equipment rental shops are available at Aspen Highlands. Their 1987-88 rental rates were:

$12 One Day
$33 Three Days
$50 Five/Six Days

Equipment provided included Head skis, Raichle-Molitor boots, Tyrolia bindings and poles. Additionally, numerous rental shops are located in the town of Aspen and at Snowmass.

Ski Tuning and Repair

Tuning and repair is available at the base area from either of the two shops. 1987-88 rates were:

$ 5 Hot Wax
$18 Flat File & Wax
$25 Complete Tune-up
$25+ P-tex

For a complete explanation of the benefits of state-of-the-art ski tuning, refer to the *Ski Tuning and Repair* section of the review of *Killington*. A list of additional shops in the area is found in the section entitled *Aspen*.

Mountain Restaurants

Two mountain restaurants and a restaurant at the base comprise the Highlands' food service. The largest mountain restaurant is the Merry-Go-Round, situated at the top of the Exhibition II lift and at the base of the Cloud 9 lift. This restaurant serves typical cafeteria-style food. The Cloud 9 Restaurant, located at the top of the Cloud 9 lift, is smaller but the food is similar to the Merry-Go-Round's. However, this restaurant has something no other mountain restaurant has: ski patrol members jump over its outdoor deck daily at noon. Thrill to the patrolmen's antics as they soar over the restaurant's 65-foot long deck! For a bird's eye view, try to catch a ride up the Olympic lift while they are performing; they will appear to almost land in your lap!

Day Care

See the chapter on *Day Care* in the section of this book dealing with Aspen. There are no day care facilities located at Aspen Highlands.

For children who ski but who are not in day care, the Aspen Highlands "Snowpuppies" is available. This program is for children aged three and one-half to six. The all day classes include lessons, lift tickets, and lunch. During the 1987-88 season, enrollment in the Snowpuppies was $45 per day or $195 for five days.

Cross-Country

There are no cross-country tracks at Aspen Highlands. See the chapters dealing with this subject in the *Aspen* and *Snowmass* sections of this book.

Special Events

As mentioned previously, the ski patrol's deck jump at the Cloud 9 Restaurant is unique to the Highlands and is held daily, weather permitting. Every Friday at noon skiers can watch a free-style exhibition on Scarlett's Run. It is easy to view this incredible event from the Merry-Go-Round Restaurant.

For additional information regarding special events, see the chapter entitled *Special Events* in the section dealing with Aspen.

Accommodations

See *Aspen* and *Snowmass*.

Restaurants

See *Aspen*.

Activities

See *Aspen*.

Services

See *Aspen*.

BRECKENRIDGE SKI AREA

Breckenridge Ski Area
Box 1058
Breckenridge, CO. 80424

(303) 453-2918 Reservations
(303) 453-2368 Information
(303) 453-6118 Snow Report

Transportation

Breckenridge is served by all major airlines through Denver's Stapleton International Airport.

All major car rental agencies are represented at Stapleton. At the airport proper, visitors will find:

Avis
Budget
Dollar
Hertz
National

Other car rental agencies are located outside airport property and offer free airport pickup and drop-off; among them are:

Alamo
Enterprise
AI
Thrifty

Breckenridge is 85 miles from Stapleton and a two hour drive in clear weather with dry roads. From Denver, take I-70 west to the Frisco exit at Highway 9. Follow Highway 9 until it becomes Main St. in Breckenridge.

All rental agencies provide their clients with free maps. Due to possible road restrictions, the traveler to Breckenridge is advised to always rent a car that is *skierized*, i.e. equipped with snow tires and ski racks. For a slightly higher price, many rental agencies can provide four-wheel drive vehicles. The traveler is cautioned to reserve these vehicles far in advance, because the demand for them is great.

Several companies offer shuttle service to Breckenridge from Denver's Stapleton Airport. One of the most reliable services is Schuss Transportation. Round-trip fare during the 1987-88 season was $43. Reservations are required and can be made by telephoning (800) 999-1967. All major credit cards are accepted.

Once the skier reaches Breckenridge, the mountain and most accommodations are within walking distance. Additionally, free shuttle transportation to the mountain's two base areas is offered. Transportation is either by the Breckenridge Free Shuttle, owned and operated by the Breckenridge Ski Area, or the Free Town Trolley, which is owned and operated by the town of Breckenridge. The Free

Shuttle operates from 8:00 A.M. to 5:30 P.M., and the Free Trolley operates from 10:00 A.M. to 11:00 P.M. Free schedules are available at all lodging accommodations and from the Chamber of Commerce. For more information, telephone (303) 453-2368, Ext. 272.

The Summit Stage also operates a free shuttle service throughout Summit County which encompasses Breckenridge, Copper Mountain, Keystone ski areas and the towns of Breckenridge, Dillon, Frisco, and Silverthorne. For more information on the Summit Stage, telephone (303) 668-0715.

Mountain Statistics

Aspen Skiing Company, the parent company of Breckenridge Ski Area, has spent millions of dollars in the last few years improving the resort's mountains, facilities, and equipment. Because of its foresight, Breckenridge has grown tremendously. Not only has Aspen Skiing Company increased the amount of skiable acreage, but it also has improved the immense intermediate terrain by widening numerous runs, expanding snowmaking capabilities, and purchasing additional grooming equipment.

Breckenridge is a large resort; there are more than 1,480 skiable acres (599 ha), consisting of 107 trails. Twenty-three percent of the trails are classified as "easiest" (beginner), 28% as "more difficult" (intermediate), and 49% as "most difficult" (expert). It is easy to understand how skiers of all ability levels can enjoy Breckenridge for more than a week.

The longest run is from the top of Peak 8 to the village at the base of the mountain. It is a beginner run named Four O'Clock and is 3 miles (4.8 km) long. Centennial and Crystal are the longest intermediate runs, each at 1.3 miles (2 km). The longest expert run is Cimarron at two-thirds of a mile (894 meters).

Three mountains comprise Breckenridge Ski Area: Peak 8, Peak 9, and Peak 10. From a base of 9,600 feet (2,926 meters) to a summit of 12,213 feet (3,723 meters), there are 2,613 vertical feet (796 meters) of wonderful skiing. All the mountains are interconnected by fifteen lifts which include three Quads, one Triple Chairlift, nine Double Chairlifts, and two Surface Lifts and give the resort an uphill lift capacity of 22,650 skiers per hour. The total skiable terrain divided by the uphill lift capacity is .065. This is a relatively high number, and indeed, Breckenridge can become crowded.

One of the joys of Breckenridge is the ability one has to move around the three mountains. This mobility assures intermediate and expert skiers of uncrowded slopes and fresh snow. However, it takes some time to learn how to use the lift system to best advantage. The ideal place to begin the day is at Peak 8. This base area is less congested than Peak 9, and it provides the most diverse runs of all three peaks.

Ride The Colorado Superchair first thing in the morning and ski to the #6 Lift. From the top of this lift, numerous choices for skiing are offered. Experts will want to test the Contest and Horseshoe Bowls; intermediates will enjoy taking Four O'Clock to Columbine. The next runs along the T-bar's Pika, Ptarmigan, White Crown, or Forget-Me-Not are short and can all be skied in just an hour or two. After skiing these runs, the morning can be finished off by skiing to the bottom of The Colorado lift via Duke's Run, Northstar, or High Anxiety, Boreas, or Little Johnny.

After skiing the top of Peak 8, it will be time to journey to Peak 9. From the top of The Colorado SuperChair, experts will relish any of the double black diamond runs which lead to the C-Lift. Runs with names like Mach 1, Goodbye Girl, Tiger, and Southern Cross offer challenging terrain. Intermediates will enjoy Frosty's. From the C-Lift's terminus, acres and acres of intermediate terrain are accessible. Super runs such as Upper Lehman, Cashier, Bonanza, and Peerless are long, wide, and groomed nightly. Experts will enjoy the North Face of Peak 9 where all the runs are double black diamonds. Similar to the back bowls along the #6-Lift, these are gladed runs whose northern exposure insures the snow will always be good. These glades are especially nice on spring afternoons when conditions on the less sheltered runs begin to deteriorate.

After spending some time on Peak 9, move to Breckenridge's newest mountain, Peak 10. Centennial is Summit County's equivalent of Snowmass's Big Burn: a wide, groomed, cruising run. Test your stamina by trying to ski top to bottom without stopping. Experts should concentrate on The Burn. Steep, moguled, and gladed, the Burn is only open late in the ski season when the snows have accumulated enough to cover fallen trees that litter the area. If there is not enough snow, ski Cimarron, Mustang, Spitfire, or Corsair.

With the exception of the double black diamond areas, the single black diamond runs are generally not beyond the ability of moderately strong intermediates. Of course, conditions do change a trail's particular characteristics and this should be taken into account before attempting a new run for the first time.

Individuals skiing for the first few times will find a great deal of beginner trails on the face of Peak 9. Long runs on which to practice skills learned in lessons include C Transfer, Red Rover, and Lehman.

Breckenridge's abundant snowfall totals over 320" (813 cm) annually. The monthly totals over the last several years have averaged:

Nov.	36"	(91 cm)
Dec.	31"	(79 cm)
Jan.	32"	(81 cm)
Feb.	45"	(114 cm)
Mar.	58"	(147 cm)
Apl.	54"	(137 cm)

Average mid-mountain high temperatures are:

Nov.	26°	-3°C
Dec.	21°	-6°C
Jan.	21°	-6°C
Feb.	23°	-5°C
Mar.	29°	-2°C
Apl.	34°	1°C

Lift Ticket Prices

Lift ticket prices during the 1987-88 season were:

$ 30......Adult, All Day
$ 56......Adult, 2 of 3 Days
$ 78......Adult, 3 of 4 Days
$100......Adult, 4 of 5 Days
$115......Adult, 5 of 6 Days
$126......Adult, 6 of 7 Days
$ 23......Adult, Half Day P.M. Only
$ 13......Child, All Day
$ 26......Child, 2 of 3 Days
$ 39......Child, 3 of 4 Days

$ 52......Child, 4 of 5 Days
$ 65......Child, 5 of 6 Days
$ 78......Child, 6 of 7 Days
$ 9......Child, Half Day P.M. Only

A child is anyone under the age of 13. Seniors aged 59 - 69 ski for the same price as children. Persons over 70 ski free.

Discounting of lift tickets for the entire Summit area is rampant. Each area has made its own arrangements with retailers in the county and along the front range. These tickets are sold at a discount to each of the merchants who will resell them. The prices for the discounted tickets will vary from one location to another, and it is possible to shop around for the best rate. During the 1987-88 season, Albertson's, Safeway, and Breeze Ski Rentals sold Breckenridge Ski Area lift tickets for $21 per day.

"Ski the Summit" passes may be purchased at any Breckenridge ski ticket location. Summit passes are good at Keystone, Copper, Arapahoe Basin, and Breckenridge. Prices for these passes during 1987-88 were:

$104.......Adult, 4 Day
$156.......Adult, 6 Day
$ 52.......Child, 4 Day
$ 78.......Child, 6 Day

Hours of Operation

9:00 A.M. to 3:45 P.M. daily

Lift Ticket Purchase Locations

Lift tickets may be purchased at the base of Peaks 8 and 9 or at the base of the D-Lift at Beaver Run Resort.

Crowd Control

Because Breckenridge receives so many guests each year, crowd control is a real concern. Peak 9 is the most crowded of all the mountains. No doubt this is because it has the most beginner and intermediate runs of the three mountains and also, because it is the mountain that exits directly into the town of Breckenridge. The best way to avoid crowds is to ski Peaks 8 and 10. Avoid the SuperChairs, because they will be more crowded than the conventional two and three place chairs. If one has the ability to ski only expert runs, use the #6 and #4 lifts, the T-Bar, and the E-Lift as there is seldom any waiting at these areas.

In the evening, it is important to remember to return to the correct base area. It is frustrating to have to wait to catch a shuttle from Peak 9 if your car is in the lot at Peak 8. Plan ahead and pay attention to the signage. The mountains are very well marked. All signs are color coded to identify the mountain one is skiing and to give the direction of other mountains. For example, all the trail signs on Peak 8 are blue, on Peak 9 orange, and on Peak 10 yellow. One must be high enough on the mountain at 3:00 P.M. to find trails leading to other mountains, if the ultimate destination is other than the mountain being skied at the time.

Be particularly careful in the late afternoon when skiing Sawmill, Sundown, and Silverthorn. These are the main exit points used by more than 50% of the skiers, many of whom will be flying down the hill. Most injuries today are not broken legs, but are more serious in nature and frequently are caused by out of control skiers who collide with others. Be alert and pay attention to other skiers.

Ski School

The Breckenridge Ski School's 160 instructors teach the ATS (American Teaching System) method of skiing. This is a universal system of skiing that is taught at most major ski resorts in the United States. It is, therefore, possible for students to take lessons at more than one resort without having to learn a new system at each location.

Never-ever and beginning skiers meet at the Quicksilver SuperChair at the base of Peak 9, or just to the left of the Colorado SuperChair on Peak 8. Classes commence at 10:00 A.M. and 1:45 P.M. daily.

Intermediate and expert skiers meet for their lessons either at the Peak 9 Restaurant or at the Vistahaus Restaurant at the top of Peak 8.

Lessons may be arranged at any of the ski school offices, located at the base of the Quicksilver SuperChair, D-Lift, or The Colorado SuperChair adjacent to the lift ticket windows. During the 1987-88 season, lesson prices were:

$30......All Day
$21......Half Day
$50......1 Hour, Private

In addition, special lessons are offered from time to time, depending upon conditions and demand. For example, during heavy snowfall periods, lessons in powder are offered. If enough skiers want to learn how to improve their ability on the moguls, classes are arranged to fill this need.

During the 1987-88 season, the ski school offered the Descente Star Test. This program enabled skiers to receive a free critique of their ability and advice on how to improve their technique. While useful, the program was primarily a way for the ski school to solicit business from skiers who were only marginally interested in lessons.

Special instruction is also available for handicapped skiers. Breckenridge has done a commendable job of working with handicapped persons. Blind skiers can go to the "Special Arrangement" windows at the base areas and receive complimentary lift tickets for themselves and a companion. Similarly, sit skiers affiliated with the Breckenridge Outdoor Education Center (B.O.E.C.) will be given free tickets and assistance.

Equipment Rental

Numerous rental shops are found in and around Breckenridge. If skiers plan to ski during the peak season, it is advisable to reserve skis in advance as the shops rent out their supply of skis quickly during Christmas and Easter.

One of the better shops in town is the Mountain Haus, located in Centennial Square at the corner of Main and Jefferson. This shop is convenient to the Peak 9 lifts, shops, and restaurants. Mountain Haus offers four rental packages, including Junior and Senior packages, and a cross-country ski package. The basic package designed for never-ever and beginning skiers is the called the Standard. It consists of:

Rossignol or Olin Skis
Nordica Boots
Salomon Bindings
Poles

During the 1987-88 season, this package rented for $10 per day or $6 for three or more days.

The Recreational package consists of:

Rossignol or Olin Skis
Salomon SX 60 or SX 70 Boots
Salomon 337 Bindings
Poles

During the 1987-88 season, this package rented for $12 per day or $8 for three or more days.

The Sport package is an upgrade of the Recreational package. It consists of:

Rossignol 808, Pre 1200, or Völkl Targa R Skis
Salomon SX 51 Boots
Salomon 747 Bindings
Poles

During the 1987-88 season, this package rented for $15 per day or $11 for three or more days.

The top of the line package is called, High Performance. It consists of:

Rossignol 4 SK or Völkl Targa R Skies
Salomon SX 81 Boots
Salomon 747 Bindings
Poles

During the 1987-88 season, this package rented for $18 per day or $14 for three or more days.

Equipment reservations are available by telephoning the Mountain Haus (800) 843-6864.

Another major force in the equipment rental scene at Breckenridge is Pioneer Sports, located at the base of Peak 9. Pioneer, like Mountain Haus, has four levels of equipment rentals, except that its packages are called: Economy, Sport, Deluxe, and Prestige. The rental rates charged vary according to the season. Best rates are accorded during the periods of November through December 18 and early April through the end of ski season. During the 1987-88 season, the lowest rates for this period were from $7 per day for the Economy package to a high of $17 per day for the Prestige package.

Clothing rentals are also available at Pioneer. Sample rates during 1987-88, were $6 for a parka, $5 for bibs, gloves (a pair), hats, and goggles were $3 each. For reservations, telephone Pioneer at (800) 525-3688.

Ski Tuning and Repair

Tuning and repair services are available at all ski rental shops, sporting goods stores, and Pioneer Sports located at the base of Peak 9. Pioneer has stone grinding equipment which provides a superior flat ski surface compared to other common methods of tuning. Skis must be warm before waxing.

Therefore, it is a good idea to drop the skis off at the end of the day and pick them up the next morning.

Rates for tuning:

$ 5 Hot Wax
$25 Flat File
$ 7.50 (Pair) Edges Sharpened
$30 Complete Tune-up
$15 Bindings Adjusted
$20+ P-tex

The rates quoted above are approximate for the 1987-88 season. At the time of this book's publication the shop was closed and exact rates were not available. However, the above rates were current at Precision in Keystone, which has the same equipment and ownership.

Mountain Restaurants

Two mountaintop restaurants are available at Breckenridge. Both are cafeterias and table service is not offered.

The Vistahaus at the top of the Colorado SuperChair is marginally better than the Peak 9 Restaurant located at the top of the C- and E-Lifts. The usual hot and cold sandwiches are available, as well as pizza, french fries, stews, and so forth. Bar service consists of beers, wines, and spirits.

Considering the trend among resorts to offer table service and gourmet meals at noon, Breckenridge is lacking. Hopefully, the resort will see fit to remedy this situation in the near future. Meanwhile, if a quality luncheon is desired, the skier will have to try one of the restaurants located at the base of Peak 9 or in the town of Breckenridge.

Day Care

The Kinderhut Children's Center is located at the D-Lift near the Beaver Run Resort. This is a fine, clean facility that accepts children one to three in the day care program and children three to six in the children's ski school.

Children enrolled in the day care program are treated to indoor and outdoor activities. Snow play and sledding are the main outdoor attractions, while indoors, the children participate in creative painting, crafts, listening to stories and music. A quiet time, lunch and snacks were included in the 1987-88 base price of $42 per day. Children may be left for half days for $32.

The Kinderhut opens at 8:30 A.M., and parents are expected to pick up their children between 3:30 P.M. and 4:00 P.M.

Those children enrolled in the ski program may arrange for rental equipment through any of the town's rental establishments or directly from the ski school. Actual ski instruction is two hours each morning and two hours each afternoon. Lunch features children's favorite foods such as spaghetti, hot dogs, grilled cheese sandwiches, as well as the old reliable peanut butter and jelly sandwiches. The daily rate for children enrolled in the ski program is the same as for those enrolled in day care.

Younger children from two months through six years are accepted at the Breckenridge Ski Area's

Peak 8 base facility. Its rate during the 1987-88 season was $32 per day or $22 per half day. Naturally, parents of infants must supply diapers and formula for their children.

Reservations for the Kinderhut should be made by telephoning (303) 453-0379. For reservations at Peak 8, telephone (303) 453-2368.

Medical Facilities

The Breckenridge Ski Patrol will only render emergency aid for skier injuries. The patrol will administer trauma treatment, stabilize broken bones, and transport the injured skier downhill by sled to the clinic, located at the base of Peak 8 or Peak 9. The clinic, located at the base of Peak 9, is well equipped to treat ski emergencies. Should an injury or illness be more serious than the clinic can handle, arrangements will be made for ambulance transportation to the Summit County Medical Center in Frisco where the patient will be stabilized and then flown via helicopter to one of Denver's major hospitals.

For medical emergencies not related to skiing, dial 911 on the telephone for assistance. Two additional medical emergency centers in Breckenridge are: Breckenridge Medical Center at 410 French St, (telephone (303) 453-6934) and Parkway Medical Clinic at the Parkway Center, (telephone (303) 453-4336).

For eye injuries telephone (303) 453-4300. There are two dentists in town: Dr. Edgar Downs at (303) 453-4244 and Dr. John Warner at (303) 453-9615.

Cross-Country Skiing

Cross-country skiing is very popular in Breckenridge. In fact, the town may even be considered a mecca for Nordic skiing.

The Breckenridge Nordic Ski Center is located midway up Ski Hill Road, the main road to the Peak 8 parking lot. Owned and operated by Gene and Therese Dayton, the Center boasts 24 km of groomed tracks meandering through open meadows and dense woods. There are three loops: an easier loop, a more difficult loop, and a most difficult loop. From these loops, the skier experiences numerous beautiful views of the town below and the Alpine ski runs above.

The lodge where the Nordic ski school is located, as well as the trail head, was formerly the base area at Peak 8. It is quaint and contains a retail store, rental shop, as well as basic food and beverage service. The lodge's setting is very picturesque nestled between tall pines and away from the hustle and bustle of Breckenridge's crowded streets and Alpine slopes.

Trail passes are available for full day or half day use. The fee during the 1987-88 season for an adult was $6 per day or $4 for a half day. Children twelve and under could ski for $4. Group ski lessons were $16 and private lessons were $28. Rental equipment was $8 per day for adults and $6 for children.

Special Events

Breckenridge's calendar is always full of special events. The largest and most popular event is the Ullr Fest, honoring the Norwegian god of winter. Staged in mid January, the event features ice sculptures, parades, fireworks, and a torchlight parade down the mountain.

Other special events include Women's Ski Seminars, held four times each year for one week periods. These programs are for women, by women, and attempt to bond the ski experience with the emotional needs of the participants. The Swatch Freestyle World Cup may become an annual function. This snowboard event is new to skiing, and Breckenridge is on the forefront of its promotion.

In the spring, the annual Telemark Returns are staged. This is a 10 km race benefiting the Breckenridge Outdoor Education Center. Classic telemark turn competition and dual slalom telemark racing are featured, along with an 1880's costume contest.

In addition to the above events, there are Pro Mogul Tour contests, a Snow Beach Party, Figure 8 Contest, and the Breckenridge Bump Buffet.

Accommodations

Hotels

The best Breckenridge hotel accommodations are to be found at the Beaver Run Resort. Located only fifty feet from the D-Lift on Peak 9, Beaver Run's location is perfect. This is a large complex resembling a college campus more than a hotel. Accommodations run the gamut from simple hotel rooms to large suites. Some rooms even boast their own spas, while others have fireplaces, kitchens, and balconies with views of the town or of the slopes. Constructed of concrete and pine, the facility epitomizes the power of the surrounding mountains in much the same way as The Cliff Lodge at Snowbird defines its terrain. During the 1987-88 season, a hotel room rented for between $95 and $125 per night, while a four bedroom suite, capable of sleeping up to ten persons, rented for between $390 and $480 per night, depending upon the season.

Tastefully appointed and well-maintained, the Beaver Run Resort is a village unto itself. It is entirely self-contained with shops, restaurants, swimming pool, disco, miniature golf, and hot tubs.

Across the street from Beaver Run is the Breckenridge Hilton, which offers accommodations similar to Beaver Run. The 208-room Hilton has all the services and facilities one expects from a large hotel. The rooms are cheerfully furnished with natural oak furniture and contemporary fabrics and have wet bars and refrigerators. Color TVs, stereos, and in-room movies are also provided. Guest facilities include a deli, formal dining room, and a discotheque. During the 1987-88 season, rooms containing either a king-size or a queen-size bed rented from a low of $55 per night to a high of $110 per night, depending upon the season.

Situated at the base of Peak 9 across from the Maggie Pond ice skating rink is a hotel called The Village At Breckenridge Resort. It is large like Beaver Run. However, the similarity ends there. This hotel does not appear to be as well managed as the Hilton, nor is it as clean. In fact, anyone booking unknowingly into The Village of Breckenridge may feel deceived by its literature and claims.

Breckenridge, as stated earlier, seems to attract more than its share of large groups of young persons. Something seems to happen to people's behavior when they join into groups. Group members become more gregarious and outspoken, their manners deteriorate, and the group becomes the center of their existence. Because there are so many of these young groups in Breckenridge, the entire town, and particularly its lodging, takes on an ill-kept appearance. The area in and immediately around the Village of Breckenridge epitomizes the worst of group behavior. This is a sorry state and hopefully, in the future, the Chamber of Commerce can reorganize and begin to exert a positive influence on its member merchants much the same as The Aspen Resort Association has done in recent years. The town of Breckenridge recently has permitted some extensive renovations and new construction in its historical district. Unfortunately, it has not allowed unattractive and poorly maintained structures along Main St. to be torn down. As a result, the town appears tacky rather than historical in the classical sense of Williamsburg or Crested Butte.

Condominiums

The condominium situation in Breckenridge is not much better than its hotel situation. There are no truly great condos here such as are found in Aspen, Vail, Telluride, Sun Valley, or Keystone. There are, however, a great number of average units suitable for most visitors' needs. During the 1987-88 season, there were nearly forty property management companies, representing literally hundreds of properties. It is very difficult for first-time visitors to Breckenridge to weave their way through the labyrinth of available properties in order to locate the facility best suited to their needs. Most of the properties for rent are different from one another, even if located within the same complex. Generally, most properties are over five years old; many are substantially older. The majority of individual property owners have not made a conscientious effort to remodel and upgrade the units. Most of the units need updating and their furnishings have become shop-worn.

One of the better condominium complexes is a ski-in/ski-out development situated just above the base area of Peak 8. The Ski Watch condos offer covered parking and hotel type furnishings. The living areas are small but comfortable, and feature wood burning fireplaces. Although there is no dining area, a large service counter separates the kitchen from the living area. The kitchens contain a Jenn-Air range, disposal, microwave, and adequate utensils for preparing meals. During the 1987-88 season, Ski Watch condos rented for $199 per night.

Located at the corner of Ski Hill Road and Park St., the Ski Hill Condominiums offer covered parking and elevator service to the units. Many of these condos have bright kitchens and earth tone decors. Fireplaces with glass doors radiate heat during cold, snowy evenings. Spiral staircases lead to upstairs sleeping lofts with spacious sleeping accommodations, a full bath, and a small balcony. Adjacent to the dining area is the master bedroom, complete with private bath. During the 1987-88 season, these accommodations rented for $159 per night.

The Cedars Condominiums, located across the street from the Hilton, appropriately derive their name from their cedar exterior. All units include private garages with electronic garage door openers. The first floor of the two-floor layout contains a living area, kitchen, and bath. The living area offers a fireplace, stereo, and cable TV. Some of the interior walls are cedar sided. The kitchen contains most necessary amenities such as an ice maker, disposal, microwave, and dishwasher. A washer/dryer is also included. These are ski-in/ski-out units located just below the D-Lift and just above the Quicksilver SuperChair. Some units seemed to have trouble with melting snow, and the balconies off some of the bedrooms are not usable because plastic sheets had been draped over the sliding glass doors. During the 1987-88 season, The Cedars rented for between $150 and $279 per night.

Restaurants

Spencer's at Beaver Run is a quality restaurant featuring American cuisine. Located on the mezzanine level of the hotel, its lackluster ambience belies the creativity of its chef and variety of his offerings. Typical appetizers may include tortellini pesto, escargot Milan, or oysters Rockerfeller. Entrées feature roast prime rib of beef, filet mignon béarnaise, tournedos Chesapeake, roast honey lemon duck, seafood pasta, vegetarian delight, fresh Pacific salmon, fresh Rocky Mountain rainbow trout, and shrimp scampi. Prices are moderate. Credit cards are accepted and a children's menu is available.

Weber's, located in a renovated Victorian house on Main Street, serves American and German dishes. All entrées served are accompanied with rolls, homemade soup, tossed green salad with poppy seed dressing or marinated herring in sour cream, red cabbage or sauerkraut of vegetable, spaetzles or baked potatoes, dessert and coffee.

The German specialties of the house include sauerbraten, wienerschnitzel, kassler rippchen, and bratwurst. American dishes include calves liver, pork chops, filet of sole as well as a variety of steaks.

Entrées during the 1987-88 season were priced from $9.95 to $17.95.

Above Main Street on Ridge street is Fatty's. This is a ramshackle pizzeria loaded with ambience, and it features excellent pizza and sandwiches. Fatty's is an institution in Breckenridge, and no visit would be complete without dining there at least one evening. Reasonably priced, it is a great place to take the family.

Other fine restaurants in Breckenridge include Mi Casa, Polo Bar, St. Bernard, and the Whale's Tail.

Activities

Reportedly, more than 50% of Breckenridge's visitors during the ski season do not ski. In response to these needs, numerous non-skiing activities are available, including:

Ice Skating on Maggie Pond
Ballooning
Snowmobiling at Tiger Run
Dinner Sleigh Rides
Movies at the Village Cinema
Shopping
Live Theatre
Walking Tours of the Historical District

Several health clubs are also available in Breckenridge including the Breckenridge Athletic Club, located on French St. This full-service club offers daily aerobics classes, racquetball, Nautilus, Olympic free weight training, hot tub, steam room, tanning, massage, and men's and women's locker rooms. Monthly and annual memberships are available.

Services

A full complement of sporting goods stores, apparel shops, pharmacies, grocery stores, liquor stores, furniture, bath, and specialty shops are within the immediate Breckenridge area. In addition, there are antique stores, massage services, art galleries, bakeries, beauty shops, book stores, florists, movies, live theatre, banks, churches, alterations, dry cleaning, optical repair shops, and baby-sitting services.

COPPER MOUNTAIN RESORT

P.O. Box 3001
Copper Mountain, CO. 80443

(800) 458-8386 Reservations
(303) 968-2882 Information
(303) 968-2100 Snow Report

Transportation

Copper Mountain is served by all major airlines through Denver's Stapleton International Airport.

Visitors will find the following car rental agencies at the airport proper:

Avis
Budget
Dollar
Hertz
National

Other car rental agencies are located outside of airport property and offer free airport pickup and drop-off, among them:

Alamo
Enterprise
AI
Thrifty

Copper Mountain is seventy-five miles from Stapleton on I-70, a one and a half hour drive in clear weather on dry roads.

All rental agencies provide free maps to their clients. Due to possible road restrictions, travelers to Copper Mountain are advised to always select a car that is *skierized*, i.e. equipped with snow tires and ski racks. For a slightly higher price, many rental agencies can provide four-wheel drive vehicles. The traveler is cautioned to reserve these vehicles far in advance because they are very popular.

Mountain Statistics

Copper Mountain comes about as close as any mountain to being described as a "perfect mountain." In terms of topography it faces north and its skiable terrain progresses from expert on the east to beginner on the west. This mountain is just naturally divided into three segments of expert, intermediate, and beginner topography.

Copper Mountain has 2,760 vertical feet (841 meters). Its base is located at 9,600 feet (2,926 meters) and its summit is at 12,360 feet (3,768 meters). The skiable terrain consists of 1,180 acres (477.5 ha) and is serviced by:

1 High-Speed Quad Lift
6 Triple Chairlifts
9 Double Chairlifts
4 Drag Lines, i.e. Poma

The longest beginner run at Copper is actually composed of two runs, Soliloquy and Roundabout, whose total length is more than two miles.

The longest intermediate run is Andy's Encore at 1.6 miles (4.1 km) which begins at the top of the B-1 lift and descends to the base of the B lift.

There is no single longest expert run at Copper Mountain, although several trails parallel one another in length on the mountain's A lift side. Far East, Too Much, and Triple Treat all afford excitement for expert skiers.

The number of skiable acres divided by the maximum number of skiers transported per hour on Copper Mountain is .043. This is a high figure and indicates that the mountain may become crowded. However, it will not be as crowded as Killington. Because Copper is located so conveniently to Denver, a great deal of day-skier business results, especially on weekends and during vacation periods when maximum occupancy of the slopes should be anticipated.

Of the 1,180 acres comprising Copper, 25% of the trails are for beginner skiers and 40% are for intermediate skiers. A full 35% of the skiable acreage is dedicated to experts' use.

The definitions of beginner, intermediate, and expert are closely adhered to by Copper. Guests should not have difficulty skiing any of the slopes by relying on Copper's trail markings. The only area where the skier can get into trouble is below the F lift, which tends to ice-up due to the heavy skiing received daily. The F lift, located at the center of the resort, tends to receive more than its share of the action. Skiers who look for soft, packed powder, intermediate runs should seriously consider spending the majority of their slope time skiing the runs off the I and J lifts. These are long, well-maintained runs that challenge intermediate skiers without intimidating them. The expert skier who does not have much powder experience should try to ski these runs early in the morning following a "big dump." It is an exceptional area in which to learn powder skiing because it is just steep enough to propel the skier downhill without creating uncontrollable fear.

The beginning skier at Copper Mountain is treated to one of the most expansive beginner areas in the country. In order to avoid any crowds, the beginner should make a beeline to the Union Creek base facility. This is the terminus for the H and K lift systems that provide acres and acres of barely tracked, broad runs as gentle as the backside of a baby and as long as two miles.

For the expert, Copper offers several areas of unique skiing. One such area, Union Bowl, is similar to the skiing found in the finest California resorts centered around Lake Tahoe. By taking the S lift to the top of Union Bowl, one skis along a ridge and finding a suitable place, drops off the cornice into broad fields of snow and bumps. Some of the areas serviced by the S lift are also lightly gladed which the expert might prefer. All the runs have triple fall lines, of course, due to being situated in a bowl.

From the top of the B-1 lift it is a short distance to the Storm King drag line which takes expert skiers to the top of Copper Mountain, and from there down into Spaulding Bowl, and thence into some of the greatest gladed, expert skiing anywhere. Runs such as Widowmaker, Highline, Cabin Chute, and Sawtooth comprise this bowl.

Copper Mountain receives an annual snowfall of about 255 inches (648 cm). Its average monthly snowfall is:

Nov.	40"	(102 cm)
Dec.	51"	(130 cm)
Jan.	38"	(97 cm)
Feb.	38"	(97 cm)
Mar.	49"	(124 cm)
Apl.	36"	(91 cm)

Copper Mountain's snowmaking capabilities are substantial. As many as 270 acres (109 ha) can be covered with artificial snow. Most of this snowmaking equipment is situated along the beginner and intermediate areas. However, during the summer of 1987, Copper did add snowmaking equipment along the B lift.

Average daily temperatures during the season are:

Nov.	26°	(-4° C)
Dec.	19°	(-7° C)
Jan.	16°	(-9° C)
Feb.	18°	(-8° C)
Mar.	23°	(-5° C)
Apl.	33°	(0° C)

Lift Ticket Prices (1987-88)

$ 30 Daily
$ 54 2 Day Consecutive
$ 72 3 Day Consecutive
$ 92 4 Day Consecutive
$110 5 Day Consecutive
$126 6 Day Consecutive
$ 15 Ages 62-69
$ 10 Beginner
Free—Over 70

Ski the Summit pass

$104 4 Day
$156 6 Day
$ 5 Cross-Country Track Only
$ 10 Cross-Country and K lift

Copper Mountain represents one-third of the available skiing in Summit County, Colorado. The other Summit resorts are Keystone and Breckenridge. While the three mountains do not honor each other's lift tickets, they all honor "Ski the Summit" passes. So if you anticipate skiing at more than one Summit resort, buy the "Ski the Summit" lift ticket. It is only slightly more expensive.

Lift tickets for children 12 years and under are priced at reduced rates.

Hours of Operation

8:30 A.M. to 4:00 P.M. at the base
Upper lifts close at 3:30 P.M.

Lift Ticket Purchase Locations

Lift ticket sales are conveniently located at the Clubhouse situated at the base of the B lift, at The Center near the base of the F lift, and at Union Creek near the base of the H lift. During peak periods such as Christmas through New Year's and Easter, additional ticketing locations are opened at the base of the A lift and in Copper's Transportation Center.

The most congested area in which to purchase lift tickets is The Center. During peak periods, generally from 9:00 A.M. to 10:30 A.M., the wait can be as long as a half hour. Waiting can be avoided altogether if tickets are purchased after 3:00 P.M. the previous day or at any of the other mentioned ticket locations.

Crowd Control

Crowds at Copper should be a concern to skiers because of the mountain's proximity to Denver and two other major ski resorts. However, crowds can be avoided if skiers use some judgment about where they ski. The worst crowding always occurs around 10:00 A.M. and between 1:00 P.M. and 2:00 P.M. During these times or during major holidays, avoid skiing runs serviced by the following lifts: F, G, I, J, B. Abundant skiing is available for skiers of all abilities without utilizing these lifts.

It should also be noted that in order to avoid a long walk in skis, do not ski Treble Cliff to its end. Just before the end of this run there is a large swale; stop here and observe a track to the left through the trees. This path is created each year and makes it easy to cut through the trees and exit onto the lower portion of Rosi's Run, thus avoiding the long hike back to B lift. By all means do ski Treble Cliff, especially during or just after a large snowfall as it is an excellent powder run for the expert.

Ski School

Copper's Ski School meets in three locations daily: The Center, Union Creek, and Solitude Station. Solitude Station is the mid-mountain restaurant located at the end of the F lift and at the base of the E lift.

These locations are convenient to the slopes, mountain restaurants, ski rental shops, ski repair shops, apparel shops, transportation, and day care facilities.

Adult classes are scheduled to begin promptly at 10:00 A.M. (lasting until 2:30 P.M.) or at 1:45 P.M. (lasting until 3:45 P.M.). They are designated for persons twelve years and older. The rate for group lessons during the 1987-88 season was $30. Private lessons were available anytime between the hours of 10:30 P.M. and 2:30 P.M. or from 2:30 P.M. through 4:00 PM. Classes were for one and a half hour or one-half day. A full-day private lesson was also available in 1987-88 at $250 and consisted of no more than five persons. This class option was an excellent way for a family to learn the mountain and to get tips on their skills at the same time.

Copper offers various lesson plans which include lessons, equipment, and lift tickets. There are also special classes available for advanced and expert skiers.

Copper Mountain guarantees its students complete satisfaction with their lessons, or it will do whatever is necessary to achieve their satisfaction.

Equipment Rental

Copper provides rental equipment at all Plaza locations where equipment such as Rossignol, Salomon, Nordica, Pre and Scott is rented. Prices varied during 1987-88 from a low of $12 per day to a high of $20 per day. Cross-country skis were available from $9 to $12. Children's rates were discounted from the adult rate.

Several private sporting goods stores are located conveniently at The Center, the B lift base, and at Union Creek. Christy Sports, located at The Center, has a particularly large inventory of high-performance skis and abundant ski apparel to meet various price points.

Ski Tuning and Repair

Tuning and repair services are available at Breeze, located at the base of the B lift, or at Christy Sports in The Center. In addition all ski rental shops and sporting goods stores in the near-by towns of Frisco, Breckenridge, Silverthorne, and Dillon offer ski tuning and repair.

Gorsuch, Ltd., located in The Village Square, has ski tuning machinery manufactured by Montana of Switzerland. This is among the finest ski tuning equipment on the market today. Properly used, this equipment can structure the ski's base and bevel the edges from 1° to 3° assuring enhanced performance. During the 1987-88 season, the fee for a complete tune-up was $25, $10 for sharpening edges, and $5 for hot wax.

All rates quoted are for the 1987-88 season and are provided by Gorsuch, Ltd. However, rates are competitive from all sources.

Mountain Restaurants

Unlike many major ski resorts, Copper Mountain has the majority of its long ski runs situated along its lower lifts. Because of this unusual arrangement most of the restaurants are situated at the various base points. There is one true mountain restaurant situated at the top of the F lift called Solitude Station. Its food service is typical ski resort fare. Food service is cafeteria-style, served hot and fresh. Anything from fresh, homemade pizza to hot dogs, hamburgers, and wine and beer is available. Breakfast is served at all base restaurants.

During warm clear days, the staff at Solitude will set up an outdoor barbecue and grill hamburgers and bratwurst.

Numerous excellent restaurants are situated throughout the Copper complex; these are discussed in the section entitled *Restaurants*.

Day Care

Copper's day care and particularly its children's ski program have been nationally recognized by *Ski* magazine as some of the country's best.

For children aged two months to two years there is the Belly Button Babies program. Copper provides special care and low supervisor ratios to insure parents that their children will receive adequate and caring attention. Persons planning to enroll their children in this program should be prepared to provide their own formula, diapers, and wipes. It is also important that reservations be made early. It is best to make day care reservations at the same time accommodations are being booked. To book day care reservations call: (303) 968-2882, ext. 6345.

Children two years and over can be enrolled in the Belly Button Bakery. This innovative program incorporates snow play and skiing (for children over three years). Lunch is included and snacks are provided in the afternoon. This class meets daily at 8:30 A.M. and children must be picked up by 4:30 P.M. It is always a good idea to provide the children with an extra change of clothing.

All day care facilities are located in the lower level of The Center. The Center is the Core 10 steel building with the clock tower. It is easily identifiable and convenient to all adult ski class meeting places, shops, restaurants, and rest rooms.

Copper offers special ski programs for juniors. There is the Junior Ranch for ages four to six and the Senior Ranch for ages seven to fourteen. Both of these programs are truly wonderful. Children are treated to races and barbecues each Thursday while they become familiar with the wintertime outdoor environment. It is great fun for parents waiting to ride the G lift to watch their children frolic in a nearby special training area.

Baby-sitting in the evenings is available by making early reservations at the Belly Button Bakery. The rate for this service during the 1987-88 season was $5 per hour plus $.50 per child.

Medical Facilities

Copper Mountain maintains a complete medical facility in order to handle emergencies or family medicine. Located in the Bridge End Complex close to The Center, it is open daily during the season.

For serious illness or injuries that cannot be handled by the clinic, there is a helicopter pad adjacent to the facility and air ambulance service to any of the Denver hospitals is available. Ground transportation via commercial ambulance can also be arranged if needed. Prescription drugs on a limited basis are available from the clinic if prescribed by one of the staff physicians. Other prescription needs can be filled by the pharmacies located in the towns of Frisco, Silverthorne, Breckenridge, or Dillon.

Cross-Country Skiing

Nordic enthusiasts will have to go a long way to find a better place to ski than Copper Mountain. Copper maintains 25 kilometers of trails, commencing at the Union Creek Base and meandering up and through the Arapaho National Forest. All of the cross-country tracks work their way up Vail Pass through beautiful glades and past roaring streams. For the beginner, there are one and a half hour lessons available for $18 including the fee for using the track. Rental equipment is available at the Union Creek base.

Special Events

Each year Copper Mountain hosts a long list of featured events. A staple among the events, however, has always been its NASTAR racing program. Located at the top of the G chairlift and running parallel to Loverly the NASTAR course is open from early December between 1:00 P.M. and 4:00 P.M. daily.

Also on Loverly is a self-timer practice race course which operates with tokens that can be purchased from the ski desk at The Center.

Copper Mountain is the only official training center in Colorado for the U.S. Ski Team and is the home of the Subaru U.S. Alpine Championships. Each month during the ski season at least one event is always featured, whether ski team training, snowboard racing, or one of numerous sponsored cup series.

Other events include ice skating, sleigh rides, candlelit dinners atop the mountain at Solitude, snowmobiling, and movies.

Accommodations

Copper's largest hotel is the Mountain Plaza Hotel. Located in The Center, the Plaza is convenient to the slopes, shops, and restaurants. Typical of many of Copper's older properties, the Plaza is beginning to show its age. These are good, standard facilities not unlike accommodations found in countless hotels throughout the United States. The rooms are arranged in modules of three, i.e. two standard hotel rooms with a studio between them. This affords management the option of renting a single room or a two bedroom unit from the same module. Similar accommodations may be found at the Copper Mountain Inn and at the Spruce Lodges.

Condominiums

Recently, Copper Mountain has begun a condominium expansion program near the base of the B lift and the golf course. Unlike the existing condos, these are being built and managed by Copper Mountain. Copper's management believes it is imperative to provide a consistent, high-quality housing environment. In response to this perceived need, it has constructed two new projects: The Woods at Copper Creek and The Greens at Copper Creek.

Of the two developments, The Woods is the premier property. Each unit shares no more than two common walls with other units. These are essentially stand-alone two or three bedroom units tastefully furnished and equipped with all the amenities one would expect from a property of this type. The views from this project's windows are of the spectacular Ten-Mile range and the A and B lift serviced runs, a vista without parallel. These accommodations include cathedral ceilings, parquet entries, fireplaces, master bath suites, and garage parking. Kitchen appliances include ice makers, self-cleaning ovens, dishwashers, and garbage disposals. Many units also have washer/dryers, whirlpool tubs, and microwave ovens.

The Greens are designed for sale as interval ownership property. However, until all the units are sold, they are available for rent. Tastefully decorated, these efficiency units offer the same views as the Woods. Enclosed parking is also available, and the kitchens are completely appointed with appliances and cooking utensils. Two bedroom, one bedroom, and studio units are available. In the two bedroom units one of the bedrooms may be converted to a sitting room. Fireplaces are constructed of stucco in the style of the Southwest. Southwest colors are represented with the use of warm greens, teals, peach and similar colors. Neither of these projects offers swimming pools nor hot tubs because management believes that the need for such amenities is filled by the Copper Mountain Racquet and Athletic club.

Restaurants

There are enough restaurants in the Copper Mountain complex to satisfy all but the most discriminating gourmets. The best restaurant is The Plaza located across from the lift ticket kiosk at The Center. Its luncheon and dinner menus offer wide varieties and the daily specials are worth considering. The Plaza's modern decor of warm woods and kelly green ultra-suede wall treatments is enhanced by many indoor plants. Service is attentive and prices are moderate.

Tuso's, located at the base of the B lift, is a very active after-ski watering hole and an excellent noon and evening dining spot. Informal and furnished in mountain chic, this is the place to go for entertainment. Meals at Tuso's tend to be very filling because of the large portions served. During the afternoon the restaurant features outdoor cooking at its front door. All ski country favorites such as hot dogs and hamburgers are served just steps from the B lift.

Across from Tuso's is The Clubhouse, a short-order restaurant. This facility, interestingly enough, doubles as the golf pro shop in the summer. The Clubhouse is open for breakfast and has outdoor dining during good weather.

Also at the base of B lift is Barkley's, named after the owner's dog. Barkley's is only open for dinner. From time to time it will open for lunch, but one should not count on it because the schedule is erratic. Barkley's is a cozy, informal restaurant featuring American cuisine. There is a similar restaurant just down the street in Frisco called Charity's which is also under the same management. It is unclear if the owner's also had a dog named "Charity."

Another fine restaurant located in Copper Mountain's Racquet and Athletic Club is appropriately named "Rackets." Situated at the top of an impressive staircase, the restaurant offers a civilized respite from the rigors of Alpine skiing and other athletic activities. Rackets is decorated in what is best described as mountain traditional. Blue and white table linens are complemented by the lovely silver service and classical le Corbusier seating. A large fireplace and oak bar complete the ambience. Because the restaurant is not located conveniently to the slopes, it is not open for lunch. It is open, however, for dinner every evening. Entrées include broiled salmon, Bar-B-Que scallop kabob, skewered lamb medallions, and roast prime rib au jus.

Numerous other restaurants scattered around Copper feature regional dishes such as Mexican and home-style cuisine. A current listing of all restaurants will be available upon checking into accommodations.

It must be noted, however, that there are additional excellent restaurants in the nearby towns of Breckenridge, Keystone, Silverthorne, and Dillon. The best restaurant in the entire area is probably The Ranch at Keystone. The best steak is found at The Blue Spruce in Frisco. The best German food is at Weber's in Breckenridge. The best Italian food is found at The Snake River Saloon located in Keystone; the best seafood is at The Navigator, also at Keystone.

In near-by Frisco and Silvethorne there is a full selection of fast food establishments such as Arby's, McDonalds, Wendy's, Pizza Hut, Kentucky Fried Chicken, and Dairy Queen.

Activities

In addition to the 35 shops and restaurants found at Copper Mountain, there is a $3 million athletic club with racquetball courts and two indoor tennis courts, a twenty-five yard, four lane lap pool, complete Nautilus, free weights, aerobics and exercise classes, tanning salon, hot tubs, saunas, steam rooms, a massage therapist, nursery, and restaurant. All guests of Copper Mountain may use the facilities which are open from 6:00 A.M. to 10:00 P.M. weekdays and from 8:00 A.M. to 10:00 P.M. weekends.

Services

A full complement of sporting goods stores, apparel shops, pharmacies, grocery stores, liquor stores, furniture, bath, florist, ice cream, and other specialty shops is located in The Center. The Center is, as one might expect, at the hub of the resort complex adjacent to the Mountain Plaza hotel and the Plaza restaurant.

CRESTED BUTTE

Crested Butte Mountain Resort
P.O. Box A
Mt. Crested Butte, CO. 81225

(800) 525-4220 Reservations
(303) 349-2211 Information
(303) 349-2323 Snow Report

Transportation

Crested Butte is located 230 miles from Denver, 196 miles from Colorado Springs, and 160 miles from Grand Junction. The drive to Crested Butte from any direction is one of the most beautiful in Colorado. From Denver take Colorado Highway 285 south to Highway 50 in Pueblo; follow this until it intersects Highway 135 in Gunnison; turn north and follow the road to Crested Butte. Once in Crested Butte, be sure to note that the town is not the same as Mt. Crested Butte. Mt. Crested Butte is the ski resort where most of the accommodations are located and is only about two miles from the town of Crested Butte. The directional signage is very good.

From the West take Interstate Highway 70 to Grand Junction; turn south on Highway 50 to Gunnison. Be careful to notice that Highway 50 makes a ninety-degree turn east in the town of Montrose. Once in Gunnison, take Highway 135 north to Crested Butte. If the weather is suspect, stop in Montrose and check on the road conditions to Gunnison. During storms Highway 50 will frequently be closed around the Blue Mesa Reservoir, and there are no accommodations between Montrose and Gunnison.

Flying into Crested Butte is easy. During the 1987-88 ski season, United, Delta, and American Airlines offered direct service to Gunnison. United's service included non-stop flights between Chicago and Gunnison every Saturday. United Express offered daily service through Denver.

Delta Airlines scheduled non-stop service from Salt Lake International Airport on Wednesdays and Saturdays.

American Airlines had two flights each weekday and three per day on weekends from Dallas/Ft. Worth to Gunnison. All service provided by these airlines was on 737 or 727 aircraft.

Both Continental Express and United Express offered daily commuter service to Gunnison from Denver as well. It is anticipated that these airlines will expand their service during the 1988-89 season.

Crested Butte is a scant twenty-eight miles from Gunnison and the road (Highway 135) is good. At the time accommodations are booked, guests should also request ground transportation and indicate to the reservationist their flight number and time of arrival. Transfers during the 1987-88 season were about $24 round trip.

Major car rental agencies are represented at the Gunnison Airport. Full-size cars, vans, and four-wheel drive vehicles are available. To reserve a car, telephone Budget at (303) 641-4040, Hertz at (800) 654-3131, or National at (800) CAR-RENT.

A car, though a convenience, is not necessary because Crested Butte is the only ski resort in the area and all activities center around it or the town of Crested Butte. A free daily shuttle runs every thirty minutes from 7:15 A.M. until midnight.

Mountain Statistics

Mt. Crested Butte is an extremely versatile mountain, with 53% of its area classified as intermediate, 27% classified as beginner, and 20% classified as expert. The intermediate and beginner terrain is intermingled nicely, and the runs are long. Most beginners who are not in classes usually gravitate to the Keystone Lift. The long, gentle runs in this area provide just enough downhill slope to keep moving without worrying about falling hard.

The intermediate skier will love the long, wide runs off the Paradise and Teocali lifts. Trees which line the sides of all the trails provide good visual contrast even in poor light. All beginner runs and most of the intermediate runs are groomed if not nightly, at least every other night. Take a run down Treasury. This intermediate trail is the longest in the resort and has enough challenging terrain to test one's skills on moguls, soft pack, and steep slopes.

One of the most unique features, however, of this mountain is its notoriously underrated expert terrain. The North Face (not to be confused with the Front Face) provides some of the best skiing found at any resort!

The Extreme Limits is unique because it receives no attention from the resort's mountain maintenance people. The patrol limits its involvement to avalanche control, emergency rescue, and a nightly sweep. Otherwise, the area is skied as nature created it. Although there is lift service to the general area, many of the specific runs can only be reached by climbing.

Under no circumstances should skiers attempt to ski the Extreme Limits the first few times without a guide. It is possible to make a wrong turn which could put the skier at extraordinary risk. The North Face is best described as a series of small bowls arranged contiguous to one another. Of these runs, the easiest is probably found in The Glades. The Glades is moderately moguled at the top. Bumps have been formed by good skiers with long skis, and the troughs associated with skiers traversing are nowhere in evidence. The most difficult are Phoenix Steps, Staircase, Slot, and Cesspool. The primary reason a guide is necessary is so skiers can learn the way out of the bowls without having to exit through one of these extremely tight, steep, rocky chutes.

In order to reach Spellbound Bowl's summit, it is necessary to climb from the top of the North Face Lift for about one-half hour. It is worth the effort, however, since you can usually find some powder somewhere on it. From this bowl, you can ski into Phoenix Bowl. From there, more walking is required until the skier finally exits onto Black Eagle. If the skier is not inclined to walk to the top of Spellbound Bowl, it is possible to enter just below the summit via Million Dollar Highway. This is a cut between the rocks which separate Hard Slab from High Life. The map identifies this cut as Phoenix Entrance, and it usually is too rocky to be used without damaging your skis.

On the Front Face is a run called Horseshoe Springs identified on the map by a single black diamond. No indication of its short length is given. Horseshoe Springs is also extremely steep! Those who have enjoyed the exhilaration of The Wall at Aspen Highlands or Mach One at Breckenridge will love Horseshoe Springs.

For those skiers who do not shy away from hiking, runs such as Peel and Upper Peel, to the right of the Silver Queen Lift, are very steep and challenging. A word of caution, however; this area does not hold snow very well and tends to become skied off quickly. Try Upper Peel and Peel if they are open, though—Wow!

Many skiers at Crested Butte begin their morning by taking the East River Lift. This lift is the first to enjoy the morning sun and as the day progresses, many skiers follow the sun around the mountain and finish the day skiing the Silver Queen Lift.

Mt. Crested Butte's base is located at 9,100 feet (2,774 meters) and its summit is at 12,162 feet (3,708 meters). The vertical drop is 3,062 feet (933 meters). The longest beginner run is Houston at 1.8 miles (2.9 km). The longest intermediate run is Treasury at 1.9 miles (3 km), and the longest expert run is International at 1.4 miles (2.2 km).

Although located only thirty-one miles from Gunnison which is noted for its very cold weather, Mt. Crested Butte has relatively moderate temperatures. Its average in town temperatures during the season are:

	High		Low	
Nov.	36°	2°C	12°	-11°C
Dec.	28°	-2°C	-8°	-22°C
Jan.	28°	-2°C	-10°	-23°C
Feb.	32°	0°C	-3°	-19°C
Mar.	39°	4°C	5°	-15°C

Receiving over 300 inches (762 cm) of snow annually, Crested Butte does not normally have to rely on its extensive snowmaking capabilities. Snow is generally made only during the early days of the season, principally to guarantee good coverage during Thanksgiving and occasionally during Christmas. The average monthly snowfall is:

Nov.	38"	(96 cm)
Dec.	58"	(147 cm)
Jan.	64"	(162 cm)
Feb.	48"	(121 cm)
Mar.	50"	(127 cm)
Apl.	25"	(64 cm)

Compared with other destination resorts, Mt. Crested Butte is relatively small with only 827 acres (331 ha) of skiable terrain. However, it is adequate for skiers of all ability levels to ski for an entire week without becoming bored with the runs and trails. The number of skiable acres divided by the uphill lift capacity is .061. This figure is almost identical to that of Vail. Guests at Crested Butte should not expect crowded lift lines except during the peak periods of Christmas, Easter, and Presidents weekend. Even during these times the lines should not be too long, certainly no more than five to ten minutes.

Lift Ticket Prices

Lift ticket prices for the 1988-89 season are:

$ 30......Adult, All Day
$ 22......Adult, Half Day
$ 60......Adult, 2 Day

$ 90......Adult, 3 Day
$148......Adult, 5 Day
$177......Adult, 6 Day
$ 17......Child, Under 13

During the 1988-1989 ski season, Crested Butte will be expanding its ever popular "Children Ski Free" program. There is no minimum lodging stay required nor minimum number of ski days, and the offer is good for the entire season except for the periods of December 26 through January 2 and March 18 through March 31. Multi-day tickets purchased prior to December 26 or March 18 that carry over into the exception periods will be honored if the bulk of the stay falls in the non-exception period. Lift tickets purchased during the exempt period which carry over beyond it will be charged on a pro rata basis. Proof of age may be requested at the discretion of the ticket seller. Only birth certificates and passports are considered acceptable proof!

Hours of Operation

9:00 A.M. to 4:00 P.M.

Lift Ticket Purchase Locations

Lift tickets may be purchased at the Gothic Building which is located at the foot of the Keystone Lift, convenient to all lodging and to Rafter's Cafeteria. Ticket wickets open at 8:00 A.M. and close at 4:00 P.M. During busy seasons, it is a good idea to prepurchase the next day's lift ticket after 3:00 P.M.

Crowd Control

Even though crowds are generally not a concern at Crested Butte, they will occur at certain lifts during some periods and at the base area in the late afternoon.

Paradise Lift is one of the lifts that seems to develop crowds more readily than others. The best way to avoid these lines when they occur is to ski the area around the Teocalli Lift where crowding is rarely experienced. Even though the runs off the Teocalli Lift are beginner and intermediate, they are very good and should be skied in any event. After 3:00 P.M. when most skiers are making their way down the mountain, crowding occurs on the trails leading to the base of the Keystone and Silver Queen lifts. Since this is the only way down in the evening, crowds are impossible to avoid. Caution should be exercised, and fast skiers should slow down. The ski patrol is usually positioned on the slopes, urging returning skiers to slow their speed and to ski defensively.

Ski School

The Crested Butte Ski School is under the direction of Robel Straubhaar, who was recognized by *Colorado Ski Country U.S.A.* as Colorado's number one ski instructor. In addition to group and private lessons, the ski school offers lessons and services for handicapped skiers. Consistent with other major resorts the Crested Butte Ski School teaches the ATS (American Teaching System).

Group lessons meet at 9:45 A.M. and 12:45 P.M. daily. Private lessons meet at 9:00 A.M. and 3:00 P.M. All lesson participants meet at Ski Area Central, located just in front of the Keystone Lift, to the left of the Grande Butte Hotel looking uphill.

For those persons who have never skied before, the ski school offers lessons entitled *Never Ever* Lessons which include a special lift ticket good only on the Peachtree Lift. These lessons during the 1988-89 season will be $32 for all day and $21 for half day.

Group lessons are taught in two-hour increments.

$21.......1, Two Hour Lesson
$38.......2, Two Hour Lessons
$55.......3, Two Hour Lessons
$88.......5, Two Hour Lessons

Private lessons:

$ 70.....2 Hours
$115.....3 Hours
$210.....6 Hours

Special programs:

$30......Bump and Powder
$21......Snowboard

Crested Butte offers its Butte Busters program for children aged seven through twelve.

$ 48......Full Day with Lunch (lift ticket included)
$ 92......2 Full Days (lift ticket included)
$134......3 Full Days (lift ticket included)
$225......5 Full Days (lift ticket included)

Children in the Butte Busters program must register prior to 9:30 A.M. and have their own ski equipment. Sunscreen and eye protection (either goggles or sun glasses) are required. Operating hours are from 8:30 A.M. to 4:00 P.M.

Equipment Rental

Rental equipment is available from any number of shops at Mt. Crested Butte or in town. Rates for equipment are comparable. Shops typically offer three types of equipment packages: Recreational, Sport, and High Performance.

The recreational package is the most basic and is intended for novice or beginning skiers. Usually the rental equipment offered is manufactured especially for this use.

Most intermediates who want to rent equipment will select from the slightly higher-priced Sport ski package. The skis offered under this designation are almost always production skis often referred to as recreational skis. Do not confuse the designation "recreational ski" with the package designated "Recreational ski package."

For skiers who want a high-performance ski or who want to demo a ski prior to a possible purchase, the High Performance package makes the most sense.

The largest rental shop in Mt. Crested Butte is Crested Butte Ski Rental located in Ski Area Central (the same building as the ski school). Crested Butte Ski Rental offered recreational packages from

$10.50 during the 1987-88 season. This rate was discounted if two or more days rental was contracted. Children's rates for one day were $7.50 and discounted the same as adults' for extended periods.

Crested Butte Ski Rental's Sport Package consists of rear-entry Salomon boots, step-in bindings, skis, and poles. During the 1987-88 season single day rental was $14.

Crested Butte Ski Rental's High Performance Package consists of top-of-the-line skis from K2, Rossignol, or Dynastar, Salomon SX-91 boots, and Marker bindings. This package was priced from $20 per day during the 1987-88 season.

Ski Tuning and Repair

Tuning and repair services are available at any of the fine ski shops at Crested Butte. However, only one company, Butte and Company located on the Mall, has stone grinding equipment which is the preferred method for tuning skis. For a complete explanation of the superiority of this equipment, read the description under *Ski Tuning and Repair* in the chapter entitled *Killington*.

Rates for these services were not available at the time of this writing. However, rates certainly are comparable with those being charged at other Colorado ski resorts featured in this book.

Mountain Restaurants

There are two mountain restaurants at Crested Butte. Twister Warming House, located at the base of the Twister Lift, may be reached via any of the runs serviced by Twister Lift. Beginners and intermediates may reach it by skiing Peanut. Nestled among the tall pines, this is a short-order restaurant with a large sun deck.

The larger and principal mountain restaurant is located at the base of the Paradise Lift and is named, appropriately enough, the Paradise Restaurant. The Paradise features a large, common dining room with cafeteria service. This restaurant is scrupulously clean, and its furniture and fixtures are well maintained. The food offerings are creative and very good. The menu features assorted grilled dishes, deli foods, wine, beer, soft drinks, and fresh salads made daily. The staff also serves lasagna, chili, beef stew, egg rolls, prime rib, and homemade pies. The prices are very reasonable and the ambience is cordial.

Bubba's, located within the Paradise, is a full service restaurant featuring table service and an extensive menu. On Sundays it offers a buffet which includes fresh seafood, eggs Benedict, quiche Lorraine, seafood crepes, fresh fruit, homemade salads, complimentary champagne and much more. Priced at $10.50 per person during the 1987-88 season, the buffet was a real value. This excellent restaurant is equal to the Coyote on Aspen Mountain or Gwynn's at Snowmass.

Day Care

Day care is available at the Buttetopia Nursery and Day Care. Situated on the ground floor of the Whetstone Building and located only a few steps west of the Grand Butte Hotel, the Buttetopia accepts infants from six months through six years. The facility is divided into two separate areas, one for infants six months through three years and one for children four years through six years.

Care is available by the hour, half day or full day. Full day care includes lunch unless the child is still on formula, which the parents provide. Diapers for non-toilet trained children should also be provided. Snacks, such as animal crackers, are provided by the staff.

Nursery rates during the 1987-88 season were $30 for a full day and $20 for a half day. The hourly rate was $6.

Day care rates during the 1987-88 season were $28 for a full day and $18 for a half day. The hourly rate was $6.

A variation of the day care program, *ABCs on skis,* is also offered at the Buttetopia. This is a program where children aged three to six can learn to ski. Offered as half day or full day programs, the 1987-88 fee was $18 per half day and $28 for a full day. Lunch and supervised activities were included in the program, as well as ski instruction.

Medical Facilities

For injured skiers, the ski patrol will only render emergency service. The patrol will administer trauma treatment, stabilize broken bones, and transport the injured downhill by sled to a clinic located in the Axtel Building at the base of the mountain. This is directly across from the Silver Queen Lift. Should additional medical treatment be necessary, patients are transported to the hospital in Gunnison.

Cross-Country Skiing

The Crested Butte Nordic Center, located in downtown Crested Butte in the Crested Butte Athletic Club at the corner of Whiterock and Second Street, is just one short block from the Mountain Express bus stop. Operating from 9:00 A.M. to 4:00 P.M. daily, the Nordic Center has 29 km of groomed tracks suitable for general touring or race training.

Certified PSIA (Professional Ski Instructors of America) teachers provide introduction to Nordic skiing. Advanced techniques such as track ski racing, back country mountaineering, Nordic Telemark, and turns (stem christies, stem turns, parallel turns, and telemark) are also taught.

Track fees during the 1987-88 season were $5. Two hour lessons were $20, while an all day lesson was only $35. Private lessons were $40 per hour.

Complete rental equipment is available at the Center and the 1987-88 rate was $10 for touring equipment and $13 for telemark equipment. For additional information, telephone (303) 349-6201.

The Crested Butte Nordic Center hosts numerous cross-country events each year. During the 1987-88 season, it hosted 5 km and 10 km Citizens races, the Alley Loop race, Team Relay, and in association with the Crested Butte Mountain Resort, the Al Johnson Memorial Uphill/Downhill.

Nordic skiing is also available at the Irwin Lodge. Be sure to review the section entitled *Activities* for more information on this unique approach to cross-country skiing. The *Activities* section also deals with the hut system between Crested Butte and Aspen.

Special Events

In addition to the cross-country special events mentioned in the previous section, Crested Butte hosts several other events which vary from year to year. To determine which events may be staged during a particular period, call the information number at the Crested Butte Mountain Resort and request a current schedule. During 1987-88, the following events were conducted and are representative of the types of events staged annually:

Burton Snowboard Championships
Subaru U.S. Alpine Championships
Mardi Gras Ski Week
American Airlines Celebrity Ski Cup
ASA Grapenuts Ski Card Weekend
Snowfest
Coke Cup

Accommodations

The Grande Butte Hotel at Mt. Crested Butte has to rank as one of the finest mountain resort hotels in the country. It dominates the foreground of the landscape with the mountains providing a spectacular backdrop.

The 262 room structure seems to overawe the winding road which leads to a cavernous underground garage and valet parking. The reception area is on the second floor and is serviced by two elevators from the parking garage. The capacious reception area and lobby has a large moss rock fireplace which provides a central feature to the room. The plaid seating and tooled leather cocktail tables add just a hint of formality to an otherwise casual decor. The cedar siding used throughout the hotel perfumes the air with a whisper of its scent. This is an active room with people milling around the piano bar or discussing the evening's plans with the hotel's concierge. Across the lobby, Christy Sports[1] is usually busy as skis are rented or tee shirts are purchased for friends and relatives.

Another quieter lounge area is located on the floor immediately below the reception area and lobby. Group meeting rooms are located on this floor as well as a swimming pool, sauna, steam room, and exercise room. As on the main floor, the central lounge area is dominated by a large native stone fireplace.

The tastefully decorated hotel rooms offered by the Grande Butte are superior to accommodations at most other resort hotels. The double queen-size beds are comfortable, and the dressers provide enough space to store sweaters, ski pants, and so forth for a full week. A small writing table, remote control color TV, upholstered reading chairs, and foot stools contribute to guests' comfort. For guests who wish to cook, a mini-kitchen is disguised as a country French armoire. This mini-kitchen while functional is purely basic, and you should not expect to prepare large meals with its humble features.

The Grande Butte Hotel has two fine restaurants: The Roaring Elk and the Spaghetti Slope. The Roaring Elk Saloon features nightly entertainment and dancing. Separated from the main lobby by etched glass windows of "roaring" elks, it is an après-ski gathering place. The decor features a beech and brass bar, cedar ceiling, plush leather seating, and plantation shutters.

From the Grande Butte's lobby, guests will find that it is fewer than 100 steps to the mountain's lift system. In addition, many other shops, restaurants, and services are located conveniently around the hotel. The hotel is indeed the center of this resort's activity.

The Crested Butte Lodge, located near the center of the resort's activities, is also only steps away from the lifts. It boasts an indoor swimming pool found next to Jeremiah's Restaurant on the main

---

[1] Christy Sports will be relocating to a new building just prior to the 1988-89 ski season. It is anticipated that another sporting goods store will take over its space in the Grande Butte Hotel.

floor. As with most mountain properties, geraniums and ferns line every available inch of window space around the pool.

Both penthouse suites and condo units are available at the Lodge. Although each unit is furnished differently, a common theme is repeated throughout. All units have brick fireplaces, natural oak furniture in a Country French style, and a fully equipped kitchen. The bedrooms have queen-size beds with Laura Ashley print comforters. A Jacuzzi bathtub and double sinks complete the accommodations. Penthouses at the Lodge are available as one bedroom/one bath; two bedroom/two bath; three bedroom/three bath units.

Only slightly removed from the Mt. Crested Butte hub, but still close to the slopes, are the Plaza Woodcreek Condominiums. Of the properties featured in this review, the Plaza is the most utilitarian. In fact, this is the property that is most frequently rented to groups of vacationing college students.

The central lobby of the Plaza is three stories high and lighted with industrial-style mercury vapor lights. Its ceiling consists of painted duct work and steel roof tresses. On the lower floor of the lobby, an enclosed hot tub and vending machines are found.

Each condominium is well-equipped. The kitchens have most of the appliances one could ever use including a refrigerator with ice maker, microwave oven, convection oven, dishwasher, disposal, toaster, and coffee maker. The dining area comfortably seats six. The units have fireplaces and cable TV.

Bedrooms at the Plaza tend to be spartan and appointed with functional naturally finished furniture. The master bedroom contains a queen-size bed, and the second bedroom has twin beds. All condominiums contain central humidifying systems which are very welcome in the dry mountain climate.

During the 1987-88 ski season, condos at the Plaza rented from a low of $75/night for a two bedroom, two bath, to a high of $210 for a three bedroom, three bath unit. These prices included a complimentary bottle of champagne upon arrival and daily breakfast.

Restaurants

As at most Colorado resorts, the food quality and service presentation at Crested Butte is excellent. One unique restaurant located in the town of Crested Butte is The Slogar. The Slogar is situated in an historic building and decorated in Victorian style. The menu is served family-style and there are only two choices of entrées: skillet fried chicken or steak. Entrées are complemented with a sweet and sour coleslaw taken from a Pennsylvania Dutch recipe. Mashed potatoes, gravy, and fresh baking powder biscuits with honey butter and strawberry preserves make dining at The Slogar a memorable event. The 1987-88 price for this meal was $9.45. Children's portions were available, as was full bar service.

The Artichoke at Mt. Crested Butte is a typical fern bar à la California. Just off the slopes and next to the Grand Butte Hotel, it is a natural luncheon spot for hungry skiers. The menu at the Artichoke is extensive but leans toward burgers, sandwiches, salads, and soups. Typical selections include "Godfather," "Good Ol'Boy," "Guac," and "ABC" burgers. The staff also prepares chicken chimichangas, artichoke quiche, steamed artichoke, Dagwood sandwiches, bratwurst, taco salads, and many other items. With its lunches priced in 1987-88 from $3.50 to $5.75, the Artichoke is an inexpensive place in which to celebrate great snow, a terrific run, or the fantastic sunshine.

The Gulf Coast Restaurant, located at the far end of the day-skiers parking lot just north of the bus turnaround, serves fresh, well-prepared seafood. The chef and waitresses all are from Destin, Florida, and operate this restaurant during the ski season. In the summer they simply relocate to Destin. The

Gulf Coast serves excellent swordfish, grouper, stone crabs, and red snapper. The portions are ample and the service is superb.

On the more elegant side, try the Spaghetti Slope Restaurant located on the lower level of the Grande Butte Hotel. The interior is slick, modern, and crisp. The grey wool carpeting, terra cotta, and brown marble details are accented by black lacquer seating and alabaster walls.

The Spaghetti Slope specializes in Italian dishes such as scampi, fettucini, and numerous other pastas. Items are moderately priced; reservations are suggested.

On Emmons Loop just above the Grande Butte Hotel at the bus turnaround, Café Creole is situated in an antique street car. The Café features short-order items such as chicken and sausage gumbo, New Orleans-style red beans, and shrimp creole. Its baked potatoes are stuffed with shrimp, broccoli, and cheese or the more traditional bacon and cheese. Café Creole does not serve alcoholic beverages, but it does serve café au lait and assorted juices. The Café's creations can be enjoyed outside under one of the colorful "Mouton-Cadet" table umbrellas or in its quaint indoor dining area. Prices during 1987-88 varied between $2 and $5, depending on items ordered.

Many other fine restaurants and bars are found in the historical district of Crested Butte. Whether you dine at the Wooden Nickel (a local hangout), Soupçon, Le Bosquet, or The Bakery Cafe, your meal will be well-prepared and your service attentive. You will want to return to Crested Butte time and time again.

Activities

Activities at Crested Butte are extensive. There are National Standard Races (NASTAR) off the T-Bar and a Marlboro course with a coin operated self-timer. Sleighride dinners, ice fishing, live theatre, movies, snowmobiling, indoor tennis, balloon rides, nightclubs, and dancing are all available to visitors.

One of the finest activities available anywhere is Irwin Lodge's snowcat skiing. The Lodge is situated among tall pines high in the Gunnison National Forest. From its 12,500 feet (3,811 meters) ridges, Alpine and Nordic skiers of all ability levels can learn to master the abundant powder that falls on this 500-acre paradise. Runs from the ridges are typically two miles (3.2 km) in length and 2,000 vertical feet (500+ meters). The lodge, decorated in the style of the roaring 1890s, contains 25 upstairs guest rooms. Resembling a South Pacific long house, it is 60 feet X 160 feet. The main floor has common dining and lounging. All electricity is created at the Lodge by generator. The only television programs are provided by video tapes run on a VCR. At 9:00 P.M. it's lights out; if it is necessary to get out of bed or to read, it must be done with a flashlight!

Rates during the 1987-88 ski season included a room with private bath, three family-style meals each day, pickup and return to the Gunnison Airport or Crested Butte. Rates were as follows:

$475 3 nights (minimum stay)
$615 4 nights
$750 5 nights
$875 6 nights
$995 7 nights.

Just getting to the Irwin Lodge can be exciting. Transportation from the trail head to the Lodge is via snowmobile and takes almost one hour. The scene is breathtaking. The pristine beauty of the Rocky Mountains, its forests, and frozen streams provides a memory not easily forgotten. One word of caution: there probably is not a worse place to be for several days if the snow conditions are bad. There is nothing to occupy the time if one cannot ski. For additional information, telephone (303) 349-5140.

If a return to the rugged days of the old mining camps excites you, try a night in Ambush Cabin. Situated at an altitude of 9,000 feet (2,743 meters) and a two mile cross country ski from Crested Butte, the Cabin forms an important link of the Pearl Pass Route to Aspen.

The cabin, whose walls have been hewn from large logs, is surrounded by 147 acres of the Gunnison National Forest and sleeps seven. If a group consists of fewer than seven persons, and if its members consent, they will be combined with other ski groups. If this is not satisfactory, the group may wish to rent the entire cabin. During the 1987-88 season, Ambush Cabin could be rented for $76 per night.

If not all the amenities of home are provided at Ambush Cabin, certainly there are enough to make this trip worthwhile. Guests will find a gas stove, basic cooking utensils, plates, soap, cut wood for heat, mattresses, and pillows as well as a gas refrigerator. Next door to the cabin is a heated bathroom with a wood fired sauna. A caretaker is provided with the rental. This facility is run by a non-profit organization dedicated to providing guests with a wilderness experience. For more information, telephone (303) 349-6400.

During the 1987-88 ski season, the Crested Butte Athletic Club was undergoing renovation. However, it will reopen for the 1988-89 season. Located across the street from The Slogar Restaurant in downtown Crested Butte, the Athletic Club is convenient to the free shuttle bus stop. Weekly, monthly, and annual memberships are available. After the renovation, the Club will offer one racquetball court, an indoor swimming pool, Jacuzzi, free weights, Universal Gym, Life Cycles, some Nautilus, sauna and steam rooms. A special floor for aerobic classes will be installed, and high and low impact aerobics will be offered.

Services

A full complement of sporting goods stores, apparel stores, pharmacies, grocery stores, liquor stores, furniture stores, bath stores, and specialty stores is within the immediate town of Crested Butte. In addition, there are antique stores, massage services, art galleries, bakeries, beauty shops, book stores, florists, movies, a theatre, banks, churches, alterations, dry cleaning, optical shops, and baby-sitting services.

JACKSON HOLE

Post Office Box 290
Teton Village, WY. 83025

(800) 443-6931 Reservations
(307) 733-2292 Information
(307) 733-2291 Snow Report

Transportation

It once was difficult to reach Jackson Hole, but not anymore! American Airlines flies into Jackson from Chicago nine times each day and once daily from Dallas/Ft. Worth. There is also round trip Saturday service from Long Beach, California on a chartered McDonald Douglas MD-80 through U.S. Sports Adventures.

Delta Airlines offers daily non-stop service from its hub in Salt Lake City, and Continental Express flies daily into Jackson from Denver. Mesa Airlines has matching daily flights with United Airlines in Denver.

The Jackson Airport is located twelve miles from Teton Village, which is at the base of the Jackson Hole Ski Area. Flying into Jackson can be one of the most beautiful, scenic flights available anywhere in the world. The airport is situated in a long north-south valley at the foot of the Tetons and is slightly south of Yellowstone National Park. On a clear day it is easy to see Yellowstone, the Tetons, Jackson Hole, and the town of Jackson from the landing or departing aircraft. Because the airport is located in a very long and broad valley it is not a difficult airport in which to land: not even during snow storms. The reliability of the air service is quite good.

Transportation either to Jackson Hole at Teton Village, to accommodations in town, or to the Jackson Hole Racquet Club is convenient via shuttle bus service. Shuttles meet every inbound and outbound flight. Taxi service and limousine charters are also available from the airport.

Although a car is not a necessity, it is a convenience at Jackson Hole. START Bus (Southern Teton Area Rapid Transit) provides shuttle service between Teton Village and Jackson ten to fifteen times each day between the hours of 7:00 A.M. and 12:00 A.M. Car rental agencies located at the airport include:

- Avis
- Hertz
- National

It is also possible to rent cars from Budget or Nez Perce, both located in Teton Village. Budget also has an office in Jackson, as does Rent-A-Wreck and Teton Motors.

Traveling by car to Jackson is easy. Take Interstate Highway 80 to the Rock Springs interchange at Highway 191; turn north until Jackson. Once in town, it is only twelve miles to Teton Village on

Highway 390. Approaching Jackson from the West on Interstate 80, take the first exit after Evanston, Wyoming, onto Highway 189 and follow it until it becomes Highway 191 and thence into Jackson. There are no major mountain passes to climb, so weather is rarely a factor.

Mountain Statistics

Jackson Hole is located in the Bridger Teton National Forest, one of the most rugged and striking ranges in America. The ski area is among the largest in North America encompassing over four square miles (1,036 ha) of skiable terrain.

Jackson Hole has had a reputation among avid skiers as a difficult mountain with some of the best and most challenging expert runs in the world. This reputation is justified. But, on the other hand, it also has some of the best intermediate and beginner runs available. Over the years, the management of Jackson Hole recognized the need to provide substantial intermediate and beginner runs in order to compete with other American resorts. To this end, they have spent countless millions on development of the resort's skiable terrain. The first problem management had to overcome was the simple fact that over 90 inches (229 cm) of snow was required before intermediate slopes could be groomed. Management attacked this problem from two directions: first, it began a program of dynamiting the large rocks obstructing the runs which were responsible for the high quantity of snow needed. Second, it installed snowmaking equipment. These improvements have made it possible to groom the intermediate trails with only 60 inches (152 cm) of snow.

Two mountains comprise Jackson Hole at Teton Village. The lower mountain, where all the beginner and a majority of the intermediate runs are located, is called Après Vous. Adjacent to Après Vous is Rendezvous Mountain. Rendezvous is the mountain responsible for Jackson Hole's reputation of being difficult.

This is a big mountain. The base elevation is 6,311 feet (1,924 meters) and the elevation at the summit of Rendezvous is 10,450 feet (3,185 meters). A vertical drop of 4,139 feet (1,262 meters) offers skiers the most vertical feet of skiing of any major United States ski resort.

The mountains consist of:

      6 Beginner Trails
      26 Intermediate Trails
      25 Expert Trails

However, this recitation of the number of trails is misleading because all the area within the boundaries of the resort is considered open for recreational skiing. A look at the trail map shows lines which indicate runs, but they are in fact, mostly open areas with numerous ways down. For example, trails numbered 3 through 7 are referred to as the "Hobacks," and it would appear there were only five ways down. In fact, there are as many ways down as there are skiers. A person could spend several days just skiing these runs and not ski down the same way twice.

When skiing at Jackson Hole, it is imperative that one pay attention to the signs. This mountain is so big it is easy not only to become lost, but also to find oneself in an area that could be dangerous. Always pay attention to signs that alert you to cliffs. These signs are not exaggerating: the cliffs are real and are *not* skiable! There are many trails identified with signs that are not on the trail map. Do not ski any of these runs unless in the company of a guide or unless you are a very accomplished skier. If the skier wants to get an idea of the kind of runs that are not shown on the trail map without actually skiing one of them, he should ride the Upper Sublette Ridge Quad Chairlift. On the left, just before the chair arrives at the bull wheel, the skier can see Corbet's Couloir. This is an avalanche chute that goes straight down and is only about 400 cm wide. In other words, it is about twice as wide as most skis are long. Persons skiing this short run usually build up a speed close to 60 miles per hour. The Couloir used to contain a large rock just at the chute's exit. However, it was removed a few years ago because its position was considered extremely dangerous.

The mountain is so vast that on flat light days it is possible to experience vertigo even on the catwalks. There is so much vertical that several weather systems frequently exist simultaneously. It is not unusual for the temperature on Rendezvous to be 10° or even 20° warmer than temperatures in the valley. Jackson frequently undergoes weather inversions, and temperature differential is a rather common phenomeon.

Both mountains are serviced by a modern lift system that includes:

1 Aerial Tram
1 Quad Chairlift
1 Triple Chairlift
5 Double Chairlifts
1 High-Speed Poma

The hourly uphill lift capacity is 8,900 skiers. The number of skiable acres divided by the maximum number of skiers transported per hour on the lifts is .280. This very low figure assures guests the mountain will never become crowded.

Although every type of skiable terrain imaginable is available, Jackson Hole is most noted for its large bowls. There are many of them, and all offer exceptional skiing. Beginning at the top of Rendezvous Peak where the aerial tram stops is Rendezvous Bowl, a broad, wide open, steep bowl. Down the center of this bowl are black sticks with large black circles mounted on top. These are placed to aid skiers who might otherwise have difficulty skiing down during flat light or during snow storms. Looking downhill from the top, there are a few gladed runs on the left. These are the only areas of Rendezvous Bowl that develop moguls. Although the bowl is never groomed, bumps do not become very large because of the abundant snowfall.

After skiing Rendezvous Bowl, a skier can elect to continue down via Cheyenne Bowl or Larami Bowl; both are steep and exciting to ski. From the bottom of either of these bowls, one can continue to ski the upper mountain or return to the base via any of the Hobacks. The only problem with taking the Hobacks down is that this route requires another ride up the aerial tram to the top.

Jackson Hole has an unusual policy regarding its tram. A separate ticket must be purchased for each ride. The 1987-88 season cost per ride was $2. Management believes that by charging an additional fee it has successfully reduced waiting time for tram rides. There are enough other lifts at Jackson Hole that it is not necessary for one to ride the tram more than once or twice daily. Also, because all runs served by the tram are expert, the additional charge may discourage some intermediate skiers from skiing above their ability level.

The longest beginner run is Eagle's Rest. It is 2,062 feet (629 meters) long. The longest intermediate run is Gros Ventre. It is 1.4 miles (2 km) long. The longest expert run is Rendevous Bowl at a length of 2,700 feet (823 meters) long.

Jackson Hole's annual snowfall is 456 inches (1,158 cm). The monthly snowfall is:

Nov.   108"   (274 cm)
Dec.   84"   (213 cm)

Jan.   84"   (213 cm)
Feb.   96"   (244 cm)
Mar.   48"   (122 cm)

The average monthly temperature at mid mountain is :

	Low		High	
Dec.	3°	-16°C	17°	-8°C
Jan.	7°	-14°C	25°	-4°C
Feb.	19°	- 7°C	31°	0°C
Mar.	20°	- 6°C	37°	3°C

The sheer magnitude of the mountain is emphasized by the "Go for the Gold" program instituted in Jackson Hole in 1978. Visitors are encouraged to keep track of the quantity of vertical feet skied each day. In fact, they are given a scorecard. After each run or at the end of the day, skiers enter the name of the runs skied and total the vertical feet. Upon achieving 300 thousand they are awarded a bronze Jackson Hole belt buckle. After reaching 500 thousand they are given a silver buckle and after reaching the ultimate one million vertical feet, they are awarded a 14 kt. gold buckle.

Since 1978, the resort has awarded 950 bronze, 575 silver, and 62 gold belt buckles. Most skiers will require up to ten years of skiing to achieve the vaulted status of a gold buckle, but there are exceptions. One eighty-two year old skier did it in two years, and an eight-year-old girl totaled 790 thousand vertical feet in only two years.

The "Go for the Gold" program is an honorary system but must be validated by Jackson Hole's Public Relations Department. Skiers who achieve 100 thousand and 150 thousand feet in one week will be awarded achievement medals. A goal of 100 thousand vertical feet in a one week period is not out of reach for most people when one considers that the mountain is nearly five thousand feet in length. Twenty runs spanning the length of the mountain or forty runs for just half the length will enable the skier to qualify for an achievement medal.

Lift Ticket Prices

Because the mountain is so rugged, it requires more snow than many resorts in order to be skiable. Therefore, it is usually early December before Jackson Hole opens. There is not a "high" or a "low" or a "value" season here. There is only "ski season!" The 1988-89 lift ticket rates were:

$ 28.......Daily Adult
$ 21........Half Day Adult
$ 84........3 Day Adult
$108........4 Day Adult
$130........5 Day Adult

14 Years & Under/65 Years and Over

$14.........1 Day
$10........Half Day
$42.........3 Day
$65........5 Day

These rates are for chairlifts and poma only. Each ride on the aerial tram is an additional $2.

All major credit cards are accepted.

Hours of Operation

All lifts open at 9:00 A.M. The aerial tram's last departure is at 3:20 P.M. The Rendezvous Poma closes at 3:30 P.M. The Crystal Springs, Thunder, and Upper Sublette Ridge chairlifts' last departure is at 3:40 P.M., while the Casper chairlift's is at 3:50 P.M. All remaining chairlifts close at 4:00 P.M. These different closing times are necessary in order for the ski patrol to "sweep" the mountain. Closing times basically follow the sweep.

Lift Ticket Purchase Locations

Lift tickets may be purchased at the base of the aerial tram station in the center of Teton Village.

Tickets for Snow King Ski Resort in the town of Jackson are also available at the tram station.

Crowd Control

With the lowest ratio of skiers to available terrain, crowds rarely exist. Even during the Christmas holidays when there is not an extra room to be had, there are no crowds. If crowding does exist it is at the aerial tram station. However, even here the wait usually never exceeds one tram departure (approximately 20 minutes.)

Ski School

The Jackson Hole Ski School offers numerous programs. The most popular choice is the five half day package. The skier receives a lesson each morning and then is able to practice the newly acquired skills in the afternoon while becoming familiar with the mountain. These classes are available Monday through Friday.

Students who want a more comprehensive program can elect to go into the full five day package program or can upgrade at any time from the half day to the full day program. However, in order to upgrade, six or more students of the same class must upgrade as well.

Small class lessons are also available, and are limited to no more than five students. Each class is two hours in length and available either in the morning or in the afternoon. Small class lessons may be purchased by the day or by the five half day package, but are not offered on Sunday.

For those skiers who do not need lessons, Jackson Hole offers its Mountain Experience Call. These classes emphasize skiing powder, skiing steep terrain, and skiing runs not indicated on the trail map. This is a great way for skiers to learn their way around the mountain without the expense of a private instructor.

The highest level of skier education is available at Jackson Hole. The Ski Meisters program is a four-day, three hour per day package including intensive mogul, powder, and racing techniques. A video evaluation is provided.

Private lessons are also available, including skiing with Jackson's ski school director, Pepi Stiegler. In addition, racing clinics and Alpine ski guides are offered.

To encourage skiers to take lessons, the ski school offered Sunday Introductory Lessons for the nominal fee of $5 during the 1987-88 season. This program was open to anyone of any ability over the age of six.

$ 75......Adult, 5 Half Day
$ 90......Adult, 5 Half Day (small class)
$100......Ski Meisters
$ 25......Mountain Experience
$ 18......Small Class
$ 30......Small Class Full Day
$ 35......Private 1 hour, (1 Student)
$180......Private All Day, (1 Student)
$225......Private All Day, (2-6 Students)

SKIWEE CHILDREN (6-14)

$50......5 Half Day
$75......5 Full Day
$20......1 Full Day
$14......1 Half Day

Equipment Rental

There are three rental and repair shops in Teton Village. Additional shops are available in the town of Jackson at slightly lower rates, no doubt.

Jackson Hole Ski Corporation owns and operates the Kastle Ski Rental Shop which only rents Kastle skis. During the 1987-88 season, the shop offered three types of rental packages. The first, called the Recreational Package consisted of:

Kastle S 301 Skis
Nordica 720 Boots
Look Bindings
Poles.............$12 Per Day

The second package offered was called the Sport Package:

Kastle SW-1 Skis
Nordica 720 Boots
Look bindings
Poles.............$14 Per Day

The third package was actually a demo package designed primarily for persons who wanted to try different skis before purchasing them.

Kastle RX Slalom
Kastle Super G Magnesium
Kastle Magnesium Light
Nordica NR 955 Boots

Saloman 747 Bindings
Poles.................$20 Per Day
Demo Ski Only........$15

All rental packages were available at a reduced rate of $2 each day if rented in conjunction with ski lessons. Further rate reductions on packages were available if rented for more than three days.

Equipment at the other two rental shops in Teton Village was comparable in rental rates and quality.

Ski Tuning and Repair

Tuning and repair services are available at all ski rental shops and sporting goods stores. None of the shops offer stone grinding nor ski structuring. For a detailed explanation regarding the superiority of ski structuring see the *Ski Tuning and Repair* chapter in the section of this book entitled, *Killington*.

Skis must be warm before waxing. It is a good idea to drop your skis off at the end of the day and pick them up the next morning.

Kastle Ski Shop 1987-88 tune-up rates were:

$ 5 Hot Wax
$10 Edges De-burred (Pair)
$18 Minor Tune-up
$22 Full Tune-up
$22+ P-tex

Mountain Restaurants

A new mountain restaurant is located in Casper Bowl at the top of the Crystal Springs double chairlift and at the bottom of the Casper Bowl triple chairlift. This two-story nine thousand square foot facility is nicely furnished with wooden tables and chairs. Food is served cafeteria-style, and the menu includes hamburgers, hot dogs, soups, french fries, and the like. Beer and wine is available at a separate service window around the corner from the food service.

There is also a small snack bar and warming hut located at the top of the tram on Rendezvous Peak.

Day Care

Day care is provided by the Jackson Hole Kinderschule. Infant care for ages three months through three years is available on an hourly or weekly basis. To make reservations for children, telephone (307) 733-2292 and ask for the nursery. Parents are expected to provide diapers and formula for their children. The 1987-88 rates were $6 per hour, $35 per day, and $175 for five full days.

Day care without skiing for children three through fourteen years of age was available during 1987-88 at the same rate as infant care. Second children were discounted $5 per day. Day care for this group included lunch and snacks.

Medical Facilities

For ski injuries, the ski patrol will only render emergency service. The patrol will administer trauma treatment, stabilize broken bones, and transport injured skiers downhill.

Jackson Hole at Teton Village has a very complete clinic. Located adjacent to the main parking lot and next to the Mangy Moose Saloon, the clinic treats most ski related injuries. If an emergency or illness exceeds the clinic's capabilities, patients will be transferred to St. John Hospital in the town of Jackson, only twelve miles away.

Cross-country Skiing

Cross-country skiing at Jackson Hole is nothing short of spectacular. Miles of double tracked trails lead off in two directions from the trail head in Teton Village. The Rossignol Ski Touring Center is the hub of cross-country activity. From this convenient starting point, groomed trails connect with the endless back-country trails of Grand Teton National Park.

The staff at Rossignol Center offers telemark clinics, cross-country track clinics, Alpine touring, and a terrific Hot Springs Tour. Guided tours of the wilderness surrounding Yellowstone National Park are offered twice a week. A picnic lunch and a soak in one of the area's hot springs are included. Take a swimming suit!

Rossignol Center has a complete selection of ski equipment, accessories, and clothing for sale. The Center also has an excellent selection of rental equipment.

Special Events

National Standard Races (NASTAR) are held every Tuesday and Thursday at 1:00 P.M. Participants should sign up at the Ski Chalet between 8:30 A.M. and 11:30 A.M. the day of the race. The Ski Chalet is located just behind the tram station.

Coin operated Marlboro Challenge racing is also available.

The Rites of Spring are celebrated annually at Jackson Hole. Each March during the universities' break, Busch beer and Jackson Hole sponsor these exciting and inexpensive festivities. Free of charge, daily activities usually include at least five types of races, inflatable raft races, costume contests, dance contests, treasure hunts, fashion shows, and live entertainment. The "Busch Bar & Grill" tent, containing five thousand square feet of heated party space, offers short order food and barbecue.

In addition, skiers enjoy dinner sleigh rides and trips to the National Elk Refuge where nearly seven thousand elk live. Yellowstone Park is accessible by snowmobile or cross-country skis. Guided tours are available.

Special events are staged annually, but change from year to year. During the 1987-88 season, the following events occurred:

Christmas Torchlight Parade
Western Region FIS Series
Powder Eight Championships
International FIS Citizen Race
Par-Ski Championships
Spring Ski Festival

Pole, Pedal, and Paddle

During the last several years, Jackson Hole has sponsored its Iron Man Competition. This is an awesome physical event that is every bit as demanding as the Iron Man competitions held around the U.S. each year. Contestants in the Jackson Hole event begin by skiing down Cody Bowl to the top of Cheyenne Bowl where they remove their skis and run uphill to the top of the aerial tram station. Here, contestants put their skis back on and ski to the bottom of the mountain. Oh yes, they also must get down Corbet's Couloir. In 1987, only one of the contestants had the physical stamina to actually ski the Couloir: all the others had to be lowered down it on a rope! The winning time is usually just under thirteen minutes, and participants have skied close to seven thousand vertical feet when the competition is over.

Accommodations

Lodging is either located in Teton Village, Jackson Hole Racquet Club Resort, or in the town of Jackson. Hotels in town are twelve miles from the resort. There is daily shuttle service to and from Teton Village. The Racquet Club is approximately two miles from Teton Village, and it is also on the shuttle's route.

Hotels

The Inn at Jackson Hole is located on the slopes of Teton Village. A older hotel, it currently is undergoing renovation. Before booking reservations, it would be a good idea to confirm that the room being occupied will have had its face-lift. Most of the rooms here do not offer a view even though they back to the mountain. Ski lockers are located on each floor, and the guest's room key locks the lockers. The Inn has a small, heated swimming pool and spa. Bar service is available in the pool area. Cable TV is available in every room. The ice machine is located in its own room outside on the main floor.

Guido's Lounge is located on the main floor of the lounge. It is an interesting place; numerous mounted animals decorate the walls and appear to climb up posts. The food offered is adequate, but the service tends to be indifferent.

The Alpenhof, also in Teton Village, is one of the better hotels. Its rooms are clean and sound proof. Most of the rooms have king-size beds and balconies. There is a heated outdoor swimming pool, spa, sauna, game room, and laundry room. Cable TV is standard in every room.

The Alpenhof dining room is featured in the restaurant section.

Other hotels in Teton Village and the town of Jackson include: Crystal Springs Inn, Hostel, Sojourner Inn, Village Center, Antler Motel, Parkway, Rawhide, 6-K Motel, Western Motel, Wort Hotel.

Condominiums

Located a scant half mile from the aerial tram, the Wind River Condominiums are situated in a meadow, and have a wonderful view of Rendezvous Mountain. These condos have free shuttle service every twelve to fifteen minutes to the tram station. In the evenings, this service provides hourly pickup and return from restaurants in the Village.

The Wind River Condominiums are three stories high and feature impressive living areas which occupy two floors. The large fireplaces are made of native stone and the L-shaped seating is comfortable. Cable TV and stereos provide entertainment for stay-at-home guests. All condos are equipped with humidistats. Increasing humidity provides great relief from the dryness always present in the mountains. A separate, formal dining room can comfortably seat eight.

The kitchen is small but everything is very convenient. The General Electric appliances include ice maker, dishwasher, diposal, convection oven, microwave oven, and blender.

The lower floor consists of two bedrooms and two baths as well as a laundry room with washer and dryer. One of the baths is a two-person Jacuzzi.

Two other bedrooms, including the master bedroom, are located on the third floor.

The Teewinot Condominiums are named in the same French terminology as are the Grand Tetons, a Teewinot being the diminutive form of Teton. Teewinot condos are available as two or three bedroom units. The rooms are smaller than those of the Wind River and these living areas do not include a formal dining area. Each living room has a wet bar, fireplace, and TV. All appliances are GE and identical to those found in Wind River Condos.

Among the least expensive condominiums located in Teton Village are the Rendezvous next door to Teewinot and Wind River. The Rendezvous, however, may offer the best value since their furnishings are not very different from those found in more expensive units. Amenities include stone fireplaces and dining rooms that comfortably seat eight. Rendezvous units are available as either two or three bedroom condos.

Other condominiums in Teton Village include: Tensleep/Gros Ventre, Timber Ridge, Nez Perce, and Sleeping Indian.

Reservations in any accommodations mentioned can be booked by calling central reservations at (800) 443-6931.

Restaurants

The best restaurant in Teton Village is the Alpenhof Dining Room. Dining at the Alpinhof is truly a culinary treat. Furnished in a Swiss/Austrian-style decor, the walls of the restaurant are constructed from natural stone. Its exterior windows overlook tall conifers. The soft, yellow light from the windows casts cozy shadows on skiers returning for the evening, while the aerial tram station's Italian lights twinkle in the freshly falling snow.

The waiters are friendly, courteous and very knowledgeable about the extensive menu and abundant wine selection. Try the potato soup with dill for starters. The chicken picatta is recommended for a delicious entrée. It is served smothered in garlic, anchovies, and a rich tomato sauce. This is a Mobile four-star restaurant, and the award is justly deserved.

The same management that owns the Alpenhof owns the adjoining Dietrick's Bar & Bistro. This is the best place for après ski. From its warm, wood interior to its numerous baskets of hanging blooms and ivy, Dietrick's is comfortable. The central feature of the room is its carved glass window pane of a mountain climber ascending a majestic peak.

Among the beverage offerings are typical ski resort drinks such as Union Jack, Tennessee Mud, and Snow Blind! Dietrick's offers one of the better tables of complimentary hors d'oeuvres. It includes spicy buffalo wings, Mexican pizza, nachos, potato skins, tostados served with spicy or sweet salsa.

A hardy lunch featuring items such as bratwurst, tortellini primavera, and gourmet pizza is also served.

The recently expanded Mangy Moose is a Teton Village institution. The Moose is many things: a restaurant, a bar, a pizza parlor, and the only place in the Village that features live entertainment. The dining room is dominated by a large stone fireplace with a "mangy" moose mounted above its mantle. Antique barber chairs are available for those who need to sit while waiting for a table. Ceiling fans, pseudo Tiffany lamps and mirrors complete the Western motif. This is a family restaurant with large tables that encourage people to mix and meet one another.

ACTIVITIES

One of the more exciting activities available in Jackson Hole is High Mountain Helicopter Skiing and Scenic Flights. Back-country skiing in the Snake River Range and Palisade Mountains just Southwest of Teton Village can be arranged for $325 (1987-88 rates). Typically, this will encompass six runs of 12,000 to 15,000 vertical feet. One run trips are available at $95.

The Aspens Athletic Club is approximately one mile from Teton Village. It offers daily, weekly, seasonal, or annual membership rates. The facilities are clean and properly maintained. Offerings include:

- Indoor/Outdoor Tennis Courts
- Nautilus
- Free Weights
- Basketball
- Volleyball
- Aerobics (including low-impact)
- Jacuzzi/Sauna/Steam
- Ice Skating
- Cross-Country Ski Center
- Racquetball
- Wallyball
- Tanning
- Horseshoes
- Outdoor Swimming Pool

Take a scenic dog sled ride offered by the Rocky Mountain Mushers. Telephone (307) 733-7388 for reservations or information.

Ride a horse drawn sleigh to visit the National Elk Refuge. It is the largest elk refuge in the United States. Sleigh rides are continuous from 10:00 A.M. to 4:00 P.M. through the end of March.

Take a snowmobile tour of Yellowstone or Granite Hot Springs. Dress warmly but take a swimming suit and enjoy the hot, thermal waters. Telephone (307) 733-6850 for reservations.

Shop in unique downtown Jackson. There are over thirty art galleries and fine stores, including Benneton and Ralph Lauren. Visit the Million Dollar Cowboy Saloon or the arched antler entrance at each corner of the central business district's park.

Have a professional, quality videotape made of your ski vacation. Telephone (307) 733-8715 for prices and information.

SERVICES

A full complement of churches, sporting good stores, apparel shops, pharmacies, grocery stores, liquor stores furniture, bath, and specialty shops is located in Jackson.

Beginning at 10 A.M. every day and continuing on the hour, ski hosts and hostesses position themselves at the top of the tram next to the large trail map. These guides are knowledgeable about Jackson Hole and can answer most questions.

KEYSTONE RESORT

Box 38
Keystone, Colorado 80435

(800) 222-0188 Reservations
(303) 468-2316 Information
(303) 468-4111 Snow Report

Transportation

Keystone is served by all major airlines through Denver's Stapleton International Airport.

The following major car rental agencies are represented at the airport proper:

Avis
Budget
Dollar
Hertz
National

Other car rental agencies are located outside of airport property and offer free airport pickup and drop-off. Among them are:

Alamo
Enterprise
AI
Thrifty

Keystone is sixty-five miles from Stapleton via I-70. Exit in Silverthorne and take Highway 9 to the resort. The trip from the airport takes one and one half hours to drive in clear weather on dry roads.

All rental agencies provide their clients with free maps. Due to possible road restrictions, the traveler to Keystone is advised always to rent a car that is *skierized*, i.e. equipped with snow tires and ski racks. For a slightly higher fee, many rental agencies can provide four-wheel drive vehicles. The traveler is advised to reserve these vehicles far in advance because the demand for them is great.

During the 1987-88 ski season, Keystone offered free Avis car rentals with all reservations for five days and six nights, or free transportation via bus or van to and from Denver.

Mountain Statistics

Keystone has three distinct mountains. The main mountain, Keystone, has 2,340 vertical feet (713 meters). Its base is located at 9,300 feet (2,835 meters) and its summit is at 11,640 feet (3,548 meters). The skiable terrain comprises 500 acres (202 ha) and is serviced by:

1 Gondola
1 Triple Chairlift
8 Double Chairlifts
2 Poma Lifts

The longest beginner run is Schoolmarm which runs for three miles (4.8 km) from Keystone's summit to the base of the mountain.

The longest intermediate run is Spring Dipper which begins at the summit. It is 1.5 miles (2.4 km) in length.

The longest expert run is Go Devil, which is slightly shorter than Schoolmarm or Spring Dipper.

Keystone's second mountain, North Peak, is located directly south of Keystone Mountain. Access to North Peak is from the summit of Keystone Mountain via Mozart which is considered an intermediate run or via Diamond Back, an expert run.

The base of North Peak is located at 10,040 feet (3,060 meters) and it has a summit of 11,660 feet (3,554 meters). Its vertical drop is 1,620 feet (494 meters), and the mountain is served by two triple chairlifts.

The longest intermediate run is Mozart which is two miles (3 km) long. Geronimo is the longest expert run at one and a half miles (2.4 km).

North Peak has 200 skiable acres (81 ha).

Keystone's third mountain is Arapahoe Basin. This mountain is located on the Continental Divide, approximately five miles (8 km) east of the main mountain and resort accommodations. Free shuttle service is available every ten minutes between various mountains and the Keystone Lodge.

Arapahoe Basin's base is at 10,780 feet (3,286 meters) with its summit at 12,450 feet (3,795 meters). The vertical drop at A-Basin is 1,670 feet (509 meters). Access to the runs are via:

1 Triple Chairlift
4 Double Chairlifts

Keystone mountain consists of thirty-nine trails of which Keystone considers:

5% Advanced
55% Intermediate
40% Beginner

North peak's terrain consists of :

78% Advanced
22% Intermediate

Arapahoe Basin's trails consists of:

40% Advanced
50% Intermediate
10% Beginner

The number of skiable acres divided by the maximum number of skiers transported per hour on Keystone Mountain is .037. On North peak it is .057 and at Arapahoe Basin it is .056.

Keystone's annual snowfall is 200 inches (508 cm). Its average monthly snowfall is:

Oct.	9"	(23 cm)
Nov.	25"	(63 cm)
Dec.	27"	(69 cm)
Jan.	40"	(102 cm)
Feb.	17"	(42 cm)
Mar.	44"	(112 cm)

All trails' actual degree of difficulty is subject to change depending on snow conditions. However, as a general guide, the descriptions are accurate. It should be pointed out, however, that the expert and advanced trails at Keystone Mountain are not nearly as difficult as the expert and advanced slopes at Arapahoe Basin. In fact, many of the runs at Arapahoe Basin are so difficult they are identified with a double black diamond. With the exception of the lower portion of Go-Devil and Last Hoot, advanced intermediate skiers should have no difficulty handling any of Keystone's terrain. The problem with the lower portions of Go-Devil and Last Hoot is that they tend to be skied off, thus exposing base conditions which can be equated with the term "ice," though not in the same sense as experienced skiers will find on the slopes of the Eastern United States.

North Peak's intermediate runs tend to become skied off and icy. The expert runs on North Peak are usually heavily moguled and may also be icy. The moguls found on Keystone and North Peak are typically made by skiers using shorter skis. As a result, they tend to become flat on the top, and the valleys are closely arranged making it difficult for skiers with longer skis to establish a path through them.

In contrast to this, moguls at Arapahoe Basin are usually made by longer skis, and their tops are more rounded than those at Keystone. The valleys are longer making it easier for the skier to pick a path through the bumps. The expert trails at Arapahoe Basin are truly "expert," and the skier who does not have a great deal of experience should not attempt them. Most of the runs at A-Basin are either gladed (meaning among trees) or steep with triple fall lines. The intermediate runs are located mainly at the top of the mountain. There are virtually no trees on the top of A-Basin. During snow storms or periods of flat light, it is extremely difficult to "feel" which way is down. As a result, vertigo is a common complaint. It is suggested that beginner and intermediate skiers only go to Arapahoe Basin on clear, sunny days. Expert skiers will love the place under all conditions.

Although the trails at Arapahoe are narrow, steep and gladed, the opposite is true at Keystone Mountain and North Peak. Here the runs are wide, are meticulously maintained, and are ego boasters!

Keystone has installed extensive artificial snowmaking capabilities which afford it the distinction of being the first ski resort to open each year. During the 1987-1988 season, Keystone could make snow on 395 acres (580 ha) or 79% of its skiable terrain. At North Peak, Keystone was able to make snow on 100 acres (40 ha) or 50% of its skiable terrain. There are no snowmaking capabilities at Arapahoe Basin. Due to A-Basin's high altitude, snowmaking is not necessary because the area catches snow early in the season and it stays late into the spring. Frequently, Arapahoe Basin (due to its high altitude) is the last mountain in Colorado to close. When it does close it is usually not due to a lack of snow, but rather due to a lack of motivated skiers.

Keystone continually grooms its beginner and intermediate slopes. Grooming of expert or advanced trails is limited and usually does not consist of more than chopping down moguls that have grown too formidable. Each day, the mountain's management meets and decides which trails will be groomed, and this information is posted conveniently at the base of each lift. Such attention to grooming assures beginner and intermediate skiers of a consistent soft pack for skiing. At Keystone there is usually little hard pack and rarely any ice. There also is almost never any powder of consequence. If weather conditions bless the slopes with abundant powder, Keystone skiers should seek out the advanced and expert runs at North Peak and Arapahoe Basin. The powder in the Colorado Rockies is generally very light and relatively easy to ski if one understands the necessary technique.

Average daily temperatures during the season taken at the top of Keystone Mountain:

Oct.	43°	(6°C)
Nov.	31°	(0°C)
Dec.	30°	(-1°C)
Jan.	29°	(-2°C)
Feb.	28°	(-2°C)
Mar.	34°	(1°C)
Apl.	44°	(6°C)

Night Skiing

Beginner and intermediate skiers have 2,340 vertical feet available from dark until 10:00 P.M. each evening for night skiing. Tickets are available for $10, and uphill transport is via the Skyway Gondola. Full cafeteria service at the Summit is also available.

Lift Ticket Prices *(1987-88)*

$30 Adult Daily
$26 Adult Multiple Day Ticket Per Day
$12 children Daily, Under 13
$10 Children Multiple Day Ticket Per Day
All major credit cards accepted

Special lift tickets that are exchangeable for lift tickets at Copper Mountain and Breckenridge, both located within thirty minutes' drive from Keystone, are available. Free shuttle bus service is offered.

Hours of Operation

8:30 A.M. to 4:00 P.M. at Base
Upper Lifts Close at 3:30 P.M.

The Skyway Gondola and several chairlifts at Keystone Mountain are open for night skiing until 10:00 P.M.

Lift Ticket Purchase Locations

Lift ticket purchase locations are conveniently located at the base of Keystone Mountain and at Arapahoe Basin. Tickets may also be purchased at the Keystone Lodge, the Condo Registration Desk, the Activity Desk, the Ski School, and at designated locations throughout metro Denver.

If lift tickets are purchased at the base of the mountains, waiting in line usually is no longer than five minutes except during the Christmas, New Year's, and Easter weeks. During these times the wait can be as long as twenty minutes.

Crowd Control

As would be expected, the longest lift lines occur at the base of the Skyway Gondola. Other lines form at the base of the Argentine Lift, the Peru Lift, the Saints John Lift and the Exhibition Triple Lift at Arapahoe Basin. Lines at these lifts from 9:00 A.M. until 10:30 A.M. can exceed fifteen minutes. Similar delays should be expected from 1:00 P.M. through 2:00 P.M. daily.

Crowd avoidance can be achieved during peak periods by skiing at Arapahoe Basin or North Peak rather than Keystone Mountain. At Keystone Mountain proper plan to ski trails served by the Erickson, Montezuma, and Ida Belle lifts.

Ski School

Keystone's Ski School is located at the base of the gondola in River Run Plaza and at Keystone Mountain Plaza base area.

These locations are convenient to the slopes, mountain restaurants, ski rental and repair shops, apparel shops, transportation, and day care facilities.

The ski school's staff consists of 150 instructors trained in the American Teaching System (ATS) of skiing. Classes consist of no more than seven students of similar ability levels. Group lessons are from 10:00 A.M. to 12:00 P.M. and are from 1:00 P.M. to 3:00 P.M. daily.

Private lessons by the hour or day can be arranged at any of the ski desks.

Rates for group lessons are $25 per two and one-half hours. Private lessons are $50 per hour.

Special lessons are available from time to time depending on weather conditions and sufficient skier demand. These lessons include:

Handicapped
Racing Clinics
Powder

Equipment Rental

Equipment rental shops are located in both the River Run Plaza and in the Keystone Mountain Plaza as well as at the base of Arapaho Basin. These locations are convenient to the slopes, mountain restaurants, ski schools, transportation, and day care facilities.

Equipment Rental Rates (1987-88):

$15 Recreation Package consisting of Skis, Poles, Bindings, Boots.
$12 Skis Only
$12 Boots Only
$ 3 Poles Only

Rental equipment consists of Technica boots, Fischer Swinglite skis, Salomon bindings, and Scott poles.

Keystone's rental equipment is excellent. Each year new equipment is purchased. Thus, equipment renters are assured of superior rental equipment that is fitted by factory-trained technicians.

A rental deposit of $100 is required for theft and breakage protection. Upon return of the equipment, the deposit is returned. Cash or credit cards are accepted.

Prior to renting equipment, skiers are required to sign a hold harmless form relieving Keystone of liability should they be injured while using the rented equipment.

High-performance skis may be *demoed* (rented) from sporting goods stores located at Keystone for a day or a week unless snow cover is inadequate.

Ski Tuning and Repair

Tuning and repair services are available at all ski rental shops, sporting goods stores, and at Precision Tuning located at the base of Keystone Mountain. Precision has stone grinding equipment which provides a superior flat surface to the ski compared with other common methods of tuning. Skis must be warm before waxing. Therefore, it is a good idea to drop the skis off at the end of the day and pick them up next morning.

Rates for Tuning (1987-88):

$ 5 Hot Wax
$25 Flat File
$ 7.50 (Pair) Edges Sharpened
$30 Complete Tune-up
$15 Bindings Adjusted
$20+ P-tex

Mountain Restaurants

Finding good food to eat is never a problem at any of Keystone's three mountains. The Summit House, located at the summit of Keystone Mountain, has cafeteria-style service on all three levels. In addition to the usual assortment of hot and cold food, special items such as pizza, barbeque, and fresh pastries are available. The Summit House is open from 8:30 A.M. through 4:00 P.M. Breakfast is not served here. Wine and beer service is restricted after 2:00 P.M.

At the base of Keystone Mountain, similar services are available at River Run Plaza and Keystone Mountain Plaza. These locations do serve complete hot and cold breakfasts. Food and beverage service is also available at the Freewater Saloon in River Run Plaza. Gassy Thompson, located in Keystone Mountain Plaza, offers complete sit-down meals at reasonable prices. Also at Keystone Mountain Plaza is a colorful outdoor wagon where delightful hot crepes and soft drinks are sold. Spirits are available from the Last Lift Bar, located on the second floor of the Mountain Plaza building.

On warm clear days, the staff at Keystone will generally set up a grill at the base of the Santiago Lift at North Peak. This is a comfortable setting where skiers can bask in the sun and enjoy a quick hamburger or hot dog.

The food and beverage service at Arapahoe Basin, though quite adequate, is not of the same caliber as at Keystone Mountain.

Day Care

Keystone's Children's Center is located in the Mountain Plaza building near the base of the Argentine and Peru lifts; at Arapahoe Basin the Children's Center is located under the restaurant at the base of the mountain. Both locations are staffed with individuals trained and licensed by the state of Colorado. Programs are available for children to take ski instruction or to participate in play groups. Programs are available for half day or full day care. Full day care includes a nourishing meal. Ages accepted: two years through eight years. Reservations should be made at the time accommodations are booked. Telephone (800) 255-3715.

Children aged three through twelve may be enrolled in "Children Only" ski instruction programs. The classes begin at 8:30 A.M. and end at 4:30 P.M. These programs provide supervised play, ski lessons, and lunch. Equipment rentals can be included in this program. Only eight children are allowed in any one class and they have their own section of mountain to ski that is "off limits" to adults.

Medical Facilities

Keystone's medical facility is located in the Snake River Health Services building at the base of Keystone Mountain Plaza just below the Argentine Lift. This modern clinic is staffed from 8:00 A.M. through 6:00 P.M. with local doctors on call 24 hours per day. At least one doctor is an orthopedic specialist. Day surgery is available and minor or emergency surgery is possible. For serious illness or injuries that cannot be handled by the clinic, there is a helicopter pad directly adjacent to the health facility with air ambulance service to any of Denver's hospitals. Ground transportation via commercial ambulance is also available. Prescription drugs on a limited basis are dispensed by the clinic when prescribed by one of the staff physicians. Other prescription needs can be filled by the pharmacy located in the town of Dillon three miles west of the resort.

Cross-Country Skiing

The cross-country skiing point of embarkation is located at the colorful Ski Tip Lodge deep in the heart of the Arapaho National Forest. A total of 46 kilometers of trails, twenty-seven of which are groomed, make up the majority of the cross-country terrain. Equipment rentals and instruction are available from mid-November through early April.

Special Events

NASTAR races are held daily in Keystone Mountain's Packsaddle bowl. Registration can be completed at any of the ski school locations. The fee is $5 for two runs: additional runs may be purchased for $2 each.

Coin operated, self-serve slalom racing is also available in Packsaddle Bowl.

From November through June, Phil and Steve Mahre offer specialized training to skiers of all abilities. This training course consists of five day sessions which include three day intensive race camps.

Special events vary from day to day and month to month at Keystone. However, they will typically include functions such as sleigh rides, hot air balloon rides, moonlit dinners in The Summit House, snowmobiling through the beautiful Arapaho National Forest, and special interest seminars. Movies are shown nightly in Keystone Lodge and in nearby Dillon.

Accommodations

Hotel

The only hotel at Keystone is The Lodge, located approximately a half mile from Keystone Mountain Plaza. Rooms are tastefully decorated with a superior quality furniture, unusual at most ski resorts. The Lodge has been the annual recipient of the prestigious American Automobile Association's Five Diamond Award and the Mobil Travel Guide's 4-Star rating. Most of the rooms in the Lodge have private balconies from which spectacular views of either Keystone Mountain or adjacent peaks can be seen. Some rooms have separate sitting rooms and loft bedrooms. All Lodge guests have access to the heated swimming pool, therapy pool, and sauna. The Lodge is a full-service hotel with valet, room service, daily housekeeping, travel agency, and nightly bed turn-down. All rooms have color television and free HBO cable service.

Within the Lodge are two cocktail lounges and three restaurants offering a variety of service and menus.

Condominiums

All the services available to guests of the Lodge are also available to guests of Keystone's condominiums. Amenities include a central switchboard and 24 hour check-in service. All guests are given their own Keystone credit card which can be used at any of the resort's shops.

Four grades of condominiums are available: Standard, DeLuxe, Premium and Slopeside.

Standard: Key Condo, Wild Irishman, Flying Dutchman, and Keystone Gulch. All are located in varying directions about one mile from the slopes. Keystone's private coach service makes daily ten-minute runs between all the condos and the Lodge, shops, and mountain bases. All accommodations are clean and modern with fully equipped kitchens including garbage disposals and dishwashers. All units have fireplaces stocked with wood; every other day maid service is provided.

DeLuxe: Pines, Soda Spring, Soda Spring II, Homestead/Lodgepole, Quicksilver, Saints. John, and Tennis Townhouses. DeLuxe condos have the same amenities found in the premium condominiums, but instead of being located around Lake Keystone, they are situated in picturesque settings throughout the resort.

Premium: Argentine, Plaza, Mall, Edgewater, Lakeside, Willows, Montezuma, Lenawee, and Decatur. These condos are situated around Lake Keystone but are convenient to The Lodge and most of Keystone's shops. Several restaurants are also located within easy walking distance. During Christmas, a beautifully lighted Christmas tree decorates the center of the lake. Spending an evening by the fire over-looking the skaters on the lake is a moment in time to cherish.

Slopeside: Chateaux d'Mont, Lancaster Lodge. The Chateaux is Keystone's most expensive lodging. During Christmas, a two bedroom condo will rent for $400 per night. Each Chateaux unit contains its own private hot therapy pool, Jenn-Air range, Scotsman ice maker, individual room thermostats, humidity control, clothes washer and dryer, private balcony, private ski locker, and Sub-Zero refrigerator. The interiors of several units were professionally designed and furnished by world famous Ginsler & Associates. All the amenities afforded guests at the Lodge are also provided to guests at Chateaux d'Mont including use of the swimming pool, central switch board, message center, and wake up calls. Daily maid service is provided.

The Lancaster Lodge consists primarily of efficiency units complete with Murphy beds. Space is limited here, but the amenities provide a comfortable setting in which to relax after a day on the slopes.

Ski Tip Lodge

Located east of the River Run Plaza, the Ski Tip Lodge is a twentieth-century anachronism. A restored 1860 stagecoach stop, the Ski Tip is steeped in mountain tradition and lore. Guests are treated to rooms without telephones or television. Meals are served family-style in the dining room and there is a different menu each evening. Nestled among the Lodgepole pines, the Ski Tip Lodge is the center for cross-country and telemark skiing. Visitors are guaranteed their stay at "The Tip" will be a memorable vacation. Space is limited so interested individuals or groups are urged to make reservations early.

Restaurants

Among the major restaurants located within the Keystone Resort, several are owned and operated by the resort itself. Perhaps the finest restaurant in the entire county is the Ranch, located on Keystone's Robert Trent Jones-designed golf course. The restaurant itself is in an exquisite log building that was originally home to a local ranching family. The decor and ambience of the dining room are reminiscent of the ranching and mining enterprises that originally occupied the area residents. Each day a prix fixe menu consisting of seven courses is offered. The food's preparation and its presentation are peerless. The Ranch is truly a world-class restaurant. Its wine cellar is stocked with the finest vintages of rare wine, as well as a complete offering of medium priced varietals. The building, the view of the snowcapped peaks, the food, and the service definitely make the Ranch a treat for hungry skiers interested in a formal dining experience.

Located in the Lodge at Keystone is another equally enjoyable restaurant, the Garden Room. This restaurant offers fare similar to that of the Ranch, but on a menu basis. The view from its floor-to-ceiling windows is of the ice skating rink, brilliantly decorated with twinkling lights, and Keystone Mountain's brightly illuminated ski trails. The service and ambience of the Garden Room are faultless.

Also located across from the skating rink is the Navigator, a fine seafood restaurant. Privately owned, the Navigator flies fresh fish in daily. The atmosphere is less formal than at either the Ranch or the Garden Room. The Navigator's soup and salad bar is excellent, and nightly entertainment in its lounge is always quite good.

Other fine restaurants abound within the resort and without as well. Because Keystone is located in Summit County, Colorado, all the fine dining establishments located at Copper Mountain, Breckenridge, Frisco, and Dillon are convenient to visitors. Among those to be visited are: The Snake River Saloon (seafood and Italian), Weber's (German), The Blue Spruce (American), Farley's (American), Charity's (American), The Plaza (Continental).

There is also a full complement of McDonald's, Wendy's, Pizza Hut, Arby's and similar fast food restaurants to keep the youngsters happy.

Activities

Keystone's winter activities include swimming in the Lodge's heated indoor/outdoor swimming pool, tennis in its indoor facility, aerobics and Nautilus in its health facility, racquetball, ice skating, snow mobiling, hot air balloon rides, dog sled rides, sleigh rides, and tours of the mountains in snow cats. Nightly movies in the Lodge are offered for a nominal fee.

Services

A complete range of sporting goods stores, apparel shops, pharmacies, grocery stores, liquor stores, furniture, bath, and specialty shops is within the immediate Keystone area.

KILLINGTON, LTD.

Killington, Vermont 05751

(800) 343-0762 Reservations
(802) 422-3333, ext. 240 Information
(802) 422-3261 Snow Report

Transportation

Killington can be reached conveniently from the Rutland Airport, Rutland Vermont. This is a small airport located only eighteen miles from the mountain. Direct flights from Boston's Logan Field and New York's Newark Airport are via Eastern Express. These flights typically utilize commuter aircraft and can seat approximately forty persons.

Car rental agencies at the Rutland Airport include Hertz and Avis. Because the quantity of automobiles is limited, it is wise to have a reservation. Be sure to request a car with snow tires and ski racks. The ski racks provided are of a highly portable nature. They do not have a rigid construction, and it is entirely likely that upon the traveler's arrival at the car rental counter, the ski racks will be handed to him in a plastic bag. It will be up to the renter to attach the rack to the car. These racks will accommodate only four pairs of skis.

Killington is located at the junction of U.S. Highway 4 and Vermont Highway 100 in Sherburne. Both of these are good, hard surface roads, and they are kept scrupulously clean by the highway department.

Mountain Statistics

Killington is the largest ski resort in the Eastern United States. It consists of six peaks which are referred to as separate mountains: Sunrise Mountain, Bear Mountain, Skye Peak, Killington Peak, Snowdon Mountain, and Rams Head Mountain. All these peaks can be skied by skiers of all levels of ability, and it is easy for all skiers to move from one mountain to another.

Killington is the only resort on the East Coast to be included in this review because it is the only one large enough to offer all ability levels enough mountain to ski for a week without becoming bored by the terrain. Killington is also the only Eastern resort that includes all the amenities one has grown to expect at major destination ski resorts.

Killington has an awesome lift capacity considering the number of acres served. In all, there are eighteen lifts consisting of:

6 Double Chairlifts
4 Triple Chairlifts
5 Quad Chairlifts
2 Surface Lifts
1 Gondola

Interestingly, the three and one-half mile gondola is the longest in North America. Killington's total skiable area is 721 acres (288 ha) with a vertical drop of 3,160 feet (1,036 meters). There are five bases, or entry points, to the mountain with the lowest elevation at the gondola at 1,160 feet (353 meters). The highest point is Killington Peak at 4,241 feet (1,293 meters).

Killington maintaines 107 trails or open slopes. Of these, 45% are rated as beginner, 20% as intermediate, and 35% as expert. Expressed in actual numbers the total skiable trails are as follows:

48 Beginner
21 Intermediate
38 Expert

The longest beginner run is Juggernaut which spirals from the top of Killington Peak to its base at Northeast Passage. It is 10 miles (16 km) long and winds through some of Vermont's prettiest countryside. The longest continuous intermediate run is Timberline, though Chute is almost the same length. The longest expert run is Cascade.

The maximum number of skiers transported per hour on Killington's mountains is 26,027. The total number of skiable acres divided by the maximum uphill capacity is .027 which is the highest ratio of lifts to skiers of the resorts covered in this review. Clearly, Killington is crowded. It also has a policy of selling lift tickets as long as there are people willing to purchase them. Therefore, the potential for crowding at all of the base facilities is even greater than on the mountain itself. The person who is considering a Vermont ski vacation should consider the potential crowding that occurs during the peak periods of Christmas and Easter. Because Killington is close to the East's major population centers, its resultant crowding may be reason enough for skiers to consider one of the many Rocky Mountain resorts.

There are ways, however, to minimize the inconvenience of Killington's crowds. The most crowded base areas are Snowshed and Killington. Crowds are much lighter at the Northeast Passage base and the Gondola base. Likewise, Sunrise and Bear Mountains do not have as many skiers as do the other peaks. Both of these areas offer skiing for all levels of ability, though it is on the light side for intermediate skiers. Located at the foot of the Northeast Passage parking lot is Killington's most famous, some might say infamous, run: Outer Limits. This run is not found on the trail map; rather it is only identified as an expert portion of the run called Nor'eastern. This is a steep, heavily moguled run which can become icy due to the heavy skier traffic.

On cold, windy or snowy days, relief from the elements can be found by skiing Bear Mountain. This is the most sheltered part of the Killington complex and also comprises some of its best expert terrain.

During the 1986-87 season, Killington received over 288 inches of natural snow. This was considered an excellent year. Average snowfall, though, is a respectable 237 inches (602 cm). The monthly snowfall for 1986-87 was:

Nov.	27"	(69 cm)
Dec.	47"	(119 cm)
Jan.	128"	(325 cm)
Feb.	65"	(165 cm)
Mar.	22"	(56 cm)

Although Killington was open in October 1987, the skiing was done entirely on man-made snow on limited terrain.

Due to Killington's low elevation, the weather sometimes does not cooperate, and snow can turn to rain or the accumulated snowfall can turn to slush or worse, to ice! Most Western skiers condemn the East for its icy conditions. Though it is true the East exhibits more icy conditions than does the West, its negative reputation is not deserved. Killington has a very sophisticated snowmaking program and, as long as the weather is below freezing, makes abundant quantities of snow. Half of the mountain can be fully serviced with snowmaking, and an early base is always applied to help conserve the natural snowfall.

According to John Okalovich, Director of Killington's Ski School, the conditions are not considered "icy" unless one cannot "set an edge." Skiers unaccustomed to Eastern conditions should, therefore, make every effort to keep their edges razor sharp and have their skis tuned frequently since Eastern conditions are "less forgiving" than typical Western conditions.

The average daily temperatures during the season are:

Nov.	28°	(-2° C)
Dec.	26°	(-3° C)
Jan.	17°	(-8° C)
Feb.	16°	(-9° C)
Mar.	26°	(-3° C)
Apl.	34°	(1° C)

Lift Ticket Prices *(1987-88)*

$32 Daily
$55 2 Day Consecutive
$83 3 Day Consecutive
$110 4 Day Consecutive
$128 5 Day Consecutive
$154 6 Day Consecutive
$176 7 Day Consecutive

Killington has joined the trend other major ski resorts are pursuing in attempting to entice its clients to extend their visits by offering discounts for longer stays. Lift ticket prices for Killington are only slightly less confusing to figure out than the IRS's 1040! Skiers planning a visit to Killington, or any other resort for that matter, should carefully review their options regarding available packages. Typically, lodging and lesson packages at Killington reduce lift ticket prices significantly.

Lift ticket prices for children twelve years old and under are $17 during the regular season but $18 during holiday periods.

Hours of Operation

9:00 A.M. to 4:00 P.M. weekdays
8:00 A.M. to 4:00 P.M. weekends.

After Thanksgiving, Killington offers the first half hour of skiing FREE. This serves two purposes: first, it offers skiers the option of testing the mountain before investing in a lift ticket. Second, the local managers and staff of lodging establishments are encouraged to take a run or two first thing each morning so they can be knowledgeable about the conditions on a day-to-day basis and be able to answer clients' questions with confidence.

Crowd Control

As previously mentioned, Killington can become crowded. This is natural because it is the largest and the most complete resort on the East Coast. Its close proximity to New York City and Boston make it natural for skiers to frequent the resort.

There is no substitute for local knowledge. The mountain must be skied frequently in order for skiers to learn how to minimize the effects of so many people on the slopes. Prudent skiers will do everything they can to avoid the Snowshed and Killington Peak base areas. These two areas are the most convenient to the lodging and, therefore, the most crowded.

Avoid eating lunch during the traditional period of 11:30 A.M. to 1:30 P.M. This may be the best time to ski those runs serviced by the Killington Peak Double Chair because most people eat at the base or at the restaurant at the top of this lift. After 2:30, the rush to the parking lots at the bottom of these two bases can resemble the Tokyo subway. On the other hand, if skiers have parked at one of the other bases they will not be significantly inconvenienced by crowds.

Ski School

Adult classes begin at 9:30 A.M. and 1:00 P.M. daily for two hours. Class registration occurs at either the Snowshed base or the Killington Peak base. Individuals interested in lessons should make advance reservations by telephoning (802) 773-1500. The need for reservations is due, of course, to the large number of skiers who frequent Killington.

Killington has a terrific ski school that teaches what it refers to as the "Accelerated Ski Method." The ski school boasts it can teach most people enough technique in two hours for them to enjoy skiing most of the beginner runs. Indeed, Killington has made a major commitment to teaching new skiers. The ski school director has authority to demand service from the mountain maintenance crews as he feels it is needed. In addition, he controls two runs used solely for the ski school. One of these runs is a relatively long trail that runs from the Killington base to the Snowshed base. This extremely easy trail is designed to teach beginners very specific exercises. The slope is divided into twelve teaching stations. The beginner is instructed in balance and control, how to step from one ski to the other, and how to form a wedge into a turn. After completion of these exercises, students are ready to follow their instructor up the mountain and commence sharpening their newly acquired skills.

Advanced skier and family workshops are available, as are private lessons. Individual adult lesson rates are $17. Family workshop rates for up to five persons are $100. Private lessons are $37 per hour (1987-88 rates).

Equipment Rental

Rental equipment shops are conveniently located at Killington's five base areas: Snowshed base, the Gondola base, Bear Mountain and Killington bases, and the Northeast Passage base.

Rental skis are Elan. Bindings are either Look or Salomon, and boots may be either Salomon or Nordica. High-performance skis may also be rented at any of these locations, if desired. The 1987-88 rates were $21 per day for adults and $14 per day for juniors. Special rates were available for those skiers who are visiting Killington on package plans. A $100 deposit was required, as well as a valid driver's license. In lieu of cash, a credit card may be used to post the deposit.

Numerous ski rental shops are also located at the foot of Killington Mountain in the town of Sherburne.

Ski Tuning and Repair

Tuning and repair services are available at all five base areas from the same shops that provide rental skis. Tuning is critical to achieving satisfying skiing in the East. It is important to have ski edges sharp and the skis structured. The services available from the base area shops do not incorporate the latest technology; however serious skiers are advised to seek out local shops that can not only flat file and sharpen their skis' edges, but which can also "structure" skis. In order to perform this service, the shop will need to have either equipment manufactured by Montana Ski Service (marketed under the brand name "Crystal Glide Finish") or Tazzari G.L. Both of these techniques utilize a man-made stone wheel to flatten and finish the ski bottom. In many cases, this is the identical equipment ski manufacturers used when they originally finished their skis.

The use of this type of equipment for tuning the skis eliminates the "whiskers" associated with sanding. It also applies a pattern or structure to the ski's bottom which is extremely important in reducing the friction on the bottom of the ski itself. Imagine trying to separate two sheets of wet glass. It is difficult to do because the water causes suction. The same thing occurs in varying degrees when skiing. The friction caused by the ski's gliding over the snow creates heat which causes the snow to melt and become water. When this happens, suction occurs and unless it is broken up by structuring the ski's bottom, it will slow the skis down and make turning more difficult. Individuals involved in ski racing will actually determine the skis' structure on the day of the race by evaluating snow conditions, temperature, and course conditions, and then dictate the exact structure they want. Portable machines are available and tuning can take place just prior to the race.

Crystal Glide equipment performs one other important process not possible with conventional services. It bevels the edge of the ski. Beveling should be somewhere between 1° and 3°. Ideally, it will taper from 1° at the toe and heel to 3° at its center. Beveling the edges does not dull the edge but enables skiers to more easily rotate from one edge to another without exaggerated un-weighting.

Mountain Restaurants

All of Killington's mountain top restaurants are cafeterias. The facilities are neat and clean, but the food is unimaginative and served without creativity. Don't expect to find any outdoor barbecues here. State law prohibits restaurants from cooking on open flames. Apparently this is due to a fear that an errant cinder could ignite a forest fire.

Lounges serving beer, wine, and spirits are located on the second floor of the Snowshed base facility, the second floor of the Killington Peak base, at the top of the Killington Peak, and at Bear Mountain Lodge.

Fine dining and individual seating is available at the Snowshed base. Just adjacent to the cafeteria is Pogonips. This is a bright, airy dining room with a nice view of the beginner runs going down Killington Peak. The restaurant specializes in pasta which is creatively served. Try its fresh pasta with dill.

Another charming restaurant located at the foot of Northeast Passage is the "Back Behind Saloon Restaurant." Featuring steaks and fresh seafood, the chef augments each day's selections with his unique specials. The restaurant is a great place to relax and enjoy a break from the day's skiing.

Day Care

Day care is available to Killington guests at the Children's Center located in the Snowshed base area. The Children's Center is licensed by the state of Vermont as a day care center. It accepts children from six weeks to eight years of age.

Enrollment in the day care program is by reservation only, and a fifty percent non-refundable deposit is required. During holiday periods, only full day reservations will be accepted.

The Children's Center staff is trained to work with small children, and it has divided the center into specific areas of play such as the reading corner, the block building area, a gross motor skills area, and a fine motor skills area. Indoor and outdoor activity is planned, and parents are advised to make certain they bring adequate clothing. Formula and diapers for infants should also be provided by the parents.

Children three to eight years old can enroll in the beginner ski program. This includes two one hour lessons each day with the balance of the time spent on other activities. Rental equipment for these small children is available at the Snowshed ski rental desk.

The Children's Center is open every day and operates from 8:00 A.M. to 4:00 P.M. Saturday through Monday. The center opens at 8:30 A.M. Tuesday through Friday. Special rates are available for children visiting for more than one day. One day visits are $25 and include lunch. For infants (six weeks to two years) there is an additional $10 charge.

Medical Facilities

Medical facilities at Killington are limited to five first aid stations located at each base area. Injured skiers determined to need professional medical treatment are transferred to the Rutland Medical Center located only sixteen miles from the mountain. The Medical Center has a completely staffed emergency department manned 24 hours each day. This is a full service hospital whose staff is able to perform identical services to those found in any large metropolitan area hospital.

Cross-Country Skiing

The Vermont countryside is among the most scenic in the United States. Unfortunately, there is no cross country skiing available at Killington Mountain proper. However, numerous operations are adjacent to the resort. Two of the largest such facilities are Mountain Meadows and Mountain Top.

Special Events

During the 1987-88 season, Killington offered its "Complimentary Ski Week Program." It is anticipated that this will become a regular feature of the resort. The Ski Week Program was open to any skier who purchased a five, six, or seven day lift ticket. The program began on Monday with a welcoming party featuring a free buffet and live entertainment. On Tuesday there was a clinic on Alpine skiing and a presentation of ski fashions. A ski tuning clinic was run on Wednesday afternoons with movies and popcorn later in the evening. During Friday afternoons, participants were awarded trail pins signifying their completion of the program.

On Thursday evenings after the sunset, the famous Santore Brothers staged a pyrotechnical show of fireworks.

Accommodations

As a full service resort, Killington offers its guests all the lodging amenities one would expect. Hotels and condominiums abound near the lifts and base lodges. However, there are no accommodations that can be considered ski-in/ski-out. It is necessary for lodging guests to drive to one of the base areas or to take one of the complimentary shuttles that run approximately every twenty minutes between the lodging and the mountain. If a guest is not staying at Killington proper, some of the surrounding accommodations will provide transportation to the mountain's gateway points.

There are two hotels at Killington: the Mountain Inn and the Cascades Lodge.

The Mountain Inn is a contemporary building with moderate rooms, not unlike rooms in any medium priced hotel. Each room has color TV, telephone and in-house movies. There is also a whirlpool, steambath, sauna, game room, and a pool table. The Mountain Inn's literature states that it is within walking distance to the lifts. This writer believes most people will find this a bit of an overstatement. It would be difficult to walk the distance wearing ski boots and carrying skis.

The Mountain Inn has a small but very nice dining room with a delightful maitre d'hotel. Its lounge is dark, and the bartender is less than attentive. However, when it is crowded and there is entertainment, the room takes on an ambience of its own to everyone's enjoyment.

Just across the street from the Mountain Inn is the Cascades Lodge. The hallways are decorated with antique ski memorabilia which is quite interesting and charming. The rooms are not unlike those found in the Mountain Inn, but the management and service personnel seem friendlier and more caring about their guests. Dining in the Copper Penny cafe is warm and intimate. The food and service are pleasant.

The Cascades also has an indoor heated swimming pool, two whirlpools, a sauna, and a Universal Gym as well as an exercycle just in case the skier did not get enough of a workout on the slopes!

The Wooden Nickel lounge is well stocked with spirits and the affable bartender will whip up any winter favorites on request. There is a blazing fireplace and wide screen TV to cozy up to on cold wintry nights.

Killington Village has an abundance of available condominiums. The flagship of the condos at Killington is High Ridge. Constructed from New England clapboard on Killington's highest promontory and surrounded by woods, High Ridge's setting is spectacular. Many units have views of Killington Mountain. Each condo has its own sauna and whirlpool; the fireplaces are faced in Vermont marble, and the living rooms feature cathedral ceilings. Amenities include icemakers, microwaves, self-cleaning ovens, and TVs equipped with VCRs and stereos.

There is also a large, heated indoor swimming pool located in the center of the development.

A two bedroom, two bath deluxe High Ridge condo rented during the 1987-88 high season for $309 per night.

Those skiers who are vacationing with their families may want to avoid staying at the Whiffletree condominiums, as this is the only complex at Killington that rents to college groups, such as fraternities.

For a complete list of accommodations both at Killington and in nearby Rutland and its environs, telephone (800) 343-0762 or (802) 773-1330 and request their free *Accommodation Guide* and/or *Your Guide to Lodging, Dining, Entertainment & Recreation in the Killington Area.*

Restaurants

No one should ever go hungry at Killington. There are marvelous restaurants throughout the area. Whether one's taste is for burgers or exotic seafood, there is a restaurant to satisfy the most demanding patron.

Not far from the base facilities on Highway 4 is located Hemingway's Restaurant. Established in an exceptionally well renovated old farm house complete with a stone walled wine cellar, Hemingway's offers Continental cuisine, enhanced by its chef's special touch. Hemingway's is the recipient of numerous culinary awards including the Mobile Guide AAA rating and an award from *Travel-Holiday*.

On the more rustic side, visitors should eat at The Wobbly Barn Steakhouse at least once during their vacation. Located just down the hill from the Snowshed base, Wobbly Barn is a Killington institution. Featuring mesquite grilled steaks, chops, and seafood, this moderately priced restaurant is a local favorite.

Across the street from the Wobbly Barn is Casey's Caboose. Constructed from what appears to be an old railway caboose with a snowplow attached to it, the restaurant features steak, chicken, seafood, and fresh Maine lobster. The atmosphere is casual and the bar personnel accommodating.

During the holidays, all of the restaurants in the area have long waiting lines. If the restaurant takes reservations, be sure to book them at least one day in advance. If reservations are not taken expect to wait at least an hour before being seated.

All of the restaurants accept credit cards but not all take American Express. Prudence would dictate that visitors make certain to carry Master Card or Visa if planning to charge meals.

Activities

The Killington Health Club is located in the Green Mountain III condominiums. This is an excellent facility for those who want a little more from their resort. Every exercise need and desire can be fulfilled at the Health Club with its lap pool, sauna, whirlpool, racquet ball courts, and exercise room with a Universal Gym and free weights. Aerobic classes are also held daily, and a telephone call will secure a reservation.

Other activities include ice skating, sledding, sleigh rides, movies, and winter camping. Additional health clubs and an assortment of bowling alleys are found in nearby Rutland.

Services

A full complement of sporting goods, stores, apparel shops, pharmacies, grocery stores. liquor stores (state run), furniture, bath, florist, ice cream, and other specialty shops is within the immediate area.

PARK CITY SKI AREA

Park City Ski Corp.
P.O. Box 39
Park City, Utah 84060

(800) 222-PARK Reservations
(801) 649-8111 Information
(801) 649-9571 Snow Report

Transportation

One of Park City's outstanding features is its accessibility. Located thirty-two miles from Salt Lake City on I-80, an all weather, six-lane highway, Park City is accessible from the Salt Lake Airport in under one hour.

Most Park City visitors who arrive by air arrange ground transportation with Lewis Brothers Stage. Comfortable buses or vans depart Salt Lake International Airport every hour on the half hour from 9:30 A.M. to 11:30 P.M. Return trips are made every hour on the hour between 7:00 A.M. and 3:30 P.M. Lewis Brothers Stage charged $10 each way and half fare for children under twelve during the 1987-88 ski season. Telephone (801) 649-2256 to book reservations.

Taxis, limousines, rental cars, and even helicopters are available from the airport to Park City.

Car rental agencies located at the airport include:

Agency	(801) 534-1622
Alamo	(801) 539-8780
AI	(801) 322-2488
Avis	(800) 654-3131
Budget	(801) 363-1500
Dollar	(801) 569-2580
Hertz	(800) 654-3131
National	(800) 328-4567

Mountain Statistics

Park City is a wonderful family mountain with a good mix of beginner, intermediate, and expert runs. This is the only resort reviewed that is not on national forest property. The land is leased to Park City Ski Corp. by mining concerns. In fact, prior to lift installation, skiers were taken near the top of the mountain by means of underground mining carts. Once at the end of the tunnel, the carts were lifted up by an elevator. The remains of this transportation system may be still be seen. Today, the old mining shafts are filled with water which is used for Park City's artificial snowmaking equipment. During fall and early winter, the water is pumped out of the shafts and in the spring when the snow melts, it runs back into the shafts. This is a self-contained ecosystem.

Park City has 2,200 acres (890 ha) of skiable terrain. Of this, 330 acres (133.5 ha) can be covered with man-made snow. There are 82 trails varying in length from one-quarter mile (.4 km) to three and one-half miles (5.6 km). Fourteen of the trails are rated by the resort as easier (beginner), 40 more difficult (intermediate), and 28 most difficult (expert). The longest beginner run is "Easiest Way Down" at 3½ miles (5.6 km). The longest intermediate run is "Payday" at 4,890 feet (1,490 meters). The longest expert run is "Shaft" at 3,830 feet (1,167 meters).

The lift system at Park City consists of:

8 Double Chairlifts
5 Triple Chairlifts
1 Gondola

The gondola at Park City is very unusual. Not only is it the longest gondola in the Western United States, but it also makes a turn half way up the mountain. Actually, the gondola changes cables at a half-way house called "Angle Station."

Park City's base at 6,900 feet (2,103 meters) and summit at 10,000 feet (3,048 meters) yield a vertical drop of 3,100 feet (945 meters).

The lift system at Park City is capable of transporting 18,700 skiers per hour. The number of skiable acres divided by the maximum uphill lift capacity is .117. This number is high, but skiers can anticipate less crowding than one would likely find at Aspen or Vail. It is a comfortable number, and if crowds are relatively evenly spaced, the queuing for lifts should not be excessive.

The mountain will remind skiers of Aspen Mountain and Aspen Highlands. Like each of these, Park City is a mountain on which the lifts go up a ridge, and where skiers ski down the sides of the ridge. However, the expert runs off the ridge at Park City are not nearly as steep as the ones on Aspen Mountain. Mountains such as these possess a lot of character. Because the trails emanate from ridgetops, they have several fall lines. Typically, they also have long run-outs from the bottom of the runs back to the lift stations.

Park City's mountain does not require a great deal of snow to be skiable. It does not have the rocky conditions one would find at a resort such as Jackson Hole or Snowbird. Park City receives an annual average of 350 inches (889 cm) of snow, the majority of which is received late in the ski season. The late snowfall is typical of the Rocky Mountains' winter.

Average monthly snowfalls are:

Oct.	19"	(48 cm)
Nov.	41"	(104 cm)
Dec.	43"	(109 cm)
Jan.	46"	(117 cm)
Feb.	52"	(132 cm)
Mar.	59"	(150 cm)
Apl.	26"	(66 cm)

The average daily temperatures at Park City are quite temperate for a ski resort:

November	26°	-3° C
December	31°	0° C
January	27°	-3° C

February	31°	0° C
March	37°	3° C

One of Park City's nicest features is that a beginning skier can ski from almost the top of the mountain all the way to the bottom by skiing along the Gondola to Angle Station, taking a left onto Sidewinder, and following it to the gondola base station. Another interesting thing to do at Park City is to take the Town Lift up from the town of Old Park City first thing in the morning. This is an unusual and beautiful ride between the historic old homes and lodging accommodations. In the evening, skiers take an intermediate run down either Quit'n Time or Creole back to Old Park City. The intermediate runs along the King Consolidated lift are excellent. Some of the runs are always groomed for cruising while others have moderate bumps for those who want to work on technique.

None of Park City's expert runs are beyond the reach of most competent recreational skiers. That is to say, there are no double black diamonds. The best expert runs have to be the trails in the bowls, of which there are several. The largest is Jupiter Bowl. Most of the bowl trails begin on open snow fields and end on gladed runs. They are never groomed, so depending on conditions, they can have serious moguls. Another interesting expert run is Blueslip Bowl, a small bowl, but steep. It derives its name from the staff members who were terminated for skiing it before the current owners decided to expand avalanche control and open it for recreational skiing. The Blueslip was the equivalent of corporate America's "Pinkslip."

In addition to all the excellent skiing at Park City, Deer Valley is only one mile away. The runs at Deer Valley are easy to intermediate and are meticulously groomed. The resort proper is among the most beautiful in America. However, it is a small mountain and would not normally maintain one's interest for more than a few days.

In the other direction from Park City, only minutes away, is ParkWest. Primarily a day ski area, it does not have a great many amenities associated with a destination resort. However, it is worth one's time to ski there. The mountain is about two-thirds the size of Park City. Taken together, the area forms one of the largest ski resorts in the country.

Guests staying in Park City can experience a European style of skiing found almost nowhere else in America. It is possible to ski from Park City to Snowbird via the Interconnect. The 1987-88 season price for the five area tour was $85 per person. The Interconnect takes eight hours to ski. Strong intermediates to experts can qualify for this great experience. On the way to Snowbird, skiers ski Solitude, Brighton, Alta, and Snowbird. Upon their arrival in Snowbird, a van returns the skiers to Park City. Shorter variations of this trip are also possible. Telephone (801) 534-1779 for information and reservations. Trips only depart on days when there is no avalanche danger, and skiers are grouped according to ability.

Night skiing is available on Pay Day and First Time. Night skiing lift tickets are good from 4:00 P.M. through 10:00 P.M. The 1988-89 fee for night skiing is $8 per adult and $5 for children twelve and under. Night skiing is free with the purchase of an afternoon half day lift ticket or with multiple day passes.

Lift Ticket Prices

During the 1988-89 ski season, Park City will have a two-tier lift ticket pricing structure. One tier price is for tickets purchased at any of the resort's ticket windows. A second, lower priced tier is available from travel agents, tour operators, and Park City lodging facilities. Purchase of tickets at the lower price must be made at least three weeks prior to arrival at Park City.

$32.......Adult, All Day
$14.......Child, All Day
$21.......Adult, Half Day
$10.......Child, Half Day
$16.......Ages 65-69
Free......Over 70

Multi-Day Pass Packages

Pre-purchased
$ 86......3 of 4 Day Pass
$114......4 of 5 Day Pass
$142......5 of 6 Day Pass
$170......6 of 7 Day Pass

At Ticket Wicket
$ 89......3 of 4 Day Pass
$118......4 of 5 Day Pass
$147......5 of 6 Day Pass
$176......6 of 7 Day Pass

Child, 12 and Under
$ 41......3 of 4 Day Pass
$ 54......4 of 5 Day Pass
$ 70......5 of 6 Day Pass
$ 80......6 of 7 Day Pass

Multi-Area Books
$155.......Adult, 5 of 6 Days
$ 70.......Child, 5 of 6 Days
$186.......Adult, 6 of 7 Days
$ 84.......Child, 6 of 7 Days

Multi-area lift tickets are good at Park City, Deer Valley ParkWest, Alta, Snowbird, Brighton, Solitude, and Sundance. However, because each area is owned by a different company and has different lift ticket prices, it is necessary for skiers purchasing these tickets to go daily to the resort's ticket window and exchange their book's ticket for the specific area's lift ticket. At those resorts with higher fees than Park City, the purchaser must pay the difference at the time of exchange. If the area to be skied is less expensive, then the skier probably will have to accept the difference in coupons exchangeable at the resort for food or some other similar purchase.

Hour of Operation

9:00 A.M. to 4:00 P.M. daily

Lift Ticket Purchase Locations

Lift tickets may be purchased at the ticket office located near the Gondola at the Resort Center. Alternately, tickets may be purchased at the base of the Town Lift in Old Park City.

Crowd Control

Crowds are at their worst during the Christmas—New Year's holidays. They can also be bad during Spring Break and on the weekends. The population of Salt Lake City has the same effect on the ski resort on weekends that Denver has on Keystone, Breckenridge, and Copper Mountain. However, during congested times, delays can be avoided by taking the Town Lift to the Crescent lift and skiing down one of the intermediate runs on the north side of Lost Prospector lift. From the top of Lost Prospector, the entire resort opens up for skiers.

Skiers staying near the Resort Center should avoid taking the Gondola. Instead, they should take the Ski Team lift and ski down to the Lost Prospector lift. From the top of Lost Prospector, it is possible to ski the entire mountain.

However, on crowded days it is important to avoid the Lost Prospector and Prospector lifts just before and after lunch time as these two lifts then become the most popular on the mountain.

Ski School

Park City employs two hundred certified ski instructors who teach the American Teaching System (ATS) and the Graduated Length Method (GLM). The GLM is only taught to rank beginners and only until they are competent enough to handle properly sized skis.

Beginning and low intermediate skiers meet at the Resort Center Meeting Place which is easy to find as it is just behind the lift ticket windows. Intermediates and advanced skiers meet at the Summit Ski School Meeting Place located near the terminus of the Gondola. All day classes meet at 10:00 A.M., break for lunch, and regroup at 2:15 P.M. Afternoon classes meet at 2:15 P.M.

$ 29.....Adult
$ 24.....Adult, Half Day
$ 70.....Adult, 3 Day
$1186.....Adult, 5 Day
$ 50.....Adult, 1 Hour Private
$135.....Adult, Half Day Private

Park City offers its Mountain Experience to advanced and expert skiers. These classes emphasize different ski techniques for skiing assorted snow conditions. Classes meet at the Summit Ski School Meeting Place at 10:00 A.M. The classes last five hours.

$ 29......One Day
$125......Five Day

Children's Classes

$ 25.......Full Day
$ 20.......Half Day
$ 90.......Five Half Day

Equipment Rental

There are nine ski rental companies in Park City. Most offer three types of rental equipment. The basic package offered is usually termed "Recreational." It is designed for novice or low intermediate skiers who will probably spend considerable time in lessons. The second package usually offered is called a "Sport" package. This is an upgrade of the recreational ski. The boots and the bindings are usually the same. However, the ski is always different and is typically a little stiffer. The third type of ski package is called "Performance" or "Demo." There is frequently a significant up-charge for this type of equipment. Many times the rental shop will offer more than one type of ski or boot. The equipment is almost always the manufacturer's top-of-the-line. Some examples of the rentals available follow:

Breeze Ski Rentals

Skis, Boots, Poles, & Bindings
$11.50 Per Day
$47.50 Per 5 Day Package

Children's rate is slightly lower.

Equipment offered includes Pre, Rossignol, K2, Olin skis, Nordica & Salomon boots and Salomon bindings.

Cole Sport, Ltd.

$8 - $17 Per Day: 1 to 3 Day Rental
$7 - $15 Per Day: 4 to 6 Day Rental
$6 - $14 Per Day: 7+ Days

Herman's World of Sporting Goods

$10......Adult, 1-3 Days
$ 9......Adult, 4-6 Days
$ 8......Adult, 7+ Days

Ski Tuning and Repair

There are substantial differences in the charges for tuning and repairing skis throughout the Park City area. For example, Breeze charges:

$ 2.50.....Hot Wax
$ 4.00.....Iron-On Wax
$ 7.50.....Deburr
$15.00.....Complete Tune
$15.00+....P-tex

Cole Sport, Ltd., using Wintersteger stone grinding equipment, charges:

$ 6.00.....Hot Wax
$10.00.....Deburr
$20.00.....Sharpen Edges
$28.00.....Full Tune
$28.00+....P-tex

The extra money for the stone grinding is worth it if the skis have not been kept in top condition. For a complete explanation of the benefits of stone grinding and "ski structuring," consult the *Ski Tuning and Repair* section of the review entitled *Killington*.

Mountain Restaurants

Park City has three mountain restaurants. The largest is a cafeteria located at the Summit where the Gondola terminates. This is a rustic restaurant whose shelter is typical of most ski resorts. However, the restaurant located on Pioneer is different.

The Mid-Mountain Lodge was built around the turn of the century for Silver King Mining Company. Originally, the lodge was a boarding house for miners. Later for a short time, it was the U.S. Ski Team's training center. In what has to be one of the most difficult house moving jobs ever performed, the two-story structure was relocated uphill intact with the aid of five bulldozers. After extensive renovation, the former boarding house was converted to a full service cafeteria. A large outdoor deck was added to the structure and the upstairs was converted to several large rooms to accommodate groups.

It is regrettable, however, that the service and the selection of items are not as interesting as the lodge itself.

The Snow Hut is located at the base of Prospector Double Chair. Often crowded during peak periods, Snow Hut serves cafeteria-style meals and an assortment of beverages including wine and beer.

Day Care

Day care for newborn and older children is available at either the K.I.D.S. Hotel or Miss Billie's Kids Campus.

The K.I.D.S. Hotel is located in the Olympic Hotel on Prospector Square, the most convenient location for guests staying in Park City. Prospector Square is a quasi-industrial/office area, located several long blocks from the ski resort proper. Miss Billie's is located across from ParkWest Ski Area.

The 1987-88 day care rate for K.I.D.S. Hotel was $45 for an entire day or $25 for a half day. Formula and diapers should be provided by parents. Older children receive lunch with their care. Both establishments are licensed by the state of Utah. Both establishments will provide a list of baby sitters for those parents who wish to step out in the evening. Reservations are suggested.

Telephone (801) 649-2900, ext. 7-KID for the K.I.D.S. Hotel or (801) 649-9502 for Miss Billie's.

Medical Facilities

Several medical emergency services are available in Park City, as well as Holy Family Health and Emergency Center. Holy Family is affiliated with Holy Family Hospital in Salt Lake City.

Skiers injured on the slopes are cared for by the ski patrol. The patrol will treat trauma and stabilize injuries, such as fractures. Further treatment is rendered at Holy Family Health and Emergency Center. Injured skiers are taken to one of the two emergency clinics on the mountain. Selection of clinics is determined by the location where the injury occurred and the severity of that injury. The ski patrol has complete treatment centers at the Summit House and at the Resort Base. If treatment is rendered at the Summit, the skier will be transported after stabilization to the base by gondola.

If an injury or illness is too extreme for the local hospital to treat, air ambulance service to Salt Lake is available.

Cross-Country Skiing

A great deal of cross-country skiing is available in the Park City area.

White Pine Touring has track skiing, lessons, and guided tours available. The Norwegian School of Nature can provide day or night tours into the back country. White Pine's telephone number is 649-8710 and the Norwegian School of Nature's is 649-1217.

Located five miles northeast of Park City is the Jeremy Ranch Cross Country Ski Area, just off I-80. The Ranch has three tracks, including a 3 km course for beginners, a 7 km course for intermediates, and an 11 km course for advanced and expert three pin skiers. Its telephone number is 649-2700.

Just twenty minutes south of Park City is the Homestead Resort with 10 km of track on the Wasatch Mountain State Park Golf Course. There is also a one-half kilometer training track.

All cross-country areas offer complete lessons, equipment rentals, and apparel. Prices are nominal.

Special Events

Each year, Park City has a full calendar of special events. The 1987-88 season was typical of the events staged and visitors can expect a similar calendar every year.

Nov: Visa Women All-Stars of Skiing race.

America's Opening Pro Cup.

Dec: Christmas Eve Torchlight Parade.

Jan: Utah Winter Games.

Senator's Ski Cup.

Mar: Utah Special Olympics Winter Games.

Apl: Adults & Kids Easter Egg Hunt.

The town of Park City also features a United States Film Festival. This program runs for ten days and includes American and foreign films, seminars and tributes.

Accommodations

Park City has accommodations for every budget. The best selection of upper end properties is found at Deer Valley Resort one plus mile from Old Park City.

The Yarrow Hotel, with its red brick tower, is somewhat of a landmark in Park City. As visitors approach the resort, it is one of the first resort properties seen. There are 179 rooms in the Yarrow. The hotel is attempting to convert to interval ownership, so the availability of rooms may be declining.

The Yarrow is a full service hotel whose large central lobby features a fireplace and nicely appointed furnishings. A ski rental shop is on the premises, as well as a Delta Airlines reservation desk and an

Alamo car rental agency. Additional amenities include a swimming pool, sauna, hot tubs, concierge service, room service, daily maid service, valet service and a complimentary shuttle to the mountain with hourly departures.

The Yarrow is scheduled for complete renovation during 1988-89. The result should be very pleasing as the rooms will become condos and some will add fireplaces and complete kitchens.

The Silver Queen is a jewel of a hotel. With only twelve rooms, each furnished differently, it is difficult to secure reservations on short notice. Located at the corner of Main Street in historic Old Park City, the Silver Queen has one and two bedroom condos. All have Jacuzzi baths, fireplaces, and washer and dryers. The kitchens are fully equipped so entertaining is easy. During the 1987-88 season, the condos rented for between $125 and $195 per night for a one bedroom unit. The two bedroom unit was between $165 and $225 per night.

One of the nicest and most convenient hotels in Park City is the Silver King. The Silver King is only a few steps from the slopes and features abundant amenities.

The Silver King is a condominium hotel. In other words, the units are privately owned, but the facility is operated like a hotel. There is a nicely appointed lobby with a large lacquered fireplace and big bright windows. The Silver King's underground parking is really appreciated on cold snowy days. The indoor swimming pool and spa are warm and comfortable, have ample seating areas, and temperature and humidity controls so one is not consciously aware of swimming indoors.

Although the units are individually furnished, there is a commonality to them. Some units may have a blue color scheme while others have a white one. All are furnished in country French. Even the smallest studio units are unique. Dining room ceilings are constructed out of glass, providing enjoyable views of the falling snow. What a cozy setting for relaxing in front of the crackling hearth!

The largest units are two bedroom penthouses which occupy two floors and have their own private spas. Large kitchens, living areas, entertainment areas and spacious bedrooms complete these marvelous accommodations.

Silver King accommodations were priced during the 1987-88 season from a low of $55 per night for a studio to $270 per night for a DeLuxe penthouse.

Many other fine accommodations exist in the greater Park City area, notably, The Washington School Inn, Stein Erickson Lodge in Deer Valley, and the Stag Lodge.

Restaurants

Perhaps the finest dining in the Park City area is found at Philipe's in Deer Valley's Stag Lodge. The menu changes every evening except for Philipe's famous rack of spring lamb which is a constant delight. The restaurant is perched on a cantilever above the lounge. It is tastefully decorated in native clear pine and accessorized with Indian artifacts. Philipe prepares his guests' dinner in full view and frequently tours the tables soliciting comments, which are always favorable.

In addition to the rack of lamb, a typical sampling of Philipe's other entrées may include escargots Vieux-Montreux, Shaffhausen onion tart, cassolette of calves' sweetbread, Norwegian salmon in a crust, braised quails with grapes, veal saltimbocca Romana, breast of duck Alexandra, and venison with wild mushrooms. All desserts are homemade.

After dinner, enjoy a warm snifter of brandy in the lounge overlooking the lodge's swimming pool.

On the more plebian side, try Hunan Restaurant located in the Resort Center. This Chinese restaurant is relatively new, and appears to need some time to organize. The shredded pork and garlic is as excellent as the hot and sour soup is inferior. The service is attentive and the prices are moderate. A word of caution: do not accept a table near the entrance. The door's constant opening and closing makes diners at these tables uncomfortably cold.

Cisero's, a fine Italian restaurant, is located in delightful Old Park City.

After booking a reservation at Cisero's, expect to wait in its downstairs bar. The restaurant will pay the club fee mandated by Utah liquor laws to compensate for the wait. However, one is expected to pay for the drinks consumed while waiting. The bar, located in a basement, is quite typical of mountain restaurants. The noise level is about twice what normal ears can stand, and the acoustics are non-existent. All these negatives somehow work well together, and the bar is a popular gathering spot for locals.

The restaurant upstairs is furnished in eclectic mountain style with both tables and banquettes. The menu features pasta dinners, veal dishes, and seafood. Specials include stuffed lumaconi, eggplant parmigiana, lasagna, Joe's vegetarian casserole, chicken cacciatore, and New York steak. The prices are low to moderate and the service attentive.

Activities

Non-skiing activities abound in Park City. Among them:

Snow tours on snowmobiles or snow cats. Telephone High Country Adventures at (801) 649-1217 for more information.

Guided snowmobile tours through the Wasatch high country. Telephone Snow Trek Tours for more information at (801) 645-RIDE.

Helicopter skiing in some of the best country around Park City. Telephone Utah Powderbird Guides for more information at (801) 649-9739.

Facials, pedicures, massage, acupressure, manicure, and make-up applications at the Winter Works. Telephone (801) 649-6363 for more information.

Grocery shopping services from "At Your Service." Telephone them at (801) 649-6700 for more information.

Hot air balloon rides around Park City. Call Balloon Affaire at (801) 649-1217 or Park City Balloon Adventures at (801) 645-8787.

Sleigh rides to a distant mountain cabin for dinner. Telephone Park City Sleigh Co. at (801) 649-3359 or Soup's On at ParkWest at (801) 649-1217 for information.

Other activities include legitimate stage performances in the Egyptian Theater in Old Park City or Gambling Tours to Nevada. Mrs. Field's Cookies are headquartered in Park City and tours of their production facilities can be arranged.

The shopping here in one of America's finest, restored mining towns is really excellent. Everything one could want is to be found on Main Street such as art galleries, tee shirt shops, restaurants, bars, hotels, and much more.

Services

Because Park City is a year-round, self-contained city, all the services one has grown to expect in a town can be found. There is a full complement of churches, sporting good stores, apparel shops, pharmacies, grocery stores, liquor stores, indoor tennis courts, ice skating, athletic clubs, aerobic classes, movies, dentists, gas stations, and optometrists.

SNOWBIRD SKI & SUMMER RESORT

Snowbird, UT. 84092

(800) 453-3000 Reservations
(801) 742-2222 Information
(801) 742-2222 Snow Report

TRANSPORTATION

Like Park City, one of Snowbird's best features is its accessibility. Located almost against the back wall of Little Cottonwood Canyon, Snowbird is only 31 miles from the Salt Lake International Airport.

The Utah Transit Authority runs seven buses daily from the airport to Snowbird. These departures are scheduled roughly every hour, beginning at 9:30 A.M. Look for the sign identifying Route 94 outside the baggage claim area. The 1987-88 season rate was $6.00. Taxis, limousines, rental cars, and even helicopters are available from the airport to Snowbird.

Car rental agencies located at the airport include:

Agency	(801) 534-1622
Alamo	(801) 539-8780
AI	(801) 322-2488
Avis	(800) 654-3131
Budget	(801) 363-1500
Dollar	(801) 569-2580
Hertz	(800) 654-3131
National	(800) 328-4567

Driving to Snowbird for the first time is something of a challenge. The Mormon Temple is considered the center of the city. Actually, however, it is located on the north side of town and is considered as "zero" for Salt Lake's street numbering system. Little Cottonwood Canyon is south of the city center. Take I-15 south from the airport or from the Temple about three miles. Watch the brown signs that indicate the Snowbird turn off. There are only a few of these signs, so keep a sharp eye out. Turn east onto Highway 209 and follow this road through commercial and residential properties until it ends at a 7-Eleven convenience store. The streets are not marked, but it is necessary to make a right turn here. Proceed to the next traffic light and turn left. This road meanders through a residential area and is called Little Cottonwood Canyon Road. Drivers will know they are on the correct road when they see a large electronic sign indicating road conditions for the rest of the trip up the canyon. In periods of heavy snow, snow tires will be required. Due to avalanche danger, there are times when the road is temporarily closed while road crews blast the snow away. Snowbird is located in the Wasatch Range which frequently receives snow in abundant quantities, so the skier should be prepared for delays.

On clear days, the drive down the mountain back into the city is beautiful. Be sure to take a camera because there are ample opportunities to photograph Salt Lake from the roadside.

Mountain Statistics

Snowbird is a great ski mountain with character and variety. There are steep, wide open runs, gladed runs, bump runs, and there are super powder runs everywhere.

Snowbird boasts of 1,900 acres (769 ha) of skiable terrain and has a total lift capacity of 8,810 skiers per hour. The base is located at 8,100 feet (2,469 meters) and the top of the tram is located at 11,000 feet (3,353 meters). This provides a vertical drop of 2,900 feet (884 meters).
The mountain is serviced by:

1 Aerial Tram
7 Double Chairlifts

The number of skiable acres divided by the maximum number of skiers transported per hour is .215, a favorable ratio for any resort. Crowding is usually not a problem at Snowbird even though it is close to a major city. This lack of crowding is primarily because there are a number of other day ski areas in the vicinity. It must also be noted that Snowbird is not an easy mountain. Its beginner and intermediate terrain is both more limited and more difficult than at most other resorts.

The trail rating used at Snowbird can equate with those of Jackson Hole, Sun Valley, and Telluride, but not with those of areas such as Keystone, Aspen, and Snowmass.

All beginner runs are located along the lower portion of the mountain and typically are catwalks. The main beginner run and teaching hill is Big Emma, named after a famous Alta madam during the height of the mining era. Big Emma is a great beginner run. It is wide and long, with a pitch so gradual that instructors can control their students' speed by limiting how far up the hill they take them.

Most of the intermediate runs are steep. However, the resort closely monitors the development of moguls and does an excellent job of cutting them before they present problems. Any intermediate who skis Snowbird will leave a better skier. The top of Chip's run is steep. Most intermediates will be able to ski down it if they stay in control. It is an excellent run, and all intermediates should ski it several times. It will build their confidence and will open up other areas of the mountain for them.

Another intermediate run, Regulator Traverse, is located on Regulator Johnson. Like Chip's Run, it is a groomed trail down the mountain's face. Due to the unique way the mountain has been developed, it is possible for members of a family with differing abilities to ski side by side on the same runs. For example, one family member who is an expert can take the bump side of Regulator Johnson, while an intermediate member can ski the Traverse's groomed trail.

However, by and large, Snowbird is for experts and aspiring experts. It is a mountain that requires a lot of snow. Fortunately, it receives over 550 inches (1,397 cm) annually. Monthly its snowfall is:

Nov.	65"	(165 cm)
Jan.	76"	(218 cm)
Feb.	84"	(213 cm)
Mar.	107"	(272 cm)
Apl.	75"	(191 cm)

Snowbird Mountain can be skied very differently depending upon snow conditions. During lean periods of snow, the runs are heavily moguled. They are best skied immediately after a heavy snowfall when the steepness is needed in order to maintain forward momentum.

The longest beginner run is Big Emma at 550 feet (168 meters). The longest intermediate run is Chip's Run at two miles (3.2 km), and the longest expert run is Silver Fox at 1.7 miles (2.7 km).

It should be pointed out that although Snowbird considers Big Emma to be its longest beginner run, some other resorts featured in this book have selected catwalks as their longest beginner runs. If Snowbird were to do the same, it would have several runs over one mile (1.06 km) in length. Likewise, it should be pointed out that Silver Fox is expert for the entire 1.7 miles!

Snowbird's terrain varies. The Cirque near the terminus of the tram is one of the world's greatest ski runs. It is a large bowl that catches abundant snowfall. The only problem is accessibility. The Cirque Traverse is a difficult run. It is narrow and steep: its sides drop off dangerously. First-time skiers on this run should use appropriate caution and remain in control. The back side of the Cirque is locally referred to as "Anderson's." Access to it is from Regulator Johnson. Ski about one-third of Regulator and begin traversing to the right. By doing this, skiers can ski under the Gad Chutes and can enjoy exceptional tree skiing.

As with most mountains that are steep, there are many possible runs and trails not indicated on the trail map. Virtually all the area within the resort's boundaries is skiable. Many of these unnamed runs require the services of a guide until one learns the ins and outs of the mountain. Any of Snowbird's snow hosts or hostesses will assist interested skiers in locating infrequently skied areas. After major storms, it is easy to see where locals have skied, but it remains difficult to surmise how they got there.

Many first-time visitors to Snowbird spend so much time skiing the Aerial Tramway, Little Cloud, and Gad lifts that they completely ignore the runs near the bottom of the mountain. This is a mistake because many fine runs such as Blackjack, Adager, and Harper's Ferry East are well worth their time. This is especially true if the wind is blowing and the temperature is dropping. During inclement weather, the only shelter may be on the Peruvian lift, Mid-Gad, and Gad-II lift.

Snowbird's average temperatures during the winter are:

Dec.	23°	-5°C
Jan.	21°	-6°C
Feb.	22°	-5°C
Mar.	25°	-4°C
Apl.	27°	-3°C

Lift Ticket Prices

Snowbird does not have a "high" or "low" season rate. There is only one rate. During the 1988-89 season that rate is:

```
$ 32.......Adult All Area   (Includes Tram)
$ 25.......Adult, All Chairs
$ 16.......Children, 12 & Under (Includes Tram)
$ 16.......Seniors, 62 & Older (Includes Tram)
$125.......Adult, 5 Day All Area
$ 65.......Child, 5 Day All Area
$161.......Adult, 7 Day All Area
$ 77.......Child, 7 Day All Area
```

Half Day Prices

$25......Adult, All Area (Includes Tram)
$19......Adult, All Chairs
$13......Child, All Area (Includes Tram)
$13......Senior, All Area (Includes tram)
$10......Child, All Chairs
$10......Senior, All Chairs

Morning half-day lift tickets are valid from 9:30 A.M. to 1:30 P.M. Afternoon half-day lift tickets are sold from 12:30 P.M. until closing.

Hours of Operation

Snowbird's hours of operation are different from any other resort featured in this review. This is due to its location on the west side of a steep canyon which does not receive good light in winter until relatively late in the morning.

Winter

9:30 A.M. to 3:45 P.M. (Tram)
9:30 A.M. to 4:30 P.M. (Lifts)

Commencing Feb. 1

9:00 A.M. to 4:00 P.M. (Tram)
9:00 A.M. to 4:45 P.M. (Lifts)

Lift Ticket Purchse Locations

The main ticket office is located just outside the Aerial Tram station. There is also an auxiliary ticket office in The Cliff Lodge.

Crowd Control

Crowds are not really a problem at Snowbird. The only area that is subject to occasional crowding is the Aerial Tram. It is possible, however, to ski the entire mountain without taking the tram. Adequate chairlifts service the entire area.

Ski School *(1988-89)*

Snowbird employs one hundred fifty instructors certified in the American Teaching System (ATS). Classes are available seven days a week for every level of ability.

Special classes for children four and a half through five years of age are offered. The Kinderbirds meet for a two hour lesson in the morning and another two hour lesson in the afternoon. The time between the two lessons is devoted to indoor play and lunch, served in The Cliff Lodge's Children's Center. During the 1987-88 ski season, there was an extra charge of $7.00 for the lunch. Older children (6 - 15) are taught by instructors who are especially trained in working with youngsters.

Adult beginners and children meet at the Chickadee Ski School sign just west of The Cliff Lodge near the Chickadee Lift. Adult classes meet at 10:30 A.M. and 2:00 P.M., while children meet at 10:00 A.M. and 1:30 P.M. Those skiers who are strong enough to ski the major runs meet at 12:45 P.M. on Big Emma.

$ 35.....Adult All Day
$ 25.....Adult, Half Day
$ 95.....Adult, 3 Day
$140.....Adult, 5 Day
$ 50.....Adult, One Hour Private
$230.....Adult, All Day Private

Snowbird offers its Mountain Experience Program to those skiers who are advanced or expert. These classes emphasize technique and handling assorted snow conditions. Classes meet in front of the tram station on the Plaza at 10:00 A.M. These classes are five hours in duration.

$ 50......One Day
$120......Three Day
$200......Five Day

Children's Classes

$ 45.......Full Day
$ 30.......Half Day
$120.......Three Day
$180.......Five Day

Equipment Rental

There are three rental shops located in Snowbird: Sport Stalker, Breeze, and Cliff Lodge Rental Shop.

The Sport Stalker rental rates for the 1987-88 season were:

Basic Package

Pre 800 Skis
540 Nordica Boots
Salomon 647 Bindings
Poles....................$12 per Day

Sport Package

Pre 1200 Skis
560 Nordica Boots
Salomon 647 Bindings
Poles....................$16 per Day

High Performance Package

K-2 KVC or TRC Skis
560 Nordica Boots
Salomon 747 Bindings
Poles....................$20 per Day

Cliff Lodge Rental Shop offers rental equipment without specifying brands. Their 1988-89 rates are:

Recreation Package..........$14 per Day
Performance Package.........$24 per Day

Rental rates are discounted at The Cliff Lodge if equipment is rented for longer than two days.

Ski Tuning and Repair

At the end of the 1987-88 ski season, no shops offered ski structuring. For a complete explanation of the benefits of ski structuring, read the *Ski Tuning and Repair* chapter in the section of this review dealing with *Killington*.

Stone grinding is offered by the Sport Stalker. Its 1987-88 rates were:

$ 6   Hot Wax
$ 8   Hot Wax w/Iron
$24   Edges Sharpened
$12   Deburr Edges & Wax
$32   Complete Tune-up Including P-tex

Mountain Restaurants

The Mid Gad restaurant is located at the top of the Mid Gad lift. It is a relatively new structure built of native timber and is quite a handsome structure. This is a cafeteria-style restaurant featuring short-order foods and hardy dishes such as beef stew, ribs, and so forth.

The best mountain restaurant is not on the mountain itself, but rather is located next to the Aerial Tram base station. It is called the Forklift. The Forklift has table service and an excellent menu. The restaurant's floor-to-ceiling windows overlook Hidden Peak. Diners can watch the Aerial Tram or perhaps the porcupine that sometimes lives in the trees outside the windows.

Try the stir-fried shrimp and oriental vegetables. It is delicious entrée and not too filling, just right for the active skier's lunch.

Day Care

Day care for children 3 years and older is available for lodge guests at The Cliff Lodge Children's Center. Younger children can be cared for in their parents' room with advance notice. The day rate for in-room sitters during 1987-88 was $8 per hour. The evening rate was $7 per hour. Telephone (801) 742-2222, ext. 5026.

Medical Facilities

The medical emergency center is located in the Central Plaza near the Aerial Tram base station. This facility, affiliated with Alta View Hospital of Salt Lake City, has a fully staffed emergency room that can handle acute emergencies and injuries and is equipped with X-ray equipment. Serious trauma cases are transported by ambulance to Alta View Hospital. The emergency center's hours are from 9:30 A.M. to 6:00 P.M.

Cross-Country Skiing

Due to the steepness of the surrounding terrain (after all, it is a box canyon), there is no cross-country skiing at Snowbird.

Special Events

Every Tuesday, Wednesday, and Thursday at noon National Standard Races (NASTAR) are held on the Wilbere Race Course. This course, located between Big Emma and the Wilbere chairlift, also has a coin operated self-timer course set up on the same hill. It is open the entire day.

Accommadations

The Cliff Lodge is as impressive as the towering peaks which surround it. Constructed of raw, rough concrete and natural clear pine, The Cliff appears to have burst from solid rock to soar ten stories.

The winding Little Cottonwood Canyon Road leading to Entrance #4 twists down a small cliff and around The Lodge. At The Lodge's lowest level is underground valet parking available for guests.

From the lower lobby, it is a short escalator ride to the spellbinding main lobby. The massive lobby is ten stories high and furnished with quality contemporary furnishings. Oriental objets d'art complete the decoration. The sheer size of the public rooms is overwhelming, and thus its decorations, such as plants, are extremely large. Floral baskets hanging in the Cliff Restaurant are large enough to contain palm trees!

The size of everything in The Lodge dictates use of strong textures such as those found in the textiles used in its wall coverings, wall hangings, and furniture covers. As a counterpoint, the designer wisely selected warm pastel colors to complete the design. Sea foam, mauve, peach, and similar colors dominate.

The spacious rooms are well lighted and furnished with quality furniture. In fact, visitors could say the single most significant impression they receive from Snowbird is its dedication to quality. Whether it is in the furniture or the chairlifts, no corners have been cut, nor expense spared in making Snowbird a truly world class resort.

The Cliff Lodge has many amenities one normally would not expect in a ski lodge. There are coin-operated laundry facilities on each floor, and steam irons and ironing boards may be borrowed from the front desk. There is an art gallery on Level C. Cribs and roll-away beds are available from housekeeping and stamps may be purchased from the front desk. A gift shop and small variety store is located on Level C.

Skis are not permitted in the rooms, but a free ski check is provided on Level 1. Cable TV in each room receives all the networks plus ESPN and PBS. There is also a Channel 13 which contains current information regarding Snowbird. Items such as road conditions, weather, places to visit, or restaurants in which to eat are frequent features.

Condominium accommodations are available at The Lodge at Snowbird. Do not confuse The Lodge at Snowbird with The Cliff Lodge. When traveling on Little Cottonwood Canyon Road, The Lodge at Snowbird's entrance is reached prior to that of The Cliff Lodge.

The Lodge at Snowbird is twelve to fifteen years old and is beginning to show its age. The architecture is very striking and in keeping with other Snowbird properties. It seems to fit perfectly into its environment. The lobby with its large stone fireplace is very attractive. Unfortunately, the furniture has been recovered in vinyl, and the carpeting is dated by its flame stitch in shades of orange and beige.

However, the rooms in The Lodge are charming. Each has a granite fireplace and cable TV. The Danish modern furnishings need replacing, but the kitchens are well-equipped with all the appliances one could need except a microwave oven and ice maker.

Staircases to the upstairs bedrooms are exceptional and are a testament to the original architect's concept of gracious mountain living. The master bedrooms are constructed as a loft and consequently, they are open to the living area. This can be a problem if more than one family or a family with children are occupying the unit. It is inconvenient if the occupants of the master bedroom want to sleep and the other occupants want to stay up and watch TV, because the volume will be just as great in the bedroom as it is in the living room.

The units' upstairs and downstairs baths are complete with tub and showers. There are also dressing rooms attached to the bathrooms; closets are spacious.

Although The Lodge at Snowbird consists primarily of one bedroom units, some may be converted to two bedroom units by utilizing an adjoining room.

Other accommodations include The Inn with sixty-five DeLuxe rooms and the Iron Blosam Lodge. The Iron Blosam is an interval ownership condominium and, as such, rooms are rarely available.

When children twelve and under stay in the same accommodations as their parents, they can stay free. In addition, each child receives a free lift ticket for each parent who purchases a lift ticket.

Restaurants

Everything at Snowbird is first-class. This is particularly true of the restaurants. The finest dining is found at The Aerie Restaurant located on the top floor of The Cliff Lodge. This is a formal restaurant with soft lighting, unique ceilings, oriental screens, and entertainment. The tables are set with fine china on white linens. The entrance is framed with antique Japanese kimonos.

The service is attentive and the food is excellent. Consider ordering the lamb. It is raised locally in Utah, and the Dijon mustard sauce is excellent. Order the salad dressings and other sauces on the side as the chef seems to have a heavy hand when he applies them.

Less formal, though no less in quality, is the Golden Cliff restaurant located on Level B of The Cliff Lodge. Enjoy a breakfast buffet here while reading a complimentary newspaper or while looking out two-story windows at the tram's arrivals and departures.

A hot breakfast buffet is offered in The Cliff Lodge's Atrium Restaurant, also located on Level B. While enjoying breakfast and gazing out the ten-story high windows, listen for the ski patrol setting its four-pound avalanche charges. As the charges detonate, the windows reverberate.

The eleven-story Atrium is obviously an extremely vertical room due to the soaring height of the windows and the open lobby adjacent to it. Large ficus trees dressed in Italian lights establish a pleasant mood. To further enhance the ambience, soft Strauss or Vivaldi music is piped in.

Another fine restaurant has just been renovated in The Lodge at Snowbird and is called, appropriately enough, The Lodge Club. During the day, the restaurant is brightly lighted by the snow's reflections through the Club's greenhouse windows. One entire wall is a glass-fronted, climate-controlled wine cellar with several hundred bottles of very fine varietal wines.

The meals are well prepared and presented by amiable waiters and waitresses. Appetizers include such selections as escargot, Manila clams, smoked salmon, duck paté, or baked brie. The salads include fresh spinach and Belgian endive. Entrées priced between $24 and $30 include breast of chicken, Norwegian salmon, pork tenderloin, filet mignon, and rack of lamb. Wonderful desserts and after dinner drinks are also available.

Visitors have heard horror stories or exaggerated claims about the Utah liquor laws. Most of these stories are mere fabrications.

Liquor may be purchased in state-controlled liquor stores and taken into any restaurant. The restaurant may charge the diner for a setup, such as cola or 7-Up. For wines that are brought in, restaurants may charge a "corkage" fee. A package store is conveniently located in the Snowbird Center.

Some restaurants such as the Forklift and the Steak Pit are licensed by the State as "mini bottle agencies." These types of restaurants have a small room or area designated as a State liquor store which only sells mini bottles of liquor and tenths of wine. The diner who wants a cocktail or glass of wine must get up from the table and walk to the mini bottle store to purchase the bottle. Upon returning to his table, the guest must then open the bottle (the waiter is not allowed to open it and pour it). The restaurants will probably charge a setup or corkage fee.

A third way to purchase liquor in Utah is in a "private club," such as the Eagle's Nest Lounge. These establishments are allowed to serve mixed drinks and wine if the guest has purchased a guest membership. Such memberships are available upon check in at the hotels and lodges. There is a $5 fee for the membership, but it is good for two weeks, and the member may purchase drinks for up to five persons. All liquor measures are from the mini bottles, although full bottles of wine may be served.

Activities

Because Snowbird is located in Salt Lake's watershed, restrictions are imposed on the activities allowed. No dogs or other domestic animals are permitted in the watershed. Therefore, there are no sleigh rides or dog sled rides here. In fact, the laws governing activities at Snowbird are so strict that the resort is not even allowed to construct high tension lines in the valley to bring in electricity: It has had to create its own energy. Consequently, Snowbird has built one of the country's largest co-generation energy plants. Natural gas fires an electric generator to provide electricity. The excess heat produced by the gas fire is used to heat The Cliff Lodge.

One of facilities Snowbird is known for is its Spa located in The Cliff Lodge. In very spacious quarters, one can exercise, enjoy a massage, or receive a beauty treatment. There is even a café which features low calorie and low cholesterol meals. Complete packages, such as those offered by the finest spas in the world, are available to skiing and non-skiing guests.

Some of the deepest powder helicopter skiing in the country is offered by the Wasatch Powderbird Guides. Reservations can be made in the Plaza building or by telephoning (801) 742-2800. In the spring, it is a unique experience to try their Cornball Special which consists of four runs in corn snow followed by 18 holes of golf at the Wasatch State Park Golf Course.

Services

A full complement of churches, sporting good stores, apparel shops, pharmacies, grocery stores, and liquor stores is located within the Snowbird resort.

Ski Hosts and Hostesses provide free guided tours of the mountain. Meet at the "Free Guided Skiing Tour" sign at the Center Plaza. Tours leave at 10:00 A.M. and 1:00 P.M. every day.

SNOWMASS

P.O. Box 5566
Snowmass Village, CO. 81615

(800) 332-3245 Reservations
(303) 923-2000 Information
(303) 923-2085 Snow Report

Transportation

Snowmass is one of the United States' most accessible major ski resorts. Driving to Snowmass from the East is as simple as hopping onto Interstate 70 and turning left on Colorado Highway 82. The distance from Denver is 200 miles, and although weather can be a factor, the completion of the Eisenhower Memorial Tunnel several years ago relieved most of the apprehension associated with this drive.

Skiers from the North and from the South can easily drive to Snowmass by taking Interstate 25 to Denver and getting onto Interstate 70. Visitors from the West can pick up Interstate 70 in Utah.

It is also very convenient to travel to Snowmass by air. United Express and Continental Express both offer quick, convenient service from Denver's Stapleton Airport to Aspen's Sardy Field. Sardy is an F.A.A. controlled airport where instrument landings are possible. Only during the worst storms is it necessary to bus passengers from Denver.

Denver has recently made great strides in eradicating Stapleton's image as an inefficient airport with mass delays and inconvenient airline transfers. A new wing served primarily by United was completed in 1987, and renovation of Continental's annex was well underway as this book was going to press. A separate section just for mountain air shuttle services is comfortable and clean. Although it is located on the far end of the terminal, inbound Denver flights are met by hosts or hostesses who quickly assist in transferring Snowmass passengers onto buses that transfer skiers directly to the shuttle area. Baggage is efficiently handled and usually is on the same flight as the passenger. However, even if the flight is missed, it is usually not a problem because the airlines schedule several daily flights from Denver.

During the 1987-88 ski season, several direct flights to Aspen were available. Check with your travel agent or call Snowmass to confirm flight schedules for subsequent seasons. Direct flights were offered from Chicago, Dallas, Los Angeles, Long Beach, and San Francisco. These flights operated during the peak ski season which started December 17 and ran through March 28. It is anticipated that a similar schedule will be maintained every year.

Once the skier reaches the Aspen Airport, Snowmass is only 12 miles west and accessible in numerous ways, including taxi (High Mountain), limousine, courtesy van, and rental car.

Most major car rental agencies are located at Sardy Field, and they provide *skierized* vehicles equipped with snow tires and ski racks. For a slightly higher price, many rental agencies can provide four-wheel drive vehicles. The traveler is cautioned to reserve these vehicles far in advance, because the demand for them is great.

Having a car at Snowmass is not necessary and may not even be desirable because the local transportation system is so good. There are constant free shuttles running among the resorts of Aspen, Aspen Mountain, Aspen Highlands, Buttermilk, and Snowmass.

Mountain statistics

The single feature that sets Snowmass apart from most other resorts is its mountain. Snowmass is a family mountain. It contains ample, varied terrain from beginner to advanced expert and has an abundance of intermediate runs.

The Village of Snowmass is roughly arranged parallel to Fanny Hill and Assay Hill, both of which are beginner runs. It is extremely convenient for guests to leave their accommodations in the morning, drop the kids at ski school, and catch a ride up one of the longer lifts which serves the rest of the mountain. In the evening, it is equally easy to ski down to the ski school, pick up the kids, walk around the village, and then return to your lodging.

Snowmass ski area is located in the White River National Forest and contains four principal peaks: Sam's Knob, The Big Burn, High Alpine, and Elk Camp. Snowmass Mountain consists of 1,582 (640 ha) skiable acres and has over 55 miles (88 km) of trails. Of these trails, 10% are considered easiest, 62% are more difficult, 21% are most difficult, and 7% expert.

The base elevation of Snowmass is 8,220 feet (2,505 meters) and its summit is 11,835 feet (3,608 meters). This provides the skier with 3,615 vertical feet (1,102 meters) of skiing.

This abundant terrain is serviced by the following lift equipment:

3 Quad SuperChairs
9 Double Chairlifts
2 Triple Chairlifts
2 Platter Pulls

Snowmass's uphill lift capacity is 20,535 skiers per hour. The number of skiable acres divided by the uphill hourly maximum lift capacity is .077. This compares favorably with other major destination resorts such as Crested Butte at .061, Keystone at .050, and even Telluride at .066. This rating clearly places Snowmass near the top of the list of resorts which have the lowest potential for crowding during peak periods.

Snowmass is most famous for its Big Burn area. Legend has it that the Ute Indians, revolting against the white man's mining activities and establishment of towns in the vicinity, forced the white settlers to flee. In the process, the Utes set fire to the mountain and, to this day, the region has not been reforested to any appreciable degree. This has created a huge snow field which is mostly intermediate terrain. The Burn is a mile wide and a mile and a half long, and thus, truly a cruiser's paradise. Occasionally, it is possible to ski the Burn while the rest of the resort is snowed-in. It is an amazing feeling to be skiing above the clouds in bright sunshine and then to disappear into a storm, only to ride the lift out of it again and again.

Most beginner runs at Snowmass are located near the bottom of the mountain, while most of the intermediate trails are in the center. The expert terrain is at the top. Notable exceptions to this rule of thumb are the Big Burn and the runs served by the Campground Lift.

At the top of Sam's Knob is a restaurant; trails located behind it and down the right side are expert. Not, "I know I will die before I get down" expert runs, but difficult enough to let skiers know they have to work to ski them well. Those skiers who are just in their prime (thirty to sixty years old) will be particularly interested in skiing Lower Powderhorn, Campground, Bear Claw, Wildcat, The Slot, and Zugspitze. Some poling may be required to return to the lift station from Wildcat, The Slot, and Zugspitze. To minimize this, it is advantageous to take the service road near the bottom left to

Campground's base which, through a short series of washboard, deposits you at the Campground Lift. This lift closes at 3:00 P.M., so make certain to time late afternoon runs so as not to become stranded. It would be an almost impossible walk back to the village at night wearing ski boots.

The truly expert skier or the crazed teen-ager should find the Hanging Valley Glades and the Hanging Valley Wall a memorable experience! Slightly less difficult, but interesting to say the least, are KT Gully and Rock Island. These two trails will remind well-traveled skiers of Tourist Trap at Vail, before Vail Associates decided to widen it. They are also similar to Pallavicini at Arapahoe Basin.

During days when the weather is less than cooperative, the intermediate skier will want to forego the Burn because it is too windy, cold, snowy, or all of the above. This is the best time to ski the Elk Camp area or the High Alpine area. Elk Camp has been carved out of the forest, and the trees shield skiers from the wind and provide contrast in flat light. The mid-portion of High Alpine is a great refuge; runs such as Naked Lady, Lodgepole, and Bottoms Up can be very satisfying.

Snowmass receives an annual snowfall of approximately 300 inches (762 cm) at its summit and 155 inches (394 cm) at its base. Its average monthly snowfall is:

Nov.	10"	(25 cm)
Dec.	52"	(132 cm)
Jan.	41"	(104 cm)
Feb.	41"	(104 cm)
Mar.	68"	(173 cm)
Apl.	17"	(43 cm)

Snowmass has portable snowmaking equipment which it moves around as needed.

The average daily temperatures in Aspen during the season are:

Nov.	31°	0° C
Dec.	22°	-5° C
Jan.	20°	-6° C
Feb.	23°	-5° C
Mar.	29°	-2° C
Apl.	39°	4° C

No discussion of Snowmass would be complete without mentioning that Aspen Mountain, Aspen Highlands, and Buttermilk Mountain are within 14 miles of the resort. These are very large mountains in their own right, and guests at Snowmass are encouraged to ski at least one other mountain during their visit. If one considers these other mountains, the skiable terrain is more than doubled.

Lift Ticket Prices *(1988-1989)*

Snowmass has many different prices for lift tickets. Space does not permit the inclusion of all of them, other than to mention that special rates are available for groups, individuals over 65, handicapped persons, and combination lift ticket/ski lesson packages.

Single day rates:

$33 Adult
$17 Child, 12 and Under

Adult Rates 3 and 4 Mountain:

$186 6 of 7 Day; 3 Mountain
$192 6 of 7 Day; 4 Mountain
$155 5 of 6 Day; 3 Mountain
$124 4 of 5 Day; 3 Mountain
$128 4 of 5 Day; 4 Mountain
$ 96 3 of 4 Day; 3 Mountain

Childrens Rates, 3 Mountain Ticket Only (12 and Under):

$102 6 of 7 Day
$ 85 5 of 6 Day
$ 68 4 of 5 Day
$ 51 3 of 4 Day

Hours of Operation

8:30 A.M. to 3:30 P.M.
Campground lift 9:00 A.M. to 3:00 P.M.
Fanny Hill and Assay Hill close at 4:00 P.M.

Lift Ticket Purchase Locations

Visitors find it is easy to ski from their lodging to any of the lift ticket windows. Lift tickets are sold in the Village Mall which is easily identified by its unique clock tower; in the "A" parking lot; at the base of the Assay Hill lift; the base of the Fanny Hill lift; the base of the Wood Run lift; and at the base of the Campground lift. (This latter location is only approachable by automobile before the lifts open). All major credit cards are accepted.

Crowd Control

Because the ratio of skiable acres to uphill lift capacity is so favorable, crowd control is minimal. There really are not a lot of crowds at Snowmass. However, as with all resorts, some areas do become congested. In the early morning and after lunch, congestion occurs at the top of Sam's Knob as skiers line up to ski Max Park. Max Park is the major avenue to the Big Burn, so many skiers traverse it on their way to the Big Burn and Sheer Bliss lifts. Traffic can be avoided by taking the Sunnyside or Pipeline trails. These are moderately difficult to easy runs, depending on conditions.

The only other potential area of congestion, and it is slight, may be found where Dawdler and the terrain off the face of Sam's Knob converge. Around 3:00 P.M. to 4:00 P.M. many skiers of differing abilities begin making their way down to lodging, bars, or the village shops. If care is taken, traversing this short distance will not be a problem.

Ski School

Snowmass employs three hundred instructors trained to teach adults, children, and the physically challenged. Traditional group and private lessons are available daily. In addition, the Snowmass Ski School offers some unique programs. For those skiers who are good enough to get down almost any slope, but who cannot always do it with the ease and style they would like, there is the Mountain

Masters program. This approach requires four days, and the instructors utilize video, races, and other techniques to sharpen the advanced skiers' ability.

One truly unique approach for teaching teenagers to ski is The Teens' Ski Week, where instructors spend time with the teens in the evenings as well as during the day. Most teenagers who have been skiing for a while do not have trouble negotiating the slopes, but they do have trouble being entertained during the evenings. To fill this need, Snowmass provides teachers and students with after-dark activities such as sleigh rides, dances, and movies.

Younger children (3-6) can be enrolled in the "Snowbunnies Program" in the recreation building located on the Village Mall. For children who are over six but not yet teenagers, there is "Kids Week." In this program, children are assured of having the same instructor each day all week. Activities, in addition to ski instruction, include picnics and races.

Aspen Skiing Company provides an alternative program for youngsters (three through six) in the newly expanded Timbermill Restaurant located at the end of the Village Mall.

There is an active ski program available to blind skiers and handicapped individuals. Snowmass's BOLD (Blind Outdoor Leisure Development) has been training skiers since its inception.

The 1988-89 ski season prices for lessons are as follows:

Group Clinics

$ 96 All Day, 3 Days
$150 All Day, 5 Days
$ 35 All Day, 1 Day

Mountain Masters (4 days):	$230 (plus lift ticket)
Powder Workshop (2 hours):	$ 30 (plus lift ticket)
Bump Clinic (2 hours):	$ 30 (plus lift ticket)

New for the 1988-89 season, Aspen Skiing Company will offer parents of teenagers one free day of ski school with the purchase of a multi-day lift ticket. This offer is good only for the first day of ski school and only for *never ever* skiers.

Equipment Rental

During the 1987-88 season, four ski rental companies were located in Snowmass. These were Aspen Sports in the Snowmass Center, Gene Taylor's Sports, located on the mall, Sport Kaelin, and Stein Eriksen's, both also on the mall.

The prices and equipment offered by these companies varied considerably, and visitors should check out the current offerings before entering into a rental contract. For example, in 1988, Gene Taylor's is offering a Basic rental package consisting of Rossignol skis, Salomon S-51 or S-71 boots, poles and bindings for $11 per day. Skis only are $10 per day. A DeLuxe package consisting of Rossignol 4S skis, the same boots, poles, and bindings is $20 per day. Boots only are $8 per day.

Just around the corner at Stein Ericksen's, a package consisting of K2 skis, Nordica or Salomon S-61 or S-71 boots, poles, Salomon or Marker bindings is $13 per day for one to three days or $12 per day for four to six days. A Performance Package consisting of either Pre, Dynastar, or Kastle skis is $19 per day if rented from one to three days, or $18 per day if rented for four to six days.

There are also many shops in the town of Aspen. For information, see the section of this book entitled *Aspen*.

Ski Tuning and Repair

All the Snowmass rental stores will tune and repair skis. Sunset Ski Repair, located on the mall near the pop corn wagon, will also tune or repair skis.

The preferred way to tune skis is to structure the bottom and bevel the edges 1° to 3°. There are no shops in Snowmass that offer this type of service. However, Sport Kaelin will accept skis for tuning using Montana Crystal Glide tuning equipment. This equipment is located at the Ski Service Center in Aspen, and Sport Kaelin will, at no additional charge, send skis to the Ski Center for overnight service. For a complete description of the benefits of ski structuring, consult the chapter entitled, *Killington*.

The 1987-88 prices for tuning at the Ski Service Center were:

$ 4	Hot Wax
$12	Flat File
$20	Complete Tune-Up
$20+	P-tex

Mountain Restaurants

Snowmass has some truly nice and unique mountain restaurants. The quality of food is better than that found on either Aspen Mountain or Aspen Highlands.

Cafeteria service is available at Sam's Knob, High Alpine, Elk Camp, and Ullrhof. Table service is available at Gwynn's at high Alpine, CeCe's at Sam's Knob, and at Krabloonik near the base of the Campground lift. A full breakfast is available at all mountain cafeterias.

An absolute must for skiers who crave an unusual dining experience while demanding quality food and service is Krabloonik, located near the Campground base.[1] The name Krabloonik is Eskimo for "big eyebrows," which is how Eskimos refer to white men. Krabloonik is also the name of the first sled dog the restaurant's owner was given.

The restaurant is truly unusual. There is no electricity, and the only heat emanates from a wood-burning stove located in the middle of the restaurant seating area. Light is provided by individual gas lanterns hanging from the ceiling's rafters. In the evening, the glow of the gas lights and the warmth of the fire create a cozy, intimate atmosphere not easily duplicated. Here, even in the dead of winter, one can always find lush azaleas blooming, adding their touch of spring to the ambience.

The menu, complemented by an extensive wine list, includes such delicacies as smoked trout, wild game tartare, baked brie with pears and ligonberries, mussels Meunière, and smoked buffalo tongue. Typical entrées include salmon, monkfish velouté, Muscovy duck breast with red currant cassis, pheasant breast Veronica, noisettes of caribou sauce poivrade, elk loin with sage sauce, wild boar schnitzel, and for the less adventurous, tenderloin of beef with sauce Diane.

---

[1] Krabloonik is not on the Snowmass property but is within walking distance of the Campground Lift. Reservations are imperative because the restaurant is frequently fully booked for lunch. Telephone 303/923-3953.

Krabloonik is more than a restaurant; it is also a sled dog kennel. There are several hundred dogs on the premises, and the cacophony is deafening during feeding time, usually between 4:00 P.M. and 4:30 P.M. When skiing the Campground lift, you can hear the Malamute, Eskimo, and Siberians barking. Krabloonik employees manufacture dog sleds on location from pecan and hickory wood. Many of these dogs and sleds find their way to the annual Iditarod race in Alaska each year. Before or after lunch, it is possible to tour the kennels or to go for a sled ride. The countryside around Krabloonik is beautiful, and being a part of a twelve-to-fifteen dog team racing through the aspen groves on a cold, clear day is quite an experience.

On the other side of the mountain at High Alpine, Gwynn's offers more traditional fare. The restaurant's Austrian/Swiss decor, complete with chintz curtains on windows which overlook the slopes, is charming. Gwynn's tends to become crowded during the high season; therefore, it is advisable to make reservations before eating there.

At Sam's Knob, CeCe's serves cuisine typical of the Southwest. In a lovely setting overlooking Lower Powderhorn and Garret Peak, one can enjoy table service, linen table cloths, and silver service. As with Gwynn's, this restaurant can become crowded, so reservations are advisable.

Day Care

Snowbunnies, located on the mall, is the only day care facility at Snowmass. It accepts youngsters eighteen months to three years of age. Reservations are suggested. Telephone (303) 923-2000.

Limited day care facilities are also located in the Airport Business Center across from Sardy Field. See the *Day Care* section on Aspen for more complete details.

Due to the limited day care facilities, Aspen Skiing Company has announced plans to establish a day care center in the newly remodeled Timbermill Restaurant, located at the end of the Village Mall. This facility will accommodate children eighteen months through three years. Tentatively, the program is being called The Snow Cubs. For more information, telephone (303) 925-4444.

Cross-Country Skiing

Three pinners will love the trails at Aspen. They are probably the most extensive in America, comprising nearly eighty kilometers of groomed tracks. No wonder locals refer to the cross-country terrain as "Aspen's fifth mountain!"

Easy to moderate trails are located east of Aspen at the site of the Aspen Club. Meandering from open meadows through aspen groves, these trails are perfect for an afternoon's adventure.

On the other side of the valley is the Rio Grande Trail whose trail head is on the bus route, near the post office. This trail follows the old railroad right of way and during good weather, it is groomed all the way to Woody Creek.

For the beginner or for those who want to take it easy before tackling more difficult slopes, there are tracks on the Aspen Golf Course. As one would expect, this is primarily flat terrain. There are also special skating lanes for those who want to perfect the latest craze in racing technique. A bridge across Maroon Creek enables the adventuresome to travel all the way to Snowmass utilizing Owl Creek Trail.

Owl Creek Trail is considered by many as being among the most beautiful trails in the Rocky Mountains. This track ties in directly with the trail network at Snowmass. Its trails are the most demanding of the free system.

The Snowmass Club trails encompass every conceivable type of terrain, from golf course flat to steep terrain located above Owl Creek Road. Check in at the Snowmass Club Touring Center and arrange for a catered lunch to be served at Gracie's Cabin, located in an open meadow on one of the trails.

Twelve miles up Castle Creek is the Ashcroft Ski Touring Center. It features thirty kilometers of groomed and set tracks available for a nominal fee.

Special Events

Each year in mid-January, Aspen and Snowmass celebrate Wintersköl with parades, torchlight processions down the mountains, and fireworks. Mardi Gras in February is also celebrated with many skiers dressing in costume. Celebrations culminate at that evening's Mardi Gras ball.

There are also innumerable special events that change yearly but which normally include professional ski races, USSA races, and World Cup.

Accommodations

There is no shortage of accommodations of every description and price in Snowmass. Generally, however, the older properties are arranged along Brush Creek Road which runs roughly parallel to the slopes. All of these facilities are close enough to the runs to be described as ski-in/ski-out. Newer units being built along Woodrun are also ski-in/ski-out.

Upon entering Snowmass, one must clear the security gate located at the entrance to the resort which is approximately three miles from the runs and accommodations. The guard at the desk has a list of all guests' names and will give directions to lodging facilities. Parking at Snowmass is restricted, and only guests with parking permits affixed to their cars are allowed to park close to their accommodations and to the slopes. Day skiers from Aspen must park further downhill near the guard's gate and take a shuttle up to the lifts and ticket offices. This is a great convenience for the Snowmass guests. Guest cars without a parking permit may be towed or at least fined. The fine is substantial.

Hotels

One of the premier hotels at Snowmass is the Snowmass Club. Situated away from the hustle and bustle of the mall at the Touring Center, the Club includes two tennis courts protected from the weather by a huge plastic bubble. Other features are two racquetball courts; two squash courts; an outdoor heated swimming pool; a Jacuzzi; Nautilus; free weights; running machine; airdyne and Life Cycle stationary bikes; sauna; steam room; pro shop, and exceptionally well-appointed locker rooms. There is even a private nursery for guests' children. Aerobic classes are offered on a regular basis and are taught on a wood, air cushion floor.

Rooms at the Snowmass Club are decorated in country French style and all have private balconies. Each room contains a small refrigerator, coffee maker, cable TV, and bath robes. Upon arrival, the guest is treated to a complimentary bottle of champagne.

The lobby of the Club is finished in fine wood, and the furniture is upholstered in rich wool fabrics.

There are two restaurants within the Club. The finest is called the Four Corners and serves Continental dishes. A formidable wine cellar is available for diners' enjoyment. The other restaurant is more casual and is called Tenth Mountain Trail, in honor of the Tenth Mountain Division that once trained nearby.

Each afternoon, après-ski is served in the lobby and features apple strudel and hot cider. Alcoholic beverages are available from the bar and an entertainer usually plays the piano.

Transportation to the ski area is provided gratis by the Club, as is concierge service.

Country Club Villas are located adjacent to the Snowmass Club and its guests enjoy member privileges at the Club. The Villas are one, two, and three bedroom condominiums.

Prices for Snowmass Club accommodations during the 1987-88 season ranged from a low of $95 per night to a high of $290 per night. Use of the tennis courts required an additional fee.

The moderately priced Wildwood Hotel is located adjacent to the slopes, just off Brush Creek Road. All rooms at the Wildwood have a private balcony with a view of the slopes. Its DeLuxe rooms feature two queen-size beds, a refrigerator, coffee maker, and TV with remote control. The rooms are small, but nicely appointed.

There is a heated outdoor pool, as well as a men's and a women's sauna. Free transportation to and from Aspen Airport is available.

The hotel has an après-ski bar, and a restaurant specializing in classic American dishes such as prime rib, New York strip steak, rack of lamb, baked chicken breast, fresh salmon, live Maine lobster, and Australian lobster tail.

Lodging prices during the 1987-88 season were from a low of $65 per night to a high of $185 per night.

Other hotels in Snowmass include the Pokolodi and the Silvertree.

Condominiums

Among the newer condominium offerings at Snowmass is the twenty-nine unit Chamonix located along the Woodrun Chairlift. These two and three bedroom condos are run like a quality hotel, with a central lobby and concierge services. Each night, the management provides a complimentary ski wax or arranges rental skis for its guests.

Rooms at Chamonix are nicely appointed with traditional furnishings. All have balconies and sun rooms which are furnished with rattan furniture. Kitchens are completely supplied with all the utensils one could possibly need. The ranges are Jenn-Air and microwave ovens complement the regular convention ovens. Washers and dryers are provided in every condominium, as are ironing boards and humidifiers.

The master baths are well appointed with steam showers, Jacuzzi tubs, and double sinks.

From its underground parking, to its heated outdoor pool, to its soaring ceilings, the Chamoix is a great retreat—a wonderful place in which to celebrate a week or two in ski country.

During the 1987-88 season, the Chamonix rented for between $200 and $650 per night.

Woodrun Place is another new condominium complex. Located diagonally across the street from the Chamonix, it is a very comfortable lodge. Managed by Snowmass Lodging Company, the staff will bend over backwards to help guests feel comfortable. Staff will grocery shop for skiers, chauffeur them, or arrange for breakfast, lunch, or dinner to be prepared and served in their condo.

All Woodrun Place condominiums feature contemporary furnishings from quality manufacturers. The color and fabric selections are warm. Kitchens are completely equipped and contain laundry facilities as well. Fireplaces and whirlpool baths are standard features.

This fifty-five unit complex has a beautiful outdoor pool and therapy pool as well as ski locker room. Exercise facilities are located on the premises. The only drawback to Woodrun may be for the guest who books a single condominium and finds that all the other units are occupied by members of a conference. Woodrun is a conference center which attempts to book groups.

Rates for condominiums during the 1987-88 season were between $150 and $650 per night.

The Woodrun V condominiums are reached by first crossing a small bridge which may not be evident after heavy snowfalls. Entry is through a small foyer, and the living/dining, kitchen, and master bedroom are upstairs. All other accommodations are located down from the foyer on the first floor.

The interiors are constructed from brick and redwood, and the decorations are traditional. Handmade Mexican tiles provide a nice touch to each kitchen. The fully-equipped kitchens feature Kitchenaide appliances and Jenn-Air grills. There are even trash compactors. Separate formal dining rooms and step-down living rooms add dimension to theses unique condos. Off the living rooms are nicely appointed sitting rooms. The many large windows provide a panoramic view of Snowmass Resort. Guests will also find stereos, VCR's, remote controlled cable TVs, copper clad fireplaces, and a heated outdoor swimming pool

Rates during the 1987-88 season were from $250 to $800 per night.

Restaurants

If Snowmass has any shortcomings, it would be its scarcity of fine restaurants. Although there are numerous restaurants, none could be described as truly gourmet. Perhaps the Village has never been able to establish the fine dining tradition the town of Aspen nurtured years ago. Whatever the reason, to experience truly excellent dining, visitors must trek over to Aspen.

Among Snowmass's slim offerings is the Tower Restaurant, owned by singer John Denver. The restaurant is in a landmark building on the Mall and thus is visible from most places in the resort. The Tower features traditional steak dinners, pasta dishes, poultry such as Hawaiian chicken, and several fresh fish selections.

Also on the mall is Hite's. Entrées are similar to those of the Tower, although the menu selections are greater and more varied. Other restaurants are found in some of the hotels such as the Silvertree; several short-order food establishments are also conveniently located in the Village.

Chez Grandmère will be new for the 1988-89 season at the Snowmass Center on Brush Creek Road. It is reported that this will be a gourmet French restaurant with only one seating per evening and a prix fixe menu.

Activities

Because Snowmass and Aspen Mountain are so close together and the uphill lift companies are the same, it is reasonable to expect activities to be shared between the two resorts. Therefore, to learn about the activities of the area, consult the section of this book that deals with Aspen.

Services

Snowmass is a complete village. There are sporting goods stores, apparel stores, pharmacies, grocery stores, liquor stores, and specialty stores. Other services are located in Aspen.

The 1988-89 season will feature a newly expanded Village Mall. This additional space will primarily be utilized by retail shops, a transportation plaza and public restrooms.

SQUAW VALLEY USA

Squaw Valley Ski Corporation
Post Office Box 2007
Olympic Valley, CA. 95730

(800) 545-4350 Reservations
(916) 583-6985 Information
(916) 583-6955 Snow Report

Transportation

The nearest major airport to Squaw Valley is Reno Cannon International. Located 45 miles from the resort, it is served by twelve major carriers. The Reno Airport is very convenient, and because of its desert location, it is relatively immune to the variences of winter weather.

A regional airport is located in South Lake Tahoe. It services flights that primarily originate from West Coast cities such as Los Angeles and San Francisco. If travelers from Boston want to fly into Tahoe, it is necessary for them to overfly Squaw, land in San Francisco, and catch another flight to Tahoe.

Numerous car rental agencies are located in the baggage claim area of the terminal as well as just outside airport property. There are also taxi and limousine services available. Car rental agencies represented in Reno include:

- Alamo
- AI
- Avis
- Budget
- Dollar
- Hertz
- National
- Rent-a-Dent
- Thrifty
- Ugly Duckling

If skiers plan to rent a car from one of the major companies at the airport, they should plan to pick up the car from the lot without their luggage. The rental lots are located about one-quarter mile from the baggage claim area and there are no shuttle buses. Unless the skier can find one of the few porters at the airport, it can be exasperating to try and carry luggage to the car. It is much easier to drive the car around to the baggage claim area and load the luggage there. Upon returning, it is likewise extremely important to unload the luggage **before** returning the car to the rental parking area.

When arranging for a rental car, it is usually less expensive to work through the rental office in the city where the car is to be rented, rather than going through the toll-free 800 number. Rates established locally are typically lower than those established nationally. Also, it can be even less expensive if the car is not reserved in advance. Rates for rental cars are usually established daily by each local manager. Of course, potential savings have to be measured against the risk of inavailability of cars. A way to secure a better rate without the risk of not getting a car is to telephone the local rental agency 24 hours in advance of the need. By doing this, the consumer is assured of both a low rate and an available car.

Because the police in the Sierras may require that all vehicles have snow tires and chains, it is imperative that the car be so equipped. Verify the equipment before accepting the rental car.

Although snowfall in the Sierras tends to be sporadic, it is prodigious whenever it occurs. Should the skier arrive in Reno during one of these major dumps, it may be necessary to drive to Squaw via Carson City, rather than taking the more direct route on I-80. Be certain to check road conditions with the rental agency before departing.

Squaw Valley operates its own bus service from 8:00 A.M. to 6:00 P.M. daily. The fee for this service is $15 each way, and reservations are required. Telephone (800) 545-4350.

Numerous limousine services transport skiers to Squaw Valley or any of the many hotels on the Nevada side of the mountains. Following is a partial list:

Aero-Trans,	(702) 786-2376
Airport Limousine,	(702) 323-3727
Executive Limousine,	(702) 826-7776
Sierra West Limousine,	(702) 329-4310

For those skiers who wish to combine skiing with a little gambling and stay in Reno, an airport shuttle bus leaves the baggage claim area each hour on the half hour for the major hotels and casinos. The price for this service during the 1987-88 season was $2 each way.

Once in Reno, there are daily shuttles from the hotels to Squaw Valley and Alpine Meadows departing between 7:00 A.M. and 8:00 A.M. The 1987-88 round-trip price for this service was $12 for adults and $10 for juniors. To arrange for pickup, telephone Grey Line at (702) 329-1147 or pickup tickets at Bally's, Sand's, or the Nugget in Sparks. Reservations are required, and the buses depart Squaw or Alpine Meadows for the return trip between 5:30 P.M. and 6:30 P.M.

Accommodations are limited at Squaw Valley, as is true of all California ski resorts. Therefore, many skiers have to stay in lodging somewhat removed from the resort itself. To help accommodate these guests, Squaw runs free shuttle buses between the resort and hotels on the north shore of Lake Tahoe, the south shore, Tahoe City, and Truckee. Telephone Squaw Valley's toll free number, (800) 545-4350, and request a bus schedule in advance because one may not be available at the airport or at the guest's hotel.

Mountain Statistics

Squaw Valley is the largest destination resort in California. It is also among the best ski mountains in the United States—possibly the world. Every conceivable type of terrain is located at Squaw. Rather than consisting solely of trails, the entire mountain's six peaks are skiable. There is certainly adequate terrain for all ability levels.

Squaw Valley is BIG! Consisting of 8,300 acres (3,359 ha), Squaw is only slightly smaller than Vail with its huge back bowls. The vertical drop is 2,850 feet (869 meters). Squaw's uppermost summit is 9,050 feet (2,758 meters), and its base is at 6,200 feet (1,890 meters).

Twenty-seven lifts serve this extremely large area, including one aerial tram and one gondola. Twenty-five percent of the lifts service beginner areas, forty-five percent intermediate, and thirty percent expert. The mountain naturally divides itself into areas of specific ability levels, thus making it possible to position lifts to exploit this natural phenomenon. The only other mountain that comes to mind with this natural division of ability levels is Copper Mountain in Colorado.

Like all great mountains, the names and numbers of trails are insignificant because the entire area is skiable. In fact, a review of Squaw's trail map will merely reveal names of the lifts. The only list of trail names, to this writer's knowledge, exists in the ski patrol's office to help patrolmen locate and evacuate injured skiers.

One of the most unique features of Squaw is that the beginner slopes are at the top of the mountain rather than at the base. Novice skiers can access the slopes by taking either the aerial tram or gondola and exit the same way after lessons or after free skiing. The longest beginner run is off the Riviera lift[1] at 387 feet (118 meters). The longest intermediate run is The Mountain Run which is three miles (4.8 km), and the longest expert trail is KT-22 at 1,753 feet (534 meters).

KT-22 is an interesting run. It is very steep and tends to become heavily moguled. Prior to the founding of Squaw Valley, the owner and his wife were dropped by helicopter on top of what was to become KT-22. The owner's wife's name was "Katie," and she reportedly said it took her 22 kick turns to get down the hill. The name stuck! Not only is KT-22 one of the most difficult runs in America, but the chairlift may also qualify as one of the most frightening. The lift before its terminus is at least as high as the Loges Peak lift at Aspen Highlands. However, the view of Lake Tahoe is breathtakingly beautiful.

The unique and wonderful thing about Squaw is that many of its expert runs can be made relatively easy or extremely difficult depending on where one begins to ski them. For example, if one takes the Granite Chief lift and skis the runs underneath, the run is primarily easy expert. All that is required is the ability to ski bumps. A strong intermediate could competently handle this terrain. However, it takes a real expert to ride the Emigrant lift and go around Emigrant Peak to the top of Granite Chief. Once around the backside, skiers find themselves on a cornice looking at anywhere from a three or four-foot jump onto the slope to a ten-foot jump, depending on snow conditions.

Most of the intermediate runs are gathered around the area just above the gondola and tram. These are the Emigrant Peak and the Shirley Lake areas. The runs are almost always groomed, and it is possible to really cruise these trails. More adventurous intermediates will enjoy the thrills awaiting them under the Siberia Express. This is a large bowl, quite steep with moderate moguls.

Squaw Valley averages over 450 inches (1,143 cm) of snow annually. Most of this snow comes infrequently, but in prodigious amounts. Its monthly snowfall is:

Nov.	52"	(134 cm)
Dec.	54"	(138 cm)
Jan.	71"	(181 cm)
Feb.	80"	(202 cm)
Mar.	77"	(194 cm)
Apl.	35"	(89 cm)

Because of the snowfall pattern, Squaw Valley experiences really excellent powder skiing during and immediately after a snowstorm. The remainder of the time conditions are packed powder. The snow

---

[1] The longest runs can only be identified by the lift serving an area, because Squaw Valley only names lifts, not trails.

at Squaw tends to be more moist than that found in Colorado primarily due to Squaw's location relative to the Pacific Ocean. Spring snows can be very heavy; therefore, more physical conditioning is required to ski Squaw than the Rocky Mountain resorts.

Squaw Valley's average temperatures at the base are:

Nov.	31°	0° C
Dec.	31°	0° C
Jan.	31°	0° C
Feb.	33°	1° C
Mar.	34°	1° C
Apl.	41°	5° C

Squaw Valley's total acreage divided by its uphill lift capacity is .210, a relatively low figure that countradicts the most frequently heard complaint about Squaw: it's crowded! In an effort to counter this negative image, the management has done something unique. It guarantees lift lines of no more than ten minutes in duration or the cost of the lift ticket is refunded, and skiers may ski the remainder of the day free. Beware, however, of seemingly ironclad offers. Actually, in order to participate, skiers must register and purchase what amounts to an insurance policy for $1. Further, they must state their ability level because the offer only applies to lifts of similar ability. All lifts are continually monitored and waiting times noted. In reality, what happens is that all the lifts of an ability level are added together and divided by the total number of lifts to determine the actual waiting time. For example, there are ten intermediate lifts. The actual waiting times for each lift are added together and divided by ten for the average wait. If this figure exceeds ten minutes, a refund is granted. However, what often happens is that a skier may be skiing one intermediate lift and experience a fifteen minute wait. When the he goes to collect a refund, he is told that although a fifteen-minute wait existed at the lift he was skiing, there was only a five-minute lift line on another lift (even though it might be a long way away from the area being skied). However, because there was an intermediate level lift with a wait of less than 10 minutes, the skier is not eligible for a refund.

Squaw offers first-time skiers the opportunity to ski for free. This is an attempt to encourage more people to take up skiing. The program is totally free: free lift ticket, free ski rental, and a free orientation lesson. The program is offered during week days only, and a $30 deposit is required. The deposit is refunded upon return of the rental equipment. This is an excellent program to help develop new skiers, and, hopefully, it will be initated at other resorts in the future.

Night skiing is offered at Squaw Valley on Searchlight, an intermediate run. Night skiing cost $7 during the 1987-88 season. A child's ticket was $5. The lift ticket was good from 4:00 P.M. to 9:00 P.M.

Lift Ticket Prices

Lift ticket prices for the 1987-88 season were:

$ 30......Adult, All Day
$ 21......Adult, Half Day
$ 55......Adult, 2 Day
$ 78......Adult, 3 Day
$120......Adult, 5 Day
$ 5......Child, Under 13
$ 5......Adult, 65+

Interchangeable lift tickets are available at Squaw Valley and at other ski areas around Lake Tahoe including: Alpine Meadows; Northstar; Homewood; Sugar Bowl; Mt. Rose; Ski Incline; Heavenly Valley; and Kirkwood.

Hours of Operation

9:00 A.M. to 4:00 P.M. daily, except weekends and holidays when the lifts open at 8:00 A.M. The aerial tram and gondola cease up-loading operations at 3:45 P.M. daily.

Lift Ticket Purchase Locations

Entrance to Squaw Valley resembles entry to a baseball game. In order to gain access to the lift system, it is generally necessary to pass through a rank of ticket vendors who separate the main parking lot from the resort proper. No doubt, this is left over from the days when Squaw considered itself a day skier's center. Unlike many large ski areas, Squaw has only one base area.

Crowd Control

Crowd control at Squaw Valley is a serious matter. In spite of its tremendous size, there is only one way down the mountain at night and that is via the three-mile long Mountain Run. The only other alternative is to ride down in either the gondola or the aerial tram.

This is a bad situation, but it is handled as well as possible by the ski patrol. Commencing as early as 2:00 P.M., ski patrolmen, some with bull horns, are positioned along the length of the Mountain cautioning skiers to slow down and to ski in control. However, once skiers get down the mountain the confrontation with crowds is just beginning. During peak seasons, it can take more than one hour just to get out of the parking lot. If the skier's accommodations are located anyplace other than at Squaw, the skier will have to fight traffic the length of Highway 89. If the ultimate destination is South Lake Tahoe and the weather is bad, this can turn into a Steven Spielberg nightmare.

Ski School

The Squaw Valley Ski School consists of over one hundred trained professionals. These PSIA instructors teach the American Teaching System (ATS) which is almost universal in the United States. Students taking ATS lessons at any resort may confidently visit other areas where the same method is taught, thereby not becoming confused by a different approach.

All day group lessons last four hours and commence at 11:00 A.M. with a lunch break at 1:00 P.M. Two hour lessons are available and begin promptly at 11:00 A.M. and 2:00 P.M. The ski school office is located at the base of the Exhibition lift, next to the rank of lift ticket wickets.

$ 27......4 Hour Lesson
$ 18......2 Hour Lesson
Price includes use of beginner lifts.
$ 50......2, Four Hour Lessons
$ 72......3, Four Hour Lessons
$115......5, Four Hour Lessons

Private lessons are $38 for one hour, $70 for two hours, and $200 for all day. The all day rate is the same whether there is one person or a maximum of three persons.

Squaw has a Junior Ski School program for children aged six through twelve.

$ 27......4 Hour-Lessons
$ 18......2 Hour-Lessons
Price includes use of beginner lifts.
$ 40......All Day, Includes Lunch

For younger children aged three through five, Squaw Valley has its Ten Little Indians Snow School. This school introduces youngsters to skiing and to snow play. The only requirement is that the children be toilet trained. Cost for the service is $35 for all day (8:30 A.M. to 4:30 P.M.). A half day program is also offered at $25. All prices are for the 1987-88 season.

Once a month during the ski season, Squaw offers its Advanced Skiing Seminars. These clinics are designed for intermediate and expert skiers who wish to improve their proficiency in a variety of conditions. Each class is limited to five students. Skiing lasts for five days, from early morning until the lifts close in the afternoon. The 1987-88 cost for the program was $465 inclusive of lift tickets, lunch, videotaping, and a banquet on Thursday evening.

A similar program called the Woman's Way Ski Seminars is offered especially for women. All the instructors are women. The small classes consist of up to five hours of daily ski instruction, body awareness, and workshops on how to care for equipment. Wine and cheese parties that follow the classes provide a camaraderie. During 1987-88, the price for a full, five day seminar was $455. A three day abbreviated seminar was $280.

Equipment Rental

In spite of the size of the mountain, Squaw Valley Village at its foot is quite small. There are not a great deal of duplicated services here. Rental equipment is available from the Company Store located on the Squaw Valley Mall, near the entrance to the Gondola. The Company Store rents recreational and high-performance skis. The recreational package consists of skis, boots, bindings, and poles. During the 1987-88 season, this package rented for $15 per day for an adult and $10 per day for a child. The high performance package was $25. Rentals are available from a number of shops located in the immediate Lake Tahoe area and at the small shop located in the Squaw Valley Lodge. In the Lodge ski shop Atomic, Rossignol, and Dynastar skis are available. Boots and bindings are Salomon.

Ski Tuning and Repair

The Granite Chief Service Center is located on the access road into Squaw Valley. This is one of the best tune-up and repair shops to be found anywhere. The people working in this shop are all expert skiers who know Squaw Valley intimately. They have state-of-the-art Montana Crystal Glide tuning machines, and they can also expertly tune skis by hand. In 1987-88 their fees were:

$25......Tune
$50......Hand Tune
$15......Up to 6 Base Repair
$35......Base Patch
$20......Ski Straightening
$30......Repair Delaminiation
$ 5......Wax
$12......Hand Wax Du Jour
$50......Hand Race Tune

$15......Binding Adjustment

Conventional tuning is also available at The Company Store. During 1987-88 its rates were:

$ 5......Hot Wax
$20......Complete Tune-up
$ 6—8..Bindings Adjusted
$10......P-tex

Mountain Restaurants

There are two mountain restaurants located on the mountain itself. The newest restaurant, Gold Coast, is situated at the top of the new gondola. This restaurant closely resembles a stage setting for the Nutcracker Suite. One expects Prince Nutcracker to walk out at any moment. Gold Coast is an extremely large restaurant occupying three floors, and it has a considerable amount of outdoor deck area.

The cafeteria-style meal service and food are excellent. Fresh salads and "make your own" sandwiches are featured. The bright colors and heraldic flags promise to lift the spirits of even the most dispassionate skier.

The High Camp restaurant, located on the mountain top where the tram docks, is also quite large. Included in its facilities are the High Camp Delicatessen and Bar, The Cinnamon Hut, and Alexander's Bar and Grill. Even though the management of Alexander's is the same as The Oasis in the Gold Coast, the food service is inferior. The quality of the food and its presentation are excellent, however.

Day Care

Day care facilities are located in a house situated almost under the gondola, just uphill a few hundred feet from the gondola building. Day care services are provided for infants from six months to three years of age. Daily registration is from 8:30 A.M. to 9:30 A.M. and from 1:00 P.M. to 1:30 P.M. Diapers and special formulas should be provided by parents. Snacks are served, and the fee for all day in 1987-88 was $35. Half day sessions were $25. Reservations are requested: telephone (916) 583-4743.

Medical Facilities

For ski injuries, the ski patrol will only render emergency aid. The patrol will administer trauma treatment, stabilize broken bones, and transport the injured skier downhill by sled to the clinic located at the base of the mountain, two doors down from the ski school. The clinic is managed by the Tahoe Truckee Medical Group. Competent physicians and nurses are always present throughout the day. Should an illness or an injury require more than emergency care, patients will be transported nine miles to the Truckee Hospital for further treatment.

Cross-Country Skiing

The Squaw Valley Nordic Center is located near the base of the Red Dog lift system. There are 40 kilometers of dual groomed trails for every ability level. Should the skier wish to cross-country ski off groomed tracks, several kilometers of wilderness trails are also available.

In addition to the usual cross-country lessons offered at most resorts, the Nordic Center offers instruction in telemark skiing. Lessons include all the turns such as wedge, skate, parallel, step, and telemark normally executed in cross-country skiing.

For unusual ski touring experiences, consider a moonlight tour or a catered gourmet lunch tour. Contact the Nordic Center at 583-8951 for details and prices.

Regular fees for using the course during the 1987-88 season were:

$7......Adult, All Day
$4......Child, All Day
$4......Adult, Half Day
$2......Child, Half Day

Group lessons during the 1987-88 season were priced at $14, and all day rentals were $10 for adults and $6 for children.

Special Events

Although events will vary from year to year, Squaw Valley has a tradition of staging numerous annual events. When booking reservations, request a current list of events to determine what will be happening during your visit. During 1987-88, Squaw hosted the following events:

Annual Christmas Eve Torchlight Parade
Newport Ski Spree
Coors/Squaw Valley Town League Opener
Pacific Crest Telemark Race
Far West Freestyle Event
Athletic Club Ski Challenge Weekend
Buddy Werner Race
Jimmie Heuga USA Express
Legends of Squaw Valley Corporate Race
Molson Bartenders Obstacle Course RAce
Snowfest Winter Carnival
Vuarnet Race
NFL Ski Championship
Multiple Sclerosis Ski-A-Thon
Spring Daze Week
Sierra Mountain Race Triathlon
Swimsuit Slalom
Slide, Ride 'n Jibe Event

Accommodations

Squaw Valley is one of only a handful of Sierra resorts that offers on-site accommodations to its guests. The available accommodations are limited in relation to the size of the mountain being served, but the facilities Squaw has built are exceptionally nice.

The premier property is the Squaw Valley Lodge, located just under the aerial tram on Squaw Peak Road. The Lodge is within easy walking distance of all base lifts, the Olympic Village shops, and restaurants. This is a new facility built as condominiums, but run as a hotel.

Lodging consists of studios and studios with lofts. Guests may specify whether they want units with one or two baths. All units come with General Electric appliances including dishwasher, microwave, refrigerator, and disposal. Fireplaces are not included in any housing units at Squaw because local ordinances prohibit them. The rooms are comfortably furnished in earth tones and fine oak. Upon entering any room at the Lodge, one is immediately impressed with the fine oak slab flooring in the foyer and kitchen. All cabinets in the kitchen and living area are constructed from riff cut oak in a natural finish. Ski storage is in the foyer and a large, well-lighted closet is also handy. Bright throw cushions and accessories invite guests to consider these accommodations home during their ski holiday. The beds are of European manufacture and consist of a thin mattress on a box spring. Thick but lightweight down comforters make sleeping very comfortable.

While staying at the Squaw Valley Lodge, guests should be certain to use their key to lock the door behind themselves when leaving. These doors do not lock automatically upon closing. Guests should also note that thermostats in the rooms are locked and cannot be adjusted without a special key. If room temperature is uncomfortable, visitors must telephone the front desk; the staff will send a technician to adjust the thermostat to a different comfort setting.

Staying in the Squaw Valley Lodge has advantages. There is a large, heated outdoor pool, a therapy pool, covered parking, an exercise facility including aerobic instruction, on-site ski and clothing rentals, and elevator service. The spacious lobby is great place to meet with friends after a hard day of skiing. It is also comfortable to relax in front of the lobby's large fireplace while enjoying a cocktail or other beverage.

During the 1987-88 season, rates for staying at the Lodge ranged from a low of $110 - $155 for a studio suite and from $130 - $180 for a one bedroom, one bath unit.

When booking reservations, please note that the reservation office does not open until 8:00 A.M. Pacific Time.

The Olympic Village Inn, referred to locally as the OVI, was originally built for the 1960 Olympics as housing for participating athletes. Now, twenty-eight years and some $40 million later, the OVI has been renovated and greatly expanded to provide luxury accommodations for Squaw Valley guests. The old dormitory rooms have been creatively converted into guest suites with private balconies and gourmet kitchens. Although the resulting layout of the suites is unusual, they do have a charm not easily duplicated. Entrance to each suite is through the bedroom. In order to go from the bedroom to the living/kitchenette area, it is necessary to go through a small hall, off which the bathroom is located. This configuration resulted from the original dormitory's layout of two rooms sharing one common bath. In the newly configured suites, one former dormitory room has become a bedroom while the other has become a living/kitchenette area.

Each suite has been decorated with Laura Ashley prints and fine country French furniture. Although the rooms are small, they are quaint and more comfortable than many larger rooms. There are two telephones per unit, and a stereo system is pre-wired throughout. The reception desk has a library of tapes available to guests.

The complex features a heated outdoor pool with a waterfall and five hot tubs. There are two on-site restaurants, and the lobby with its large stone fireplace and comfortable seating is massive. Floor-to-ceiling windows overlook the ski slopes and surrounding countryside. In the evenings, entertainment featuring comedians, country-western, or contemporary entertainers is provided in the lobby.

Although the Olympic Village is within walking distance of the lifts, complimentary shuttle service is available every five or ten minutes.

Situated at the other end of the lift complex at the Red Dog lift is the Squaw Tahoe Resort. These are older, more traditional condominiums than either the Lodge or the OVI. Squaw Tahoe Resort has a total of thirty-two condominiums, but a third of them are time share units not normally available for rental. Accommodations consist of studios, one, and two bedroom units. All units have fully-equipped kitchens with GE appliances. Some units have fireplaces. Those units with fireplaces burn chemical logs which burn cleaner than natural wood. This is necessary in order to comply with local fireplace codes. Should a room with a view of the slopes be desired, be certain to request an odd numbered room. The even numbered rooms all face the Olympic Village or the meadows. Studio units have queen-size Murphy beds, while the full size units have queen-size beds. The Squaw Tahoe Resort has underground parking and a clubhouse with outdoor spas and an exercise room. The equipment in the exercise room consists of free weights and progressive resistance equipment.

The Squaw Tahoe Resort is located adjacent to one of the mountain's equipment barns. Light sleepers may want to request accommodations on the other side of the complex.

The 1987-88 rates for the Squaw Tahoe Resort were between $95 and $150 per night for a studio suite. The two bedroom rate varied between $165 and $195 per night.

Restaurants

Although there is considerable night life in the Lake Tahoe region, there is almost none at any of the Sierra ski resorts. Fortunately, there is activity at Squaw Valley, though somewhat limited when compared to destination resorts in the Rocky Mountains.

Dining activity at Squaw Valley revolves around the Olympic House, situated at the gondola base. This building has two levels and contains many restaurants and bars as well as other services, such as clothing stores and specialty shops. In the afternoons activity centers around Bar One. Located on the second floor of the Olympic House, Bar One contains a large outdoor deck facing Squaw Peak. In the spring many patrons sit outside enjoying the tanning power of the late afternoon sun. Another gathering spot for the après ski crowd is found on the second floor of the Olympic Plaza building. This building abutts the Olympic House and appears to be a part of it. Here the Olympic Plaza Bar features continuous Warren Miller films or other ski-related movies on wide screen TV. Its outdoor deck which faces KT-22 and Red Dog is sheltered from the wind; parts of it are in the shade of huge California redwoods.

The Olympic House and the Olympic Plaza have an arcade feel to them. Numerous fast-food restaurants feature many specialty foods such as oysters, tacos, ice cream, pizza, and deli-style sandwiches which may be enjoyed in any of the bars. Seating is also available next to the glass-enclosed gondola house. While dining next to the gondola, diners may watch the gondola cars load and revolve around the bull wheel.

Table service dining is available at Jimmy's, located on the second floor of Olympic House next to Bar One. Open for breakfast and dinner, Jimmy's specializes in California-style fine dining. In addition to daily specials, it features freshly prepared appetizers and entrées such as calamari steak; oysters Rockefeller; artichokes; sashimi; tournedos of beef; teriyaki brochette of beef; prime rib; rack of lamb; roast chicken with lemon & fresh dill; fettucini with chicken; shrimp and sausage. The wine list includes many California varietals such as Cabernet Sauvigon, Zinfandel, and Chenin Blanc. Champagnes and dessert wines are also available.

Jimmy's is the only Plaza restaurant that accepts major credit cards. Squaw's fast-food establishments accept only cash.

Locals enjoy Le Chamois bar and pizza restaurant located next to the aerial tram base station. The food is good, and the service is congenial. Paul, who has tended bar there for several years, knows the local history as well as anyone. For a taste of a regional snack, ask Paul for a "Squeeler." This is a little hot sausage that comes with its own "kit." The kit consists of a napkin, hot cajun mustard, and a stick to spread the mustard on the squeeler.

Fine dining is the specialty of the Creekside Restaurant located in the Olympic Village Inn. Its ambience is soft and warm. Lighting is diffused through an intricate, redwood ceiling lattice. Tables overlook the swimming pool and waterfall which are both illuminated in the evening.

Entrées typically include farm-raised game such as venison and seafood. The three bean soup is spicy and the green beans are al denté. The venison is excellent, and because it is farm raised, it does not have the wild taste normally associated with game.

Activities

Activities other than skiing are limited at Squaw Valley. There is a Marlboro self-timer practice race course located at the top of the Shirley Lake chairlift.

Twice each day the Tahoe Queen plies the waters of Lake Tahoe between the casinos located at South Lake Tahoe and Squaw Valley. Guests staying in South Lake Tahoe may take the 8:00 A.M. shuttle and arrive around 10:00AM in Squaw Valley for a full day of skiing. Departure in the evening for the return trip is at approximately 4:00 P.M. The 1987-88 fare was $16.50 per adult each way. Full breakfast, dinner, and cocktails are available at extra charge. The Tahoe Queen is a large, paddle wheel boat graciously furnished in Victorian style.

Services

A full complement of sporting goods stores, apparel shops, pharmacies, grocery stores, liquor stores, furniture, bath, and specialty shops is within the immediate North Lake Tahoe area. In addition, there are antique stores, massage services, art galleries, bakeries, beauty salons, book stores, florists, movies, theatres, banks, churches, alterations, dry cleaning optical shops, and baby-sitting services.

STEAMBOAT

2305 Mt. Werner Circle
Steamboat Springs, CO. 80487

(303) 879-0740 Reservations
(303) 879-6111 Information
(303) 879-7300 Snow Report

Transportation

Steamboat is served by both American Airlines and Northwest Airlines. American flies daily non-stops from Chicago and Dallas/Ft. Worth airports. It also flies six days a week from Los Angeles and three days a week from San Francisco. American utilizes Boeing 727 aircraft for the flights. Northwest serves Steamboat with three weekly flights from Minneapolis, also using Boeing 727 aircraft. All flights terminate at the Yampa Valley Regional Airport located twenty-two miles from the resort. Ground transfers during the 1987-88 season were $18 round trip. Call (800) 525-6268 for advance reservations.

Air service is also available from Denver via Continental Express's DeHavilland Dash seven 50-passenger aircraft. Continental Express flies into the Bob Adam's STOLport only five miles from the slopes. The Sheraton Hotel offers complimentary pickup from the STOLport, as do several other lodging companies. When booking accommodations, verify pickup. Should the skier's lodging company not offer pickup service, contact Alpine Taxi at (303) 879-2800 or Ultimate Limousine at (303) 879-7417.

Budget, National, and Hertz all have rental cars equipped with snow tires and ski racks and are represented at both airports. However, Steamboat is such a compact resort that a car is not a necessity and, in fact, can be a nuisance.

Traveling to Steamboat by car is easy and convenient. From Denver, travel due west on Interstate 70 through the Eisenhower Memorial Tunnel and take the Silverthorne exit at Colorado Highway 9 north. Follow Highway 9 along the Green River to Kremmling. In Kremmling, turn west onto U.S. Route 40 and proceed directly into Steamboat.

A scenic drive of 157 miles under most conditions, the trip should not take longer than two and a half hours. However, during heavy snow storms, the drive over Rabbit Ears Pass can be memorable. Should weather be a consideration on the day of travel, telephone (303) 639-1234 for road conditions. If the road should be closed overnight, ample hotel rooms are available in the town of Kremmling.

Approaching Steamboat from the West is as simple as taking Interstate 70 east to Colorado Highway 131 at the Wolcott Interchange. Turn north until the U.S. 40 Interchange then follow the signs to Steamboat. This is a very picturesque drive through low mountains and open range. Should heavy snow conditions prevail, you may want to consider an alternate route from the West. Instead of taking the Wolcott exit off Interstate 70, take Colorado Highway 13 out of Rifle and go around the mountains. In the town of Craig, take U.S. 40 east to Steamboat. This alternate route is slightly longer, but in bad weather it will be much faster and safer.

Daily express bus service from Denver's Stapleton Airport to Steamboat is available. Telephone (800) 525-2628 for current schedules and rates. During the 1987-88 season, a round trip ticket was $58.

Mountain Statistics

Situated in the Routt National Forest, Steamboat has four mountain peaks available for recreational skiing: Thunderhead Peak, Storm Peak, Sunshine Peak, and South Peak. Taken together, these peaks offer 3,600 feet (1,097 meters) vertical, the second highest vertical in Colorado. (The highest is Aspen Highlands). Base elevation is a moderate 6,900 feet (2,103 meters) and Steamboat's highest peak is 10,500 feet (3,200 meters). There are 2,500 skiable acres (1,012 ha) and over 50 miles (80 km) of trails. Of these, fully 1,551 acres (628 ha) are groomed.

Steamboat is served by twenty lifts comprised of:

1 8 Passenger Gondola
1 Quad Chairlift
7 Triple Chairlifts
9 Double Chairlifts
2 Ski School Lifts (1 Surface, 1 Double Chairlift)

The longest beginner run is Why Not at 3 miles (4.8 km). This trail begins at the top of the Silver Bullet Gondola and winds its way down to the base area. The longest intermediate run is High Noon. It is two and a half miles (4 km) long. High Noon begins at the top of Sunshine Peak, at the terminus of the Priest Creek and Sundown chairlifts. Skirting the Rendezvous Saddle restaurant, it continues down to the base of the Elkhead lift.

The longest expert run is Shadows, which runs parallel to the Sundown chairlift on Sunshine Peak. It is just under one mile (1.6 km) in length, and it is a gladed run.

Each day at Steamboat a report on the snow conditions and a list of groomed runs are posted in the lift ticket sales windows. The information includes temperature, wind, snow depth, and recently groomed trails. Special events are also mentioned. Adjacent to the tram room at the base is a large trail map which is electronically changed to indicate the current status of all runs.

Steamboat is a diverse mountain where skiers of most ability levels can ski around the entire complex and enjoy the terrain's rich diversity. Its intermediate and expert runs are spread evenly throughout the four peaks.. All beginner runs, however, are located on Thunderhead. The well thought-out lift locations make it easy and quick for skiers to find untracked powder or freshly groomed conditions. During periods of inclement weather, the mountain's even distribution of varied runs guarantees skiers good ski conditions. When the wind is blowing over Storm Peak and Sunshine Peak, it is best to ski the Four Points, Burgess Creek, WJW, Arrowhead, and Thunderhead lifts, or the Silver Bullet Gondola; all are protected from the wind.

Steamboat is as much a gentle mountain as Snowbird is a difficult mountain. In other words, Steamboat does not have many trails that are intimidating. In fact, no runs are designated double black diamonds. This is a great family mountain where the entire family can enjoy skiing together on numerous runs. However, the expert runs are not wimpy. They will challenge the expert, and in the right snow conditions (powder), they may be among the best in Colorado. Chute One and The Ridge can be very demanding!

Ski through the trees off Traverse, The Ridge, and Crowtrack or enjoy the frequent knee deep "Champagne" powder that regularly graces this mountain. The term "Champagne" is reserved for the snow at Steamboat where the flakes are small and very light: just like bubbles in champagne. This kind of snow is effortless to ski. No doubt, the powder's lightness contributes to the ski school's active powder classes. There is probably not a better place to learn to ski deep powder than at Steamboat. Once powder skills are learned under these ideal conditions, they are easily transferred to other areas where the snow may be a bit heavier.

Steamboat begins each day with a rather unusual ritual: the "rope drop." All visitors will have heard of the drop by their second day at the resort. The term refers to the literal dropping of a rope at the terminus of the Silver Bullet Gondola each morning at 9:00 A.M. The gondola begins its trips up the mountain before the runs open so skiers can have breakfast at the top of Thunderhead and begin skiing at the earliest moment. The ski patrol places a rope between the restaurant and runs. At 9:00 A.M. the patrol "drops the rope," opening the mountain for skiing. On days when the powder from the previous night is deep, the rope drop can resemble a stampede!

The total number of skiable acres divided by the maximum number of skiers transported on the lifts per hour is .087. This is a moderately low ratio. Steamboat's lift service is very adequate for the quantity of terrain served.

Steamboat's annual snowfall is 325 inches (825 cm). The monthly snowfall is:

Nov.	27"	(69 cm)
Dec.	71"	(180 cm)
Jan.	63"	(160 cm)
Feb.	56"	(142 cm)
Mar.	57"	(145 cm)
Apl.	20"	(51 cm)

Average monthly temperatures during the season are:

Nov.	28°	-2° C
Dec.	18°	-8° C
Jan.	15°	-9° C
Feb.	18°	-8° C
Mar.	26°	-3° C
Apl.	38°	4° C

Lift Ticket Prices *(1988-89)*

Like many other Colorado ski resorts, Steamboat has departed from a "high" season and a "low" season. Instead, it has established a "regular" season and a "value" season. Value season rates are $5 less expensive than regular rates. The regular season commences on or about December 17 and runs until early April.

Regular Season Lift Tickets

$ 29.........Daily Adult
$ 23.........Half Day Adult
$174.........6 Days Out of 7
$150.........5 Days Out of 6
$124.........4 Days Out of 5
$ 14.........Daily (Age 65-69)
$Free........Daily (Age 70+)

All major credit cards are accepted.

Hours of Operation

9:00 A.M. to 4:00 P.M.

Lift Ticket Purchase Locations

Lift tickets may be purchased at the Silver Bullet Gondola building located off the Plaza at the mountain's base.

Of particular interest to parents skiing with children is the "Kids Ski Free™" program. In order to be eligible for this program, parents and their children must stay in lodging booked through the Steamboat Springs Chamber Resort Association for a minimum of five days. However, once this minimum criteria is met children may stay free in their parents' room. Sorry, but if children require their own room, there will be a charge for the additional room.

Steamboat has an innovative program that allows children to ski free on a one-to-one basis. In other words, if their mother and father both purchase lift tickets, up to two children will be given lift tickets gratis. If only one parent skis, then only one child can ski free. Should parents rent skis, these same rules are in effect for the children's rental equipment.

Crowd Control

The principal areas of congestion at Steamboat occur at lower High Noon, at the base of the Elkhead lift, and in the evening along Heavenly Daze and Vagabond.

The ski patrol places gates constructed from fabric netting at trail junctions in order to slow down skiers coming off the trails. A frequent place for these precautions includes the Twister and Four Points junction where they exit onto Ego. The technique works and prevents really fast skiers from intimidating less aggressive intermediates on Ego.

Ski School

Steamboat's ski school, under the direction of Vern Greco, employs 170 instructors trained in the American Teaching System. Most, if not all, credible resorts use this teaching method. It is important that a uniform teaching method be employed because skiers tend to move around and visit different resorts. For this reason, the ATS has become an American standard.

At Steamboat, two basic group lessons are available to guests: two hour lessons and all day lessons. A two hour lesson during the 1988-89 season will be $24 while an all day lesson will be $34. Beginning skiers will be delighted to learn that lift tickets are not required while skiing with an instructor. Beginner lessons start at 10:15 each morning and continue until 3:15 each afternoon.

1988-89 Adult lessons, including lift tickets are:
$184 3 Two Hour Lessons Per 4 Days
$210 3 Two Hour Lessons Per 5 Days
$234 3 Two Hour Lessons Per 6 Days
$264 3 All Day Lessons Per 6 Days
$ 17 Per Hour Per Person Guide Service

Children's lessons, ages 6-15 are priced at:
- $ 21 2 Hour Lesson
- $ 57 3 Two Hour Lessons
- $ 38 All Day Lesson With Lunch
- $102 3 All Day Lessons With Lunch
- $172 Ski Week: 5 All Day Lessons, 4 Lunches

For children between the ages of three and five, Steamboat offers its Kiddie Corral. Enrollment in Kiddie Corral includes lift tickets and lunch.

- $ 28 Half Day Lesson
- $ 38 All Day Lesson
- $107 3 All Day Lessons
- $150 5 All Day Lessons

With the exception of beginning skier classes, all adult classes last two hours and meet daily at 8:45 A.M., 11:15 A.M., and 1:45 P.M. All day lessons meet at 10:15 A.M. and finish at 3:15 P.M. Classes meet in back of the Sheraton Village Hotel between the Preview and the Headwall lifts.

Children's two hour classes meet at 10:45 A.M. and their all day classes meet at 9:45 A.M. Classes meet either at the gondola terminal or in front of the Thunderhead Restaurant where the gondola terminates.

Kiddie Corral participants must be registered no later than 9:30 A.M., but instructors will accept children as early as 8:00 A.M. Parents return for their children at 3:00 P.M. Kiddie Corral meets at the base of the gondola building.

Special ski classes available for those who have specific skills they want to hone include the Mt. Werner Challenge Series, an intensive two day program for advanced and expert skiers. Class sizes are limited, and the 1987-88 fee was $60. Meet at the top of the gondola at 10:15 A.M. Classes are organized for adults and children.

A two hour NASTAR race clinic is offered for adults and children. These Classes meet daily at 11:00 A.M. at the Bashor Race Area; cost is $30. Take the Christie III chairlift to get to the race area; exit the chair to your left.

Bump and powder clinics are also available at Steamboat. Powder clinics are held every morning when there is at least six inches of new snow. Personally, this author does not believe the lessons are worthwhile unless there are at least nine to twelve inches of new snow. The technique for skiing six inches of champagne powder is not significantly different from that of skiing packed powder. However, at nine inches or more, the technique is definitely different and lessons would be a good investment.

Equipment Rental

Seven ski rental shops are located at or near the base of the gondola. The least expensive of these rental shops during the 1987-88 season was Clock Tower Sports located in Ski Time Square (which is within any NFL field goal kicker's scoring distance of Gondola Square). Its least expensive ski package was $8 per day, and its most expensive performance package was $16. Rates for more than two days were slightly lower. The brand names of equipment were not available at press time.

Prices at the Sport Stalker, located on Ski Time Square and on Gondola Square, were higher at $12.50 for a recreation package and $21 for a high performance package. The Stalker rents Rossignol, K-2, and Pre skis. Boots are by Nordica or Salomon.

Other rental stores with competitive prices include: Ski Haus International, Steamboat Select Inc./Pro Select, Terry Sports, Village Center Ski Rentals, and Warners' Storm Hut. All stores accept major credit cards. Either a cash deposit or credit card imprint is required.

Ski Tuning and Repair

Tuning and repair services are available at all ski rental shops and sporting goods stores. The Sport Stalker has stone grinding equipment manufactured by Montana, called Crystal Glide, which provides a superior flat surface to ski on compared to the other common methods of tuning. For a detailed explanation on the superiority of "ski structuring," review the *Ski Tuning and Repair* chapter in the *Killington* section of this book.

Skis must be warm before waxing. Therefore, it is a good idea to drop the skis off at the end of the day and pick them up the next morning.

Sport Stalker 1987-88 tune-up rates were:
$6	Hot Wax
$10	Deburr and Wax
$16	(pair) Edges Sharpened, Wax
$24	Complete Tune-up
$32	Complete Tune-up (Montana Stone Grinding Equipment)
$10	Bindings Adjusted
$3-8	P-tex Per Weld

Mountain Restaurants

A convincing argument could be made that America's very best mountain restaurants are at Steamboat. The resort's flagship has to be Hazie's, located in the gondola building at the top of Thunderhead Peak.

Hazie's broad expanse of two-story high windows gives its diners an uninterrupted panoramic view of the Yampa Valley. Diners look out across sprawling Old Steamboat Springs and see the distant mountain that locals refer to as the "Sleeping Giant." Look carefully at the mountain. Can you see his chin? His chest? His feet? The Giant is lying on his back with his head facing south and his feet pointing north.

Begin a leisurely lunch at Hazie's by having a cocktail in its attractive bar constructed from mahogany and accented by deep green carpeting. The walls are glass and the fixturing is brass. Sample the bar's exceptional hors d'oeuvres such as: sashimi, fresh yellowfin tuna, sliced thin and served raw; gravad lax—"buried salmon," Norwegian salmon cured at Hazie's; tuna grille aux poivre, fresh yellowfin tuna, rubbed with cracked black pepper, seared and served cold with a Roma tomato sauce; crab back, a Caribbean specialty; blue crab mixture stuffed into the shell and baked with lime butter; Several kinds of oysters including blue point, oysters nouvelle, or Moscow are also served. Hazie's freshly made and unusual gourmet pizzas are also worth a try.

From the bar, move to the adjoining restaurant which occupies two floors. The view from Hazie's windows is uninterrupted because the second floor is cantilevered off the interior wall over the first floor dining area. The result is spectacular. Table settings and service are first-class. Each table is decorated daily with fresh flowers, adding to the ambience.

Hazie's is open for lunch and dinner. A perfect night in Steamboat calls for an early evening ride on the Silver Bullet to dinner in the restaurant. For appetizers consider one of the following: curried Cajun seafood salad, Mozzarella salad, or Callaloo—a coconut cream-based soup of the Isles, abundant with fresh spinach and crab.

The nouvelle American cuisine dishes include such items as scallop pie in bonnet or salmon mousse. Hazie's salads often add unusual items such as calamari. Typical entrées might be veal roulette with wild mushroom stuffing or orange spicy shrimp. The menu at Hazie's is never predictable because the chef prepares different dishes each evening; all of them are very interesting and always excellent.

The diner can watch the evening lights come on in Steamboat Springs as the snow begins to fall gently, preparing the mountain for yet another day of that special Steamboat champagne powder.

Steamboat's other mountain restaurants seem to pale in comparison to Hazie's. However, these restaurants are still superior to those at most other resorts.

Located in Rendezvous Saddle at the top of South Peak is Ragnar's restaurant. This is smaller than Hazie's, and the offerings are different. Ragnar's is decorated in a style reminiscent of Old Steamboat. Weathered barnboard walls are decorated with many old photographs of the late Buddy Werner and other legendary skiers.

The menu at Ragnar's leans toward Scandinavian dishes such as Dages Fiske Ret (seafood special of the day); Grilleret Laks Norheimsund (fresh Norwegian salmon, mesquite broiled and served with light mustard dill sauce.); Stekt Lammekolle (oven baked leg of lamb served with fresh garden vegetables and drippings from the roast); Stekt Rodspaette Trondheim (fresh Sole sauteed with asparagus, shrimp and leeks in a butter lemon wine sauce).

Rendezvous Saddle Restaurant is located in the same building as Ragnar's; This is an excellent cafeteria which has menu items such as fresh fruit, pastries, and quality hot food. There is also a terrific outdoor sun deck with a bar where freshly grilled foods, including barbeque, are offered. Staff members are among the friendliest in Colorado, and they will make sure your luncheon experience is memorable.

The cafeteria at Thunderhead is called Café Thunderhead. The food service here is comparable to that of Rendezvous Saddle. The café provides a warm shelter in an occasionally hostile climate.

The Stoker Bar, located one floor below Hazie's, offers table service and is quite charming. Though not as elegant as Hazie's nor Ragnar's, it is very comfortable and a great place to grab a sandwich on those days when one does not want a full meal. Its coffee drinks are also welcome on cold, snowy days.

The B.K. Corral is located on the third floor of the gondola building. This fast service restaurant is a cafeteria and home of Charlie's Breakfast Club. The term "Club" is a misnomer because Charlie's serves a full breakfast and is frequented by those serious skiers who want to be among the first on the mountain at rope drop. At noon the offerings feature pizza, hamburgers, hot dogs, and other typical American lunch items.

In the evenings, ride the Silver Bullet to the Corral restaurant and enjoy a family-style Western barbeque, live entertainment, and dancing. The Corral features such traditional Western fare as baron of beef, Danish pork ribs, barbecued chicken breasts, baked potatoes, salad bar, dinner rolls, and desserts. Reservations are suggested.

All of Steamboat's mountain restaurants are relatively new and are meticulously maintained. Other resorts would be well-advised to visit Steamboat and emulate its excellent food service.

Day Care

The day care nursery at Steamboat is part of the Kiddie Corral located on the bottom floor of the Silver Bullet Gondola at the mountain's base. The nursery accepts children from six months through six years. Lunch is available for $4 for children over two years. Meals for younger children must be provided by parents. Diapers and other special items should also be provided by parents. Cost for nursery service is $25 for the first child and $14 for the second. Half-day care is also available at $18 for the first child and $12 for the second child. All prices were current for the 1987-88 ski season.

Medical Facilities

The ski patrol will only render emergency aid for ski injuries. The patrol will administer trauma treatment, stabilize broken bones, and transport injured skiers downhill. Actual treatment, however, will be administered at the Routt Memorial Hospital in Old Steamboat Springs. Injured skiers are transported to the hospital via ambulance. This is a full service hospital with several practicing physicians on staff.

Chiropractors, dentists, orthodontists, optometrists, pharmacies and physical therapists are available in Steamboat Springs as well.

Cross-Country Skiing

Cross-country is not available at Steamboat proper. However, the Steamboat Ski Touring Center offers 20 kilometers of groomed trails and guided tours of Rabbit Ears Pass. Also, some guide companies will take groups on moonlight cross-country tours. See the *Activities* section for more information.

Special Events

NASTAR races are held daily, except Monday, on the Bashor race course area from 10:00 A.M. to 3:00 P.M. Adjacent to the NASTAR course is the Marlboro Ski Challenge, a coin operated self-timer race course. Its hours are the same as NASTAR.

Billy Kidd offers three and six day race camps throughout ski season. Open to all ages, a typical day includes two hours of free skiing with Billy or one of his specially trained coaches, five hours of race training, and one hour of video analysis.

Although special events vary from year to year, a few are repeated annually. Among them are beautiful torchlight parades down the face of Thunderhead staged on New Year's Eve and several other times throughout the season.

The Annual Cowboy Downhill is one of the largest media events in Colorado Ski Country. Originated by Billy Kidd and his buddy Larry Mahan, the six-time, All 'Round World Champion Cowboy, the Cowboy Downhill consists of over sixty events. One event not duplicated anyplace else includes running a slalom course, lassoing a ski hostess, saddling a horse, and crossing a finish line. This event seems to always coincide with the National Winter Stock Show held in Denver.

The Winter Carnival, another annual event, happens also to be the oldest winter carnival west of the Mississippi. For one week in February, the entire town of Steamboat participates in such events as racing, ski jumping, sled racing, a cross-country hot air balloon race, a parade, and many other events including a spectacular fireworks display.

The annual Steamboat Express held in March is staged to raise funds for the Jimmy Heuga Center for Multiple Sclerosis and the United Way. More than thirty teams compete to ski as many vertical feet as possible in six hours. Last year the teams logged over 2.5 million feet!

Because Steamboat has one of only two ski jump hills in the country, it is usually the site of the National Ski Jump Championships. Over 100 jumpers compete on the 70-and 90-meter hill over a three-day period.

Accommodations

Steamboat has old and new lodging to fit all budgets. Physically, the lodging and most of the restaurants are situated around the base facility. Old Steamboat Springs is downhill about two or three miles. City bus service between the two entities runs on a half-hour schedule from early morning to late evening.

Hotels

The largest hotel in Steamboat is the Sheraton Village Hotel located across from Ski Time Square. The lift system is just off the Sheraton's lobby, and the gondola is an easy two minute stroll. The Sheraton's lobby is typical of other Sheratons and is rather nondescript. The common amenities include a heated swimming pool, whirlpool, laundry facilities, restaurants, and an après ski lounge on the premises. All rooms have cable TV. Underground parking is also available. During the 1987-88 season, rooms at the Sheraton rented for between $89 and $119 per night.

Just across the hill from the Sheraton is the Ptarmigan Inn. Located practically under the gondola cables, the Ptarmigan is managed by Best Western and is a ski-in/ski-out facility. The rooms at the Ptarmigan are spartan but clean, and the staff is very friendly. All rooms have cable TV, views of the mountain or of the outdoor heated pool. There are also individual ski lockers, a sauna, and a restaurant. Rates during the 1987-88 season ran from a low of $45 per night in November to a high of $125 per night during the Christmas/New Year's holiday period.

Condominiums

The Norwegian Log Condominiums, located up the ski hill about 125 yards, are ski-in/ski-out units. The view from one side of the condos is of the ski mountain and from the other side of the Flat Top mountains. There are a total of eleven condominiums consisting of two and three bedroom units. The fully equipped kitchens' amenities include microwave ovens, convection ovens, complete sets of dishes, serving pieces, silverware, and glasses. All accommodations have fireplaces, color TVw/HBO, balconies, and Jacuzzi bathtubs. Daily maid service, garages, and an on-site concierge add to guests' comfort.

The Norwegian Log Condominiums are about nine years old. Although all the units are decorated individually, the theme is consistent throughout. Typical of the time they were built, they are beginning to show their age. The walls are knotty pine, and the dominant color is brown. The rooms are large and nicely furnished. During the 1987-88 season, they rented for between $190 and $210 per night.

Among the nicest properties at Steamboat is The Meadows at Eagleridge. Situated in an open meadow about 500 yards from the lifts, The Meadows is among the newest offerings at Steamboat. The stucco exterior is complemented by an extensive copper-clad roof, which is just beginning to take on the green patina of aging. Access to the individual units is through the underground garage. Upon checking in, all guests are given an electronic door opener not only for their convenience, but also as a security device.

Although the Meadows has only eighteen condominiums, a concierge and daily maid service are on the premises. The complex features a beautiful, heated outdoor swimming pool and spa. Its ample deck area is a great place to have a party or to gather and meet other guests.

The condominiums are elegantly furnished, and five of the penthouse units have private elevators. Each living room has a large brick fireplace and recessed ceilings. All lighting is on rheostats so one can adjust the room's lighting to his own preference. Each dining room has its own private wet bar and Scotsman ice maker. The kitchen has grey stone flooring and contains a microwave oven, a convection oven, a Thermador grill, and an instant hot water tap. The grill is set in an attractive brick arched alcove. The view from some of the kitchen windows is of Mt. Werner. Other rooms look out on the Sleeping Giant.

The rich Zolatone colors selected for the walls are accented with quality mahogany trim. The baths include Jacuzzi tubs, double sinks, tile counters, medicine cabinets, and all are well lighted.

The master bedroom features a wood burning fireplace. The master's king-size bed has reading lights built into the headboard as well as a remote control unit for the TV. All condos have central humidity control, walk-in closets, and private balconies off each bedroom. The balcony floors are heated so it is not necessary to shovel snow off them. Thus, the balconies can be used all season.

The minimum 1987-88 season rate at the Meadows was $195 per night. The maximum rate was $325.

Many other hotels and condominiums are available. Before booking reservations, ask for a copy of *Steamboat's Travel Planner*, a free brochure with photographs of the properties and descriptions of the amenities. A review of this brochure will insure that guests know in advance the quality and appearance of the accommodations.

Restaurants

All genre of restaurants is available in Steamboat, from the finest French restaurants to modest Mexican cafés.

The "in" place for après ski is The Inferno, located downstairs at Gondola Square. This is a "down and dirty" old-west bar and grill. The barnboard walls are decorated with old gasoline station signs. The bar is dark, and when the music starts, it is the only thing anyone can hear. The central feature at The Inferno is its Wheel of Fortune. Occasionally, a bartender will spin the wheel and the number on which the arrow stops becomes the price for Corona beer! There is a small dance floor, and live entertainment is offered after 9:30 P.M. Tuesday through Thursday.

Walking through the mountain village on a cold snowy evening, one may come upon an aberration from warmer climes. Just off Ski Time Square is a little restaurant with Italian lights strung outside. Umbrella tables are in front of the entrance, and the warm light from its windows creates shadows that for just a moment can be mistaken for ruffling palm fronds. If only there were a lake in front and the grass were green, one might think of being in Italy rather than in Steamboat. Such is the charm of Steaming Jack's.

Steaming Jack's is a dinner theatre offering light comedy or musical reviews. During the 1987-88 season, dinner was $19.95 for adults and $12.95 for children and featured prime rib, chicken Marsala or the fresh catch of the day. Dinner begins promptly at 8:15 P.M. Wine and spirits are available at extra cost. During warmer months an outside deck is open and meals are available from the outdoor grill.

Many of Steamboat's restaurants are located in Ski Time Square, including one of the better Mexican restaurants called Dos Amigos. It features traditional Mexican dishes served in a warm, friendly atmosphere. The owner and host, Bill Cropper, has collected many unusual photographs from Mexico, so be sure to take a few extra minutes and walk around the restaurant to view them.

Cipriani's is Steamboat's best small Continental restaurant. It is located in the Sheraton Resort and Conference Center (not to be confused with the hotel). The Conference Center is located in the Thunderhead Lodge and Condominiums across from Ski Time Square. Cipriani's is located in the basement of the lodge.

With seating for only fifty-eight patrons within its setting of stuccoed walls and brass rails, Cipriani's has the flavor of an intimate left bank bistro. Cipriani's manager, Barry Wolfman, is justifiably proud of his wine selections. A sampling would include '86 Raymond at $28.50 per bottle; '83 Sequoia Grove at $24.00/bottle; '84 Laboure-Roi Pouilly-Fuisse at $29.50/bottle. All prices quoted were for the 1987-88 ski season.

The Italian menu features such delectables as Pesce Spada Graticola (freshly broiled swordfish topped with lemon butter, diced tomatoes, artichoke hearts, scallions, hearts of palm and shallots); Maré Alfredo (fettucini with clams, oysters, mussels, crab and Languestino topped with sauce Alfredo and bacon); Vitello con Funghi, Sugo di Galliano (Veal scallopini, sauteed with leeks and wild mushrooms, topped with butter sauce and finished with butter).

Other fine restaurants must include: The Brandywine at Eighth at Lincoln Ave in Old Steamboat Springs which serves such American classics as steak, scampi, red snapper, and king crab legs; L'Apogee, 810 Lincoln in Old Steamboat Springs which offers classic French and Continental cuisine; Panda Garden in Central Park Plaza which features excellent Chinese food.

Activities

Steamboat offers an endless variety of activities:

Balloons Over Steamboat, hot air balloon rides. Telephone (303) 879-3298

Over the Hill Gang. Skiers 45+ meet on Sundays and Mondays at their sign near the Sheraton. Participants should be intermediate skiers.

Jupiter Jones Powder Cats. Untracked powder skiing on Buffalo Pass in Routt National Forest. Intermediate through expert skills required. Free Coyote skis provided. Telephone (303) 879-5188 for reservations.

Dinner sleigh rides . Telephone (303) 879-2606 between 8:00 A.M. and 6:00 P.M. for reservations.

Snowmobile rentals. Telephone (303) 879-2062 or (303) 879-1551 for information and reservations.

Bowling, only two and a half miles from the slopes. Telephone (303) 879-9840 to reserve a lane.

Skids Club, located in Gondola Square. A place for kids and teens to meet and play video games, enjoy large screen TV, play pinball, listen to music and eat. Hambergers, french fries, pizza, soft drinks, and ice cream at reasonable prices. Open from 2:00 P.M. to 7:00 P.M.

Dogsleding. Telephone (303) 879-7199.

Ice skating. Howelsen Hill Ice Rink. Telephone (303) 879-0341 for the operating schedule.

The Steamboat Health & Recreation Company. Thirty exercise classes each week consisting of aerobics, including low impact, stretching and toning, and yoga. There is also a weight room with free weights, Universal Gym, and stationary bicycles.

Services

A full complement of churchs, sporting goods stores, apparel shops, pharmacies, grocery stores, liquor stores, furniture, bath, and specialty shops is within the immediate Steamboat area. Additionally, guests at any of the condominiums or homes may place orders for provisions directly with Nancy's Selective Shopping. Telephone (303) 879-5018 for delivery prior to arrival.

SUN VALLEY

Sun Valley Company,
Sun Valley, Idaho 83353

(800) 635-8261 Reservations
(208) 622-4111 Information
(800) 635-4150 Snow Report

Transportation

Compared to many American destination resorts, Sun Valley cannot be considered easy to reach. Its nearest commercial airport is in Boise, a distant 168 miles. A private airport in Hailey, 12 miles south of Sun Valley, is served daily by Horizon Airlines. Private aircraft can be chartered at the Hailey Airport, if desired.

Although somewhat inconvenient to reach, Sun Valley is well worth the inconvenience because once skiers reach the resort, its secluded location becomes an advantage. There are no weekend crowds, and the entire resort takes on a comfortable, family atmosphere.

The best way to reach Sun Valley by air is to fly into Salt Lake City Airport, a major airline hub. From Salt Lake, it is a short flight to Boise on scheduled airlines, followed by a three hour drive to Sun Valley. The drive is easy because the road follows mountain valleys and is virtually immune to inclement weather.

Take I-84 from either Boise or Salt Lake. This fine, all-weather divided highway bisects the Snake River Plain, and one is not even in the mountains until reaching the town of Bellevue about twenty miles from Sun Valley. In fact, the name "Sun Valley" is literal—it attests to the fact that the weather is usually sunny in the valley. Unlike many mountain resorts, Sun Valley experiences few long periods of grey sky and snowy days. Quite the contrary, it typically receives frequent, small snowstorms that assure boot deep powder on a regular basis, and it usually enjoys clear, deep blue skies during daylight hours.

Charter bus services are available from Boise, Idaho Falls, Twin Falls, and Salt Lake City. Interested travelers should contact their travel agents for a list of services and times.

Car rentals are available at all the major and regional airports. Hertz and National will rent cars that can be dropped off at Sun Valley. All other rental agencies require drivers to return the cars to their original rental location.

Although a car is not a necessity at Sun Valley, it will certainly enhance one's visit. The resort itself is self-contained, but there are many other interesting places and towns to visit. The added flexibility and mobility that an automobile provides should justify the expense.

Mountain Statistics

Sun Valley, like Aspen, has two mountains: Bald and Dollar. Dollar Mountain is situated adjacent to the Sun Valley resort, while "Baldy" is approximately two miles away. Shuttle buses run every fifteen minutes between both mountains. Shuttle service begins a half hour before the lifts open and runs until one-half hour after the lifts close. In addition, the city of Ketchum provides shuttles which run continuously between the mountains and the various hotels, condos, and retail establishments in town. For those wishing to drive between the Sun Valley resort and the mountains, ample parking is available at Dollar's base and at the River Run base of Baldy.

Dollar Mountain is considered primarily a teaching mountain. It is relatively small and very gentle. There is not a single tree on this hill, causing it to resemble Sestriere, the famous ski resort in northern Italy. Dollar's base is 6,010 feet (1,832 meters) and its summit is at 6,638 feet (2,023 meters), giving it a vertical drop of 628 feet (191 meters). The entire mountain consists of only 127 acres (51 ha) with uphill lift service for 5,000 skiers per hour.

Bald Mountain is a classic ski mountain and it is the mountain for which Sun Valley is most famous. Baldy has all the elements skiers of every ability level look forward to in skiing! There are gentle rolling slopes, steep runs, moguled trails, and bowls filled with downy powder. At first glance, the trail map maligns the enormity and the diversity of the terrain and considerably understates the quantity of runs. As at Jackson Hole, most of the terrain on the map is skiable, not just the illustrated runs. Also, the trails emanating from the upper ridge are large, completely open bowls.

Baldy's base is 5,750 feet (1,753 meters), the lowest of any resort located in the Rocky Mountains. Its summit is 9,150 feet (2,789 meters) giving it a vertical drop of 3,400 feet (1,036 meters).

During the summer of 1988, Sun Valley will completely revamp its lift services on Bald Mountain. New for the 1988-89 season will be two or possibly three high-speed, detachable quad lifts. The Forest Service has approved lifts manufactured by Lift Engineering & Manufacturing Co. (YAN), and they should be in service opening day. Assuming that three lifts will be installed, they will replace various slower chairlifts installed between 1957-1971.

One new lift, Look-Out Express, will replace the Lower Warm Springs lift and the Limelight lift. The new Christmas lift will replace the former Christmas lift and the Ridge chairlift. The third new chairlift will be named Greyhawk and will run roughly parallel to the Look-Out Express, except it will terminate at the top of the Upper Greyhawk trail. The addition of these new lifts will greatly enhance the uphill lift capacity of the mountain and will provide a total uphill lift capacity of 23,800 skiers per hour.

The total reported number of skiable acres is 1,275 (516 ha). However, Sun Valley significantly understates its skiable acreage by failing to take into consideration the entire terrain of its bowls. If Sun Valley were to include this immense bowl area in its figures, the total acreage would possibly double. Even without the additional acreage, however, the total acreage divided by the maximum up-hill lift capacity remains at a respectable .053. Actually, the Sun Valley resort is never crowded like Aspen or Vail. During 1987-88, Sun Valley's average skier days were only 3,500, significantly below its maximum capacity. This is the reward one receives for skiing at a major resort away from any substantial urban area.

Sun Valley's trail map not only understates the available terrain for skiing, but it also creates the false impression that Baldy is an "easy" mountain. This impression is created by the use of the terms "easier," "more difficult," and "most difficult." Skiers familiar with other areas, particularly Colorado, are used to associating the color green with beginner, blue with intermediate, and black with expert. At Sun Valley, however, green is easier, but definitely not beginner. Beginning or low intermediate skiers are advised to confine their skiing to Dollar Mountain. Green runs such as Gretchen's Gold, Southern Comfort, Christin's Silver, and Siggi's Bowl, to name a few, are definitely intermediate, and may be among the easiest runs on the mountain: relatively steep, but not moguled. In fact, that seems to be the major difference between the green "easier" runs and the "more difficult" blue runs. The "most difficult" black runs are upper intermediate and low expert. There are no truly "expert" runs here like the double black diamonds found at resorts such as Jackson Hole or Snowbird.

One of the greatest attractions to Bald Mountain is that it is a nearly perfectly formed mountain. There are almost no areas in or out-of-bounds that are avalanche prone. After a snow storm, many local skiers take off for the out-of-bounds areas to ski untracked powder. This form of skiing presents little danger with a guide along, and the out-of-town skier can arrange with the ski school to experience wonderful out-of-bounds areas.

Skiers who want to stay on the traditional runs after a major dump will find the best snow in Siggi's Bowl, Mayday Bowl, Lookout Bowl, Easter Bowl, Little Easter Bowl, and Christmas Ridge and Christmas Bowl. Because the wind normally blows from right to left (looking downhill), the best conditions are on the lee, or right-hand side of the bowls. During snow storms, or on rare days when Sun Valley gets flat light, stay out of the bowls and ski runs heavily lined with trees. The trees provide contrast and make it much easier for the skier to see moguls and other terrain features. Sun Valley's bowls are such broad expanses of white that contrast and definition are difficult to perceive.

Bald Mountain is located in such a way that one side is almost always in the sun. Most knowledgeable skiers will begin their day skiing the River Run side but after lunch will switch to the Warm Springs side.

Sun Valley's annual snowfall is 175 inches (445 cm): small, but adequate, by comparison with many other resorts. Neither Bald nor Dollar Mountain is excessively rocky, nor do they require extraordinary quantities of snow to cover their runs. Monthly snowfall is as follows:

Nov.	36"	(91 cm)
Dec.	60"	(152 cm)
Jan.	100"	(254 cm)
Feb.	115"	(292 cm)
Mar.	100"	(254 cm)

Average monthly temperatures during the season are:

Nov.	32°	0° C
Dec.	21°	-6° C
Jan.	19°	-7° C
Feb.	24°	-4° C
Mar.	31°	0° C

Lift Ticket Prices

Sun Valley has a two tier lift ticket price structure. The cost of a daily lift ticket for Dollar Mountain during the 1987-88 season was $19. A one day ticket for Bald Mountain during the same period was $30. However, persons purchasing a lift ticket for Dollar may purchase a Baldy upgrade at anytime. The skier who purchases a lift ticket for Baldy may also ski at Dollar.

Baldy lift ticket prices during 1987-88 were:

$ 30......Adult, Daily
$ 80......Adult, 3 Day
$130......Adult, 5 Day
$155......Adult, 6 Day
$ 20......Adult, Half Day

$ 19......Child, Daily
$ 13......Child, Half Day
$ 85......Child, Six Day

Dollar Mountain lift ticket prices during 1987-88 were:

19.......Adult, Daily
$13.......Child, Daily
$13.......Half Day

Children's rates apply to children aged eleven and younger. Throughout the season, Sun Valley stages seasonal promotions during which children may ski free, or the Ski Corporation offers various discounts for children. Interested skiers should check with the resort in advance to determine if there are any incentives or discounts to be offered during their planned ski holiday. Telephone (208) 622-4111, ext. 2431.

Hours of Operation

9:00 A.M. to 4:00 P.M. daily

Lift Ticket Purchase Locations

Lift tickets may be purchased at either the River Run Base or the Warm Springs base of Bald Mountain. Lift tickets for Dollar Mountain are available at Dollar's base. Additionally, tickets may be purchased at the Sports Desk located on the shuttle turnaround next to the Sun Valley Lodge. Tickets may be purchased any time between 8:30 A.M. and 3:30 P.M.

Crowd Control

Because Sun Valley's uphill lift capacity greatly exceeds its average quantity of skiers, there are no crowds and, consequently, no need for crowd controls. As proof of this statement, no mazes at the lift stations were evident during the 1987-88 season.

Ski School

Sun Valley's Ski School is more than fifty years old. Over the years, the ski school has honed its teaching techniques to a fine edge and offers instruction for any ability level. It offers group lessons and private lessons; instructors will even customize a program to fit specific needs such as powder skiing, bump skiing, or racing.

Over one hundred-fifty instructors are employed at Sun Valley. Sun Valley is one of the few major resorts which exclusively teaches the Graduated Length Method. Using GLM, as it is abbreviated, the novice student is started out on very short skis. As the skier's ability improves, he advances in small increments to longer skis. This technique has been criticized and largely abandoned by many ski schools because if it is not taught properly, GLM skiers do not develop the smooth grace of skiers taught by the American Teaching System (ATS). GLM students may develop a habit of "muscling" their turns. Some skiers who then progress to longer skis take the muscling habit with them and never advance their ability to ski varying conditions such as powder.

Novices and low intermediates are taught to ski on Dollar Mountain. Strong intermediate skiers are taught on Seattle Ridge or College, located on Bald Mountain. Advanced ski instruction is at the instructor's option and can take place on any of the runs on Bald Mountain.

Enrollment in the ski school is easy. The main office is located next to the Sports Center on the shuttle turnaround next to the Lodge. Skiers also can enroll at Dollar Cabin situated at the base of Dollar Mountain or at the North Face Hut at the base of Baldy's Warm Springs. Those skiers who decide on last minute lessons can enroll at the Look Out Restaurant atop the Limelight lift.

The 1987-88 ski school rates were:

$ 42......One Day (4 Hours)
$ 98......Three Days (12 Hours)
$129......Five Days, (20 Hours)
$ 42......One Hour, Private
$208......All Day, Private

The above prices do not include lift tickets. There are no class lessons available at Bald Mountain on Saturday or Sunday, except during the Christmas holidays.

Equipment Rental

There were twelve equipment rental shops in Sun Valley during the 1987-88 season. One of the larger shops, Sturetevants of Sun Valley, has two locations: 314 N. Main Street in Ketchum and in the Greyhawk Alpine building located at the base of the Warm Springs lift. At the Main St. store, skiers can rent recreational ski packages consisting of:

Blizzard Skis
SX 61 Salomon Boots
Salomon Bindings
Poles

The cost of this package was $12 per day, or $11 per day if rented for between three and four days. The price is further reduced to $10 per day when rented for five days or longer.

Sturetevants's other rental option is its Sport Package. Whereas the Recreation Package is designed for beginners or low intermediate skiers, the Sport Package is designed for intermediate and expert skiers. This package consists of: Rossignol or Blizzard Scirocco skis, Nordica 725 rear entry boots, Look bindings and poles for a base rate of $17 per day. Multi-day rentals are reduced similarly to the Recreation Package.

The High-Performance Package is primarily a demo rental program, considered a means for the store to generate equipment sales. Under this program, a skier can rent any brand or ski size in either shop for $20 per day.

All packages must be accompanied by a $3.50 damage waiver which is actually an insurance policy. Also, at the time of rental the renter's credit card number is noted as is its expiration date. Neither an imprint nor a deposit is required.

Another major shop in Sun Valley is Snug, located on the Mall in Sun Valley Resort at 680 Sun Valley Road, across the lobby in the Elkhorn Resort. Snug rented ski packages during the 1987-88 season starting at $7 per day for a Recreation Package consisting of Pre 1200 R skis, SX 31 Salomon boots, Salomon 647 bindings and poles. An upgrade to Pre Electra SX skis, Salomon SX31 boots, Salomon 647 bindings, and poles was $12 per day. Its High Performance package included Pre 1200 Special Edition skis, Salomon SX 91 boots, Salomon 747 bindings, and poles for $15 per day.

Demo skis were available for $18 per day or $25 per day for an entire package consisting of boots, bindings, and poles. A damage waiver had to be purchased at a varying cost of between $1 to $1.50 per day. A credit card voucher had to accompany each transaction.

Ski Tuning and Repair

Tuning and repair services are available at all ski rental shops and sporting goods stores. Sturetevants of Sun Valley has WinterSteiger stone grinding equipment which provides a superior flat ski surface compared to other common methods of tuning. For a detailed explanation on the superiority of "ski structuring," review the *Ski Tuning and Repair* chapter in the *Killington* section of this book.

Skis must be warm before waxing. Therefore, it is a good idea to drop the skis off at the end of the day and pick them up the next morning.

1987-88 Sturetevants tune-up rates were:

$ 5	Hot Wax
$20	Edges Sharpened
$30	Complete Tune-up
$30+	P-tex

Sturetevants tries to be as cooperative as possible, and its staff will, therefore, be pleased to deliver customers' skis to either store for pickup.

Snug does not have stone grinding equipment at any of its three stores. Its staff will hand tune all skis left over night. In fact, its store located on Sun Valley Road has a glass enclosed tune-up area where skiers can watch as their skis are being tuned. Snug's 1987-88 prices were:

$ 5	Hot Wax
$ 6	Iron-on Wax
$15	Edges Sharpened
$25	Complete Tune-up
$ 5	Each Base Weld

Mountain Restaurants

There are two mountaintop restaurants on Bald Mountain. Lookout Restaurant, situated at the top of the Christmas and Limelight lifts, is a cafeteria. A large, clean, and nicely furnished restaurant, Lookout can be a refuge for skiers on cold, stormy days. On bright sunny days, dining is available outside on a broad deck with a fantastic view of the Sawtooth National Forest.

The other mountain restaurant is situated at the top of the Cold Springs lift and the base of the Christmas lift. This is a unique structure named after its shape: "Roundhouse." Cafeteria-style meals are available here, as is table service. The table service part of the restaurant is by far the best of all the mountain restaurants reviewed. This part of the Roundhouse is named "Averell's" after Averell Harriman, former Chairman of the Board of Union Pacific Rail Road and ambassador to the Court of

King James. Averell Harriman was responsible for both Sun Valley's development and the Roundhouse restaurant, which dates back to 1939.

At Averell's, the diner is treated to a magnificent view of the Sun Valley resort, the town of Ketchum, and the entire Sawtooth range. The food service is prepared on site; a uniformed chef typically slices and serves leg of lamb, roast beef, turkey, or baked ham. Sliced squaw bread is a local specialty that must be tried. Other items include: bouquet of fruit, seafood bouchee, Alpine chicken salad, gourmet fromage, quiche du jour, smoked trout, homemade pastries, Kahlua parfait, and ice cream.

The Carte de Vin at Averell's is peerless. Among the many varietals offered during the 1987-88 season were: Grand Cru/Cabernet Sauvignon; Sterling/Cabernet Sauvignon; Rutherford Hill/Merlot; Glen Ellen/Proprietor's Reserve Chardonnay; Kendall Jackson, Charardonnay; Trefethen/Pinot Chardonnay; Callaway/Fumè Blanc; and Pouilly Fuisse. Additional wine selections are also available by the bottle or by the glass. Domestic and specially selected foreign beers, coolers, and mineral waters can also be purchased. Dining at Averell's is definitely a treat not to be passed up!

Other restaurants are located at the base of Dollar Mountain and at the base of the Warm Springs lift on Baldy.

Day Care

Day care in Sun Valley is available from three firms: Warm Springs Day Care at the base of Baldy, Potato Patch Kids in Ketchum, and Tiny Tots Playschool behind the post office on the Sun Valley Resort Mall.

Tiny Tots accepts infants and children up to six years of age. However, during peak seasons such as Christmas and President's Weekend, space may be limited to children of Sun Valley Resort guests only. The facility can handle up to thirty children and reservations are strongly suggested. Its rates vary from $4-$5 per hour or between $30-$35 per day, with the higher rate charged for infants.

For children still on formula, parents should provide the formula marked with the child's name. Clothing should be clearly labeled. Disposable diapers are required. Lunches are available at a slight extra charge.

Reservations at Tiny Tots can be made by telephoning (208) 622-4111, ext. 2288.

Medical Facilities

The Sun Valley ski patrol will only render emergency service to injured skiers. The patrol will administer trauma treatment, stabilize broken bones, and transport injured skiers downhill by sled or helicopter.

After evacuation, skiers are transported to Moritz Community Hospital for actual treatment. The hospital is full service and has a 24 hour emergency room.

Cross-Country Skiing

Some of the greatest cross-country skiing in the country is available at Sun Valley. Principally, there are four companies that offer cross-country experiences.

The Sun Valley Resort's Nordic Center is located just behind the indoor ice rink at the Lodge. Nordic skiers have complete use of the resort's two heated swimming pools, indoor and outdoor ice skating rinks, as well as all the amenities offered by the Lodge.

The terrain at the Center's trail head is quite gentle, but as it continues on its 40 kilometer trek, it increases in difficulty. Three-pin skiers usually are not subject to high altitude sickness, the fatigue, or other ailments normally associated with Rocky Mountain Nordic skiing because of the area's relatively low elevation. Groomed tracks direct skiers through snow-covered meadows where they can either ski tour or experiment with the diagonal skating so in vogue today.

It is possible to rent or purchase all the equipment necessary for cross-country skiing at the Nordic Center. The Center also has a wax room and shop with all the necessary accessories needed for waxing and tuning. In addition, those Alpine skiers who have purchased a multi-day ticket may exchange one day for a cross-country ticket. This is a good program for skiers who have never tried cross-country but who think they might like it. Pick a clear day and try skiing the green beginner course or better yet, take a lesson from one of Hans Muehlegger's certified staff: a one and a half hour group lesson was only $14 during the 1987-88 season.

The daily trail fee during 1987-88 was a modest $6 and only $3 for children six to twelve. Senior citizens can ski for only $4.

The Nordic Center at Warm Springs Ranch has 12 kilometers of groomed creekside tracks. One kilometer of track is even lighted for night skiing! A complete pro shop, day lodge, lessons, rentals, and off-track tours are available at Warm Springs Ranch. There is even a doggie track for those skiers who cannot bear to leave Fido at home. A word of caution, though: most resorts and condos will not allow dogs in their units.

Located only twenty-two miles from Sun Valley and situated in the Sawtooth National Forest is the Galena Lodge. A chef in the recently remodeled kitchen turns out freshly-baked biscuits daily and offers complete breakfast and luncheon menus. The 40 kilometers of tracks are groomed daily by a newly-acquired Piston Bully 170, assuring skiers of a smooth, firm surface regardless of weather conditions.

Galena Lodge charges $7 for adults using its tracks. Children's rates are $4.50. The Lodge has a complete rental shop stocked with accessories and an excellent ski school. Transportation to Galena is provided Tuesday through Friday for a nominal charge.

For the cross-country skier who is really into experiencing the mountain environment, there is not a better way to do it than to arrange a tour to a Mongolian Yurt. Sun Valley Trekking Company offers a four to six hour tour over easy trails to its Fishhook Yurt. Once at the Yurt, skiers will be treated to a lunch of culinary delights. This trip is especially memorable on New Year's Eve. New Year's Eve 1988 was celebrated by an evening tour to the Yurt where the host served a hot and spicy golden punch, homemade cream of chestnut soup, crème fraîche, and boned shoulder of lamb. For dessert a Bûche Noël cake was served as a yard-long chocolate roll.

Special Events

Like most major ski resorts, Sun Valley has a full calendar of special events. The actual dates of the events vary, so persons interested in attending special functions should check with the resort prior to booking reservations. A sampling of events during the 1987-88 season included:

Sawtooth Series Telemark Dual Race; Christmas Eve Torchlight Parade; New Year's Eve Glenn Miller Celebration; USSA Masters Race; Duchin Cup Invitational; Allan Patterson Memorial

Downhill; Huega Express; Sun Valley Winter Carnival; Sun Valley Ski Club Reunion; Sun Valley Ski Club Bradford Cup; Annual Reidy Memorial Cross-Country Race; Sun Valley Pro Am; Sun Valley Cross-Country Biathlon; Sun Valley International Master's Race; Smokey Mountain Nordic Race.

Accommodations

There are inadequate adjectives in the English language to describe the graciousness and ambience that surround Sun Valley Resort's guests.

If arrival is in the evening, the guest is greeted upon entering the town of Sun Valley by a large lighted wreath on the side of a barn. The road leading to the resort itself is lined with split rail fencing; its lighting creates a fairyland atmosphere. Upon entering the grounds of the resort, one is immediately awestruck by towering pines that frame the entrance. The main building of Sun Valley Resort and the guest's first stop is the Lodge. Under an immense porte cochère, a valet will help unload the car and park it. One enters the reception area and lobby through large double doors. High tea is served in the afternoon while guests sit in front of the fireplace and watch skaters on the outdoor ice skating rink. The room is large and elegantly decorated from its hardwood floors with sculptured carpet in rose, flaxen, and silver to the rich, wood picture frame paneling, and gold-tone chandeliers. In a far corner of the room, a tuxedoed pianist plays show tunes and traditional favorites.

Adjacent to the lobby is the Peter Duchin Room. The natural oak paneling and plush seating is reminiscent of a fine bar in New York City, rather than a mountain lodge. The bar is constructed of fine inlaid grey/brown marble and the service here is excellent. The spirits and wines offered are exceptional. However, the guest is cautioned to ask for the price before ordering the better varietals. It is not uncommon to order a glass of wine only to find out that it has cost as much as $9 a drink for a bottle that sells for $12 in a liquor store.

The Peter Duchin Room features piano jazz after 4:00 P.M. Later in the evening, a band plays dance music. On occasion, a big name entertainer is presented and there is never a cover or up-charge.

The corridors leading to the rooms resemble a well kept museum. Photographs of Hollywood notables and Washington politicians abound, as do full cases of trophies won by many of Sun Valley's residents and visitors.

The rooms in the Lodge are tastefully decorated with traditional flair. Not large by most standards, they include amenities such as towel warmers and closets whose light goes on when the doors are opened. All the services of any world class hotel are as near as the telephone: room service, massage, valet, and so forth.

The grounds of Sun Valley are meticulously maintained. Many of the evergreens are lighted, and walkways are always cleared of snow. A stroll through the picturesque village is delightful as one passes by the Opera House and the Mall with its tony shops. Sun Valley is probably the only resort where a skier can purchase a custom-made ski parka or ski pants. Staying at Sun Valley Resort is so pleasant one does not even have to put ski to slope to know this is as good as it gets!

Although Sun Valley Resort is the premier place to stay while skiing at Sun Valley, there are several other accommodations. Very nice accommodations at that! Not far from Sun Valley Resort is the new Elkhorn Resort. Managed by Amfac Resorts, this should prove to be a major destination stop for skiers. Elkhorn is comprised of over 300 hotel rooms and condominiums. The style is Tyrolian modern and appears very comfortable with its surroundings. A small village is located in a semi-circle emanating from the lodge. Restaurants, shops, and galleries are all within walking distance of the accommodations.

A deluxe bedroom at the Elkhorn Lodge during the 1987-88 season rented from a low of $90 during the value season (Oct. 1 - Dec. 18) to a high of $130 during the regular season. Less expensive rooms were available and two bedroom condos ran from $120 to $220 per night.

If staying at the base of the lifts is a consideration, pickings are limited at the River Run base. Within walking distance is the Tyrolean Lodge managed by Best Western. This is a medium priced hotel and its location is somewhat removed from town and other resorts in the area. During 1987-88, rooms rented for between $70 and $95 per night.

Numerous condominiums are available at the base of the Warm Springs lift. To arrange for rentals and to find out what accommodations are available, telephone Warm Springs Property Management at (208) 726-8274.

The area around the base of Warm Springs is very congested. Parking is limited; therefore, guests staying in this area should make certain when booking their reservations that parking is included in the rental cost. Skiers staying in areas other than Warm Springs should not drive to this area, but should take one of the shuttles provided by Sun Valley Resort or by the city of Ketchum. Should parking be unavoidable, expect to pay as much as $15/day for the privilege.

Restaurants

If the skiing on Baldy and the beauty of the Sun Valley Resort are not enough to entice skiers to Idaho, then the restaurants will. Although restaurants are plentiful around Ketchum, none is finer than the Lodge Dining Room found on the second floor of the Sun Valley Lodge. Those skiers who have been fortunate enough to enjoy the cuisine at The Ranch in Keystone will be delighted to discover another restaurant equally worthy of their praise. Evening dress and a coat and a tie are **strongly** suggested for dining in the Lodge Dining Room. Beautiful table settings, attentive service, and outstanding food make an evening at the Lodge a treat. Diners should sample the trout meunière and some of the sinfully sweet confections. On Sunday, rest and attend the Lodge's buffet laid out among beautiful ice sculptures. Enjoy a leisurely meal accompanied by harp music and more delectable dishes than one could possibly eat.

For less formal occasions, there are numerous restaurants located around the resort, principally on the Mall.

One such restaurant, The Ram, is decorated in Swiss/Austrian decor with scythes, ox yokes, and cowbells on the walls. Chandeliers constructed from antlers complete the image. The chef labors over guests' orders on an open brazier. Waitresses are costumed in Bavarian attire, and the menu offers a complete list of meat and fish dishes. Naturally, a restaurant of this type offers several game dishes on its menu, including elk with lingonberries. The native trout with pea pods, cauliflower, cherry tomatoes, baby carrots, and wild rice is excellently prepared. The vegetables are always al denté, and the rolls are served hot with honey butter.

An even less formal restaurant is the Konditorei. Featuring its own takeout bakery, the Konditorei is a comfortable establishment. While waiting to be served, one can read a complimentary newspaper and catch up on the world's events. Order one of the ice cream specialties or just enjoy a hot cup of coffee. The Konditorei is a New York City hotel's equivalent of a snack bar or short-order grill.

Located on a side street in downtown Ketchum is Peter's Restaurant. Peter's is a modern Tyrolian restaurant. Its white stucco interior is subtly lit with track lighting, making it warm and inviting. The walls are sparsely decorated with local artists' water colors which are for sale. Many of the veal dishes featured are typical of the mountain regions of eastern Europe. The Gulyas soup is a Hungarian dish prepared with tomatoes, beef strips, and paprika. Try the excellent watercress salad with orange tarragon dressing. For an entrée, taste the veal with paprika complemented with spitzel, red cabbage, and fresh green beans with almonds. The meal service is well-paced, and some of the waitresses have a theatrical air which is very pleasant. Although the acoustics could stand some improvement, Peter's rates an "A" for food and service.

All told, twelve quality restaurants are located on Sun Valley Resort property and over fifty other restaurants are found throughout Ketchum. Meals of every type and description from hot dogs to fine Continental dining are available. Try any of the restaurants; very few will be disappointing.

Activities

For skiers who would like to find out just how good they really are, National Standard Races (NASTAR) are held on Baldy every Tuesday through Friday on the face of Warm Springs. A coin operated Marlboro self-timer practice race course is also located on Warm Springs Face.

Sun Valley Helicopter Ski Guides will fly powder hounds to back country skiing. Five full runs per day totalling 15,000 vertical feet are achievable. Too much? Try three runs and 9,000 vertical feet. For more information, telephone (208) 622-3108 or 788-4884.

Mulligan Snowmobile Tours offers tours with catered lunches everyday of the week. Telephone Mike Mulligan for more information at (208) 726-9137.

Ice-skate to the sonorous strains of Bolero on either of Sun Valley's two ice skating rinks. Admission during the 1987-88 season was only $4.75, and skates could be rented for $1.25.

Take a dinner sleigh ride in the Sawtooth Mountains. Telephone R. J. or Glenda Lewy for reservations at (208) 622-5019.

Beautiful, clear sunny days in Sun Valley were made for soaring! Scenic soaring tours in a glider are available from Soar Sun Valley. Telephone (208) 788-3054 for information and costs.

The Comedy Club at the Ram Bar in Sun Valley Resort is a fun place to check out in the evenings.

The Sun Valley Health Club on First Avenue in Ketchum is the place to flex the plex. This is a new, modern facility featuring all the amenities one expects from a first-class health club. Nautilus, free weights, aerobic classes, karate, ballet, stairmaster, stationary bicycles, treadmills, and rowing machines are all there. A complete pro shop can provide any items needed but forgotten at home. There is even a twenty yard, four-lap indoor pool complemented by a sauna and steam room.

No need to let small children interfere with an exercise schedule: the Athletic Club will entertain them right on the premises with toys and trained supervisors. Telephone (208) 726-3664 for more information.

Finally, enjoy fabulous shopping in the Sun Valley Mall. Among the many fashionable shops you will find are The Kitzbühel Collection and Panache, specializing in ladies' clothing and furs.

Services

A full complement of sporting goods stores, apparel shops, pharmacies, grocery stores, liquor stores, furniture, bath, and specialty shops is within the immediate area. In addition, there are antique shops, massage services, art galleries, bakeries, beauty salons, book stores, florists, movies, theatre, banks, churches, alterations, dry cleaning, optical shops, and baby-sitting services.

TAOS

Taos Ski Valley, Inc.
Taos Ski Valley, NM 87571

(800) 992-7669 Reservations
(505) 776-2291 Information
(505) 776-2916 Snow Report

Transportation

Taos Ski Valley is located in the southern Rocky Mountains' Sangre de Cristo Range. It is 143 miles north of Albuquerque and approximately 20 miles from the picturesque town of Taos. Because most of the area around Taos is high desert, the roads are usually clear. On occasion, however, wind-driven storms can cause hazardous road conditions. If driving and weather conditions are suspect, it is always a good idea to check road conditions before setting out.

With today's interstate highway systems, it is easy to reach even a secluded area like Taos. Arriving from Texas, use I-40 out from Amarillo to Albuquerque and take I-25 north to Santa Fe. From Santa Fe, take Highway 84/285 to Taos. Go through town to Highway 150 and turn right. The road ends at the Ski Valley.

From farther North and East, take the interstate system to Denver and then follow I-25 south to exit 18 (the second Walsenburg exit). Continue west on Colorado Highway 160 over La Veta Pass, a well maintained all-weather highway to Fort Garland. At Fort Garland turn left onto Colorado Highway 159, which becomes NM Highway 522 as the New Mexico state line is crossed. Continue on NM 522 through Questa until you see a blinking yellow light, then turn left onto NM Highway 150. Highway 150 will end at Taos Ski Valley fifteen miles later.

From the West, take I-40 east to Albuquerque and then I-25 north to Santa Fe. From Santa Fe, take Highway 84/285 to Taos. Go through town to Highway 150; turn right and you will arrive at Taos Ski Valley in about twenty minutes.

Reaching Taos by air is as easy as booking a ticket on any of the major airlines to Albuquerque's International Airport. At the airport, a car can be rented, or Mesa Airlines offers commuter service to the Taos Municipal Airport. At the time of this writing, Albuquerque's airport was undergoing extensive renovation and expansion. In a word, it was a mess. If tickets are booked directly to Taos, you can at least avoid baggage handling problems and arrive sooner than you could by driving from Albuquerque.

All the major car rental agencies at the Albuquerque Airport are located near the baggage claim area on the terminal's lower level. It is a good idea to have a car in Taos. Without one it is difficult to enjoy the town of Taos, due to its distance from the ski valley. And, because Taos is the oldest continually-occupied city in the United States, it has a great many features which visitors to the area will surely want to enjoy. Car rental selections in Taos are more limited than they are in Albuquerque.

When renting a car, be sure to insist that it has been *skierized*, i.e. with snow tires and ski racks. Vans and four-wheel drive vehicles are also available. Due to the latter's popularity, however, it is prudent to reserve one far in advance. Most rental agencies, and resorts for that matter, begin accepting reservations in August. For peak holiday seasons, the availability of cars and accommodations can become limited by September.

During the 1987-88 ski season, Mesa Airlines flew skiers to Taos from Albuquerque in thirty-six minutes for a one-way fee of $59; with a seven day advance purchase, the round-trip fare was $106. A ticket purchased thirty days in advance was only $83 round trip. There were three daily departures: 12:00 noon, 2:30 P.M., and 5:00 P.M. Check with your principal airline to confirm current year departure times, or call Mesa direct at (800) 637-2247.

Shuttle service to Taos Ski Valley from the Taos Airport and from the Albuquerque Airport is provided by Faust's Transportation. In 1987-88, Faust scheduled departures from Albuquerque at 3:00 P.M. and 5:45 P.M. From Taos they departed at 8:00 A.M., 11:30 A.M., and 3:15 P.M. One-way fare from Albuquerque was $25, round-trip $40. For current rates and information, telephone (800) 345-3738 in New Mexico and (505) 758-3410 from outside the state.

Mountain Statistics

Taos enjoys a justly deserved reputation as an expert's mountain. However, it is so much more! Taos is an experience not to be found at any other American ski resort. This resort, more than any other, was built from the dreams of one man, Ernie Blake. Taos was founded just after World War II when Ernie and his family single-handedly developed the mountain and its village. The resort has maintained its quaint and unique style right into the 1980's.

Taos's guests are strongly encouraged to enroll in a week-long ski program of instruction in the morning and free skiing in the afternoon. Taos's ski instructors teach skiers of all ability levels. During a February 1988 visit, the author witnessed a class of middle-aged skiers learning to ski an avalanche chute! Unless guests are staying in a condominium, all the accommodations are American plan. This means that guests take all meals in their lodge. A camaraderie is quickly developed among skiers, many of whom return year after year for the same weeks. The same camaraderie is fostered during lessons. Instructors encourage people to learn together and to develop friendships that will last throughout the week. Refusal or non-participation in this program will make guests feel like "odd man out." Everyone else at the resort will be making friends and enjoying their holiday, while non-participants will still be trying to understand the trail map.

Taos is unlike those mountain resorts that illustrate all available runs on a trail map. Many of Taos's runs are not illustrated at all! Just like at Snowbird and Jackson Hole, there is an entire group of runs not shown on the map. In fact, after disembarking the # 2 Lift, you will notice a table manned by one or two ski patrolmen. Whereas at most resorts this chairlift would be considered at the top of the runs, at Taos it is located only two-thirds of the way up the mountain. Walk up to the desk and notice other skiers signing a form. This form states "The undersigned represent that they are experienced and expert skiers and expressly recognize and assume both the particular and general risks involved; and hold harmless Taos Ski Valley, Inc. and the U.S. Forest Service for any mishaps which may befall them. They shall ski on the chute signed for below." This form must be signed and dated; the choice of run must also be indicated. In order to identify the run to be taken, skiers are given a new trail map with twenty-nine runs that are not shown on the usual trail map. A short hike uphill and a leisurely walk along the ridges opens fantastic terrain to the experienced skier. The level of expertise required to ski these runs varies widely. It is much better to ski them for the first time with instructors who will make certain skiers do not find themselves on slopes beyond their ability level. Instructors will also help skiers improve their technique. By the end of one week, skiers will inevitably be better than they were prior to enjoying the Taos experience.

However, Taos is not only for expert skiers. Absolute novices who have never skied before are taught to turn very early, because this is the best method to slow down. Taos's beginner hill is similar to Big Emma at Snowbird and is one of the steepest beginner hills of any resort. Nonetheless, Taos is an excellent resort at which beginners can learn to ski. Not only is ski instruction among the best available anywhere, but the natural steepness of the terrain forces people to become competent skiers sooner than would be possible at a resort with more gentle topography.

Taos also boasts a good deal about its intermediate terrain. The designation intermediate equates with intermediate elsewhere. So, one need not fear that all Taos's skiing will be tough. Some of the best intermediate cruising grounds are found off Kachina Peak. Runs like Shalako, Hunziker Bowl, and Honeysuckle are terrific! Powderhorn which runs the entire length of the mountain is a long, dream run. All intermediate runs are continually groomed and errant bumps are scrupulously removed.

The elevation of Taos at its summit is 11,819 feet (3,602 meters). With its base at 9,207 feet (2,806 meters), the vertical drop is 2,612 feet (796 meters). Of the seventy-one runs illustrated on the trail map, thirty-six (51%) are classified as expert, eighteen (25%) as intermediate, and seventeen as (24%) beginner.

The longest beginner run, Whitefeather, is 3.1 miles (5 km); the longest intermediate run is Honeysuckle/Rubezahl at 5.25 miles (8.4 km). Honeysuckle/Rubezahl is actually one run, but was given two names to facilitate the ski patrol's need to quickly identify injured skiers' location. The longest expert run is Longhorn which is 2.05 miles (3.3 km).

Taos is a mountain of extremes: when it snows it usually snows prodigious amounts, and when it is not snowing, the weather is usually clear with bright, warm sunshine. Receiving over 323 inches (820 cm) of snow annually, its monthly average totals are:

Nov.	40"	(102 cm)
Dec.	36"	(91 cm)
Jan.	58"	(147 cm)
Feb.	37"	(94 cm)
Mar.	63"	(160 cm)
Apl.	39"	(99 cm)

Taos's southern location gives it a rather temperate climate. The average monthly temperatures at the base are:

Nov.	27°	-3°C
Dec.	21°	-6°C
Jan.	22°	-5°C
Feb.	28°	-2°C
Mar.	32°	0°C
Apl.	39°	4°C

The United States Forest Service will not allow Taos to sell more than 4,500 lift tickets per day. With an uphill lift capacity of 7,000, the slopes are never very crowded. Because there are only 900 beds at Taos Ski Valley, it is essential that most guests stay in the town of Taos and drive to the resort. Once there, however, adequate facilities accommodate the skiers. The 400 acres (162 ha) of skiable terrain divided by the uphill lift capacity is .057. This figure is similar to Vail and assures skiers of hassle-free lift lines. In fact, it is interesting to note that the uphill lift capacity is almost twice the number of skiers the Forest Service permits to ski each day. It should also be noted that the actual number of skiable acres open, which is not necessarily represented by the official trail map, is 1,100.

Lastly, it should be pointed out that Al's Run is indeed as formidable as previously reported by others. First, it is steep; second, it has some of the largest moguls that skiers will ever see. The mogul field is most formidable at the top. As skiers work (and it is work) their way down Al's run, the severity of the bumps diminishes. Near the top, however, the bumps are frequently waist-high with their backs chopped off. Hopefully, Taos will find the funds in the near future to purchase a winch cat and begin cutting these moguls.

Lift Ticket Prices *(1988-89)*

The lift ticket prices reported at Taos are day ski rates. Actual rates for guests staying in one of the lodges will be lower because multi-day lift ticket discounts are included in the lodging and lesson packages.

$29......Adult, All Day
$27......Adult, Multi-Day
$16......Child, All Day
$14......Child, Multi-Day
Multi-Day tickets are for a minimum of three consecutive days. A child is anyone 12 or younger.

Hours of Operation

9:00 A.M. to 4:00 P.M.

Lift Ticket Purchase Locations

Lift tickets may be purchased in the Ski Valley near the parking lot shuttle bus stop in the center of the village, just below the #1 Lift, and in the town of Taos through the Olympic Ski Shop located on North Pueblo Road.

Crowd Control

Most crowds at Taos will be encountered in the day skiers' parking lot as visitors leave after a day of skiing. This is not as bad as at Squaw Valley, but during holiday periods, it can be annoying.

Crowding on the mountain is rare; however, the potential for crowding exists on lower Whitefeather and Rubezahl. Both of these runs are low on the mountain and form the most convenient routes down the mountain at the end of the day. The only way to avoid crowding on these runs, should it occur, is to take Al's Run down in the evening.

Ski School

The Taos Ski School is justifiably acknowledged as one of the best, if not the best, ski school in the country. No doubt, this reputation is due to the large numbers of expert skiers it trains daily. Under the direction of Ernie Blake, the ski school is a family affair. All family members share teaching responsibilities with the hired staff. Ernie believes it is imperative that the owners of Taos constantly be in touch with their clientele. One of the best ways to achieve this goal is by active participation in the daily teaching agenda.

The 200 PSIA certified instructors teach their own technique which is similar to the American Teaching System (ATS). The Taos system differs only in small details. Because so many Taos students are advanced, many of the lessons are actually refinements of techniques for learning how to ski specific conditions or situations. For example, a class may work on moguls, powder, chutes, or whatever the instructor and class agree is needed on a particular day.

Because most of the guests staying at Taos are participants in the "Learn to Ski Better Week" program, six days of intensive instruction are included in their lodging package, which also includes three meals per day and seven nights' accommodations. For those not participating in this program, group or private lessons are available.

Group lesson participants meet daily at 10:00 A.M. and at 2:00 P.M. Lessons are two hours, and during the 1988-89 season, cost is $20 or $18 if a multi-day lesson is purchased.

Private lessons are $45 per person per hour. All day is $280, or $190 for one half-day private lesson.

For the *never-ever before* skier, Taos offers its "Yellow Bird Program." Under this program, beginners receive four hours of daily instruction, use of the Poma, and rental equipment for $40 per day. Cost of the program without rental equipment is $33 during the 1988-1989 season.

Taos's Kinderkafig, the children's ski school, is open to children aged three through six. A very well-conceived program, it typifies the individual attention skiers of all ages receive from Taos's instructors. It is important for parents to register their children in advance, particularly during the holiday seasons.

Children enrolled in the Kinderkafig should arrive at the indoor facility (located just below the Kändähar Condominiums and close to the Poma) at 8:45 each morning. The first hour is spent getting the children organized and providing them with a small snack. At 9:30 A.M., they are ready to hit the slopes! They ski until noon and then have lunch followed by a quiet time which usually consists of hearing a story or listening to music. By 1:45 P.M., everyone is ready to ski again. Another snack is served around 3:30 P.M., and the kids are ready to be picked up by their parents at 4:00 P.M. During the 1988-1989 season, the fee for the Kinderkafig is a reasonable $29 per day, or $168 for the six day week.

For children aged seven through twelve whose parents are enrolled in the Ski Week Program, there is a parallel program called the Junior Elite. Children spend the morning in classes and are free in the afternoon to ski with their instructor. The afternoon sessions are particularly rewarding for the students as they become very familiar with the mountain, and their abilities rapidly improve due to the non-structured sessions. The Junior Elite Program includes lift tickets and costs $39 per day.

Equipment Rental

Two rental shops are located at Taos Ski Valley and numerous others are found in the town of Taos.

At the resort proper, Taos Ski Valley Rental is located at the base area, just below the #1 Lift. During the 1988-1989 season, two rental packages are offered. The first is the Recreation Package designed for beginning and intermediate skiers which includes Atomic, Head, or K2 skis, Tyrolia bindings, Nordica or Raichle boots, and poles. The fee for this equipment is $12 for the first day and $10 for subsequent days.

The other package offered is called the High-Performance Package. The skis are the same kind as those in the Recreational Package, but the models have been designed for more accomplished skiers. These rent for $16 the first day and $14 for subsequent days.

Children's rentals are $7 the first day and $6 each additional day from both rental shops.

Ski Tuning and Repair

The finest tuning is available at Taos Ski Valley Rental, which has Montana Crystal Glide ski structuring equipment. For a complete explanation of the benefits of this type of tuning, read the *Ski Tuning and Repair* section in the *Killington* review.

During the 1987-1988 season, tune-up rates were:

$ 5......Hot Wax
$15......Flat File
$25......Complete Tune-up
$25+.....P-tex

Mountain Restaurants

Taos has one and "one-half" mountain restaurants. The full restaurant, located at the base of the Kachina Lift, is a relatively new facility designed to blend in with the towering pines of the Carson National Forest. Constructed of rough-hewn timbers and enhanced by numerous windows, the Phoenix Restaurant is always bright and pleasant. The cafeteria-style food service is presented well, and there is ample variety. The lack of a sit-down dining area is regrettable, particularly because so many skiers at Taos do not stay in Ski Valley lodges. The Phoenix is really the only place on the mountain where skiers can go for a full meal.

The other restaurant, mentioned with tongue in cheek, is the Whitefeather Whistlestop, located at the base of the #6 Lift. This small facility offers pizza, sandwiches, hot and cold drinks, and snacks. It also has the only sanitary facility on the upper front side of the mountain.

The St. Bernard Hotel, located directly to the right of the #1 Lift looking uphill, is primarily for lodging guests, but it also has a small, excellent food service adjacent to the dining room. If someone should suggest lunch at "the Dog," the St. Bernard Hotel is what is being referred to.

There is one additional cafeteria located at the base facility, and, as of this writing, it was truly grim. However, management has promised that by the beginning of the 1989-1990 season it will be replaced with a new three hundred-seat cafeteria and a new one hundred-seat table service restaurant and lounge. Judging by the commitment the Blake family has made to Taos during past years, this restaurant will be a well-planned and appropriately furnished facility.

Day Care

Taos's management is concerned that all its guests enjoy themselves. This concern is readily apparent in the lengths to which the owners have gone to provide excellent day care.

The independently owned and operated Peek-a-Boo Day Care Center, located about one hundred-yards from the lifts in the Hide 'n Seek Building, accepts children from six weeks through three years of age. Parents must supply formula and disposable diapers. All clothing should be labeled.

Due to the size of the facility, reservations are a must. They can be made by telephoning (505) 758-9076 anytime after October 1. The 1987-88 season rate was $28 per day and did not include lunch. Again, because many of the guests are enrolled in the Ski Week Program, the children take their noon meal at their parents' lodge. If meals are required, parents should make appropriate arrangements with the Peek-a-Boo staff.

There are also in-home day care facilities available in the town of Taos. Reservations may be made at Home Day Care at (505) 776-2652 or (800) 433-1321 or at Trudy's Discovery House at (505) 758-1659.

If baby-sitting services are needed, guests should check with their lodge's receptionist for a current list of sitters.

Medical Facilities

The ski patrol at Taos Ski Valley renders emergency service to injured skiers. The patrol will administer trauma treatment, stabilize broken bones, and transport injured skiers downhill by sled to the First Aid Station located at the base of the #1 Lift. From the clinic, injured skiers will be taken by ambulance to Holy Cross Hospital in the town of Taos.

For illnesses other than ski injuries, there are numerous doctors and clinics in the town of Taos. Consult the local Yellow Pages for listings.

Cross-Country Skiing

There are no cross-country skiing tracks nor lessons available at the Taos Ski Valley. Telemark skiers are welcome to ski on the mountain, however.

Special Events

Taos is a small resort compared to mega resorts like Vail and Aspen. Professionally staged races can cost as much as $100 thousand to sponsor. It is therefore unrealistic to think that a small, privately held company such as Taos Ski Valley with its restrictive capacity could compete for major events. Not that the mountain would not lend itself to such competition! If the moguls were cut on Al's Run, it would become an awesome downhill course, and several areas could accommodate slalom races, such as Powderhorn or Maxie's in the Kachina Basin.

In spite of not hosting World Cup nor professional race events, Taos has managed to create its own brand of events, including the Plymouth All-American Ski Races, Taos Pueblo Deer/Buffalo Dance, Taos Pueblo Turtle Dance, and Christmas Eve Torchlight Parade. At the end of the season, Bump/Bolt/Bike Races are staged.

NASTAR races (National Standard Races) are held almost daily under the #7 Lift, which is also the site of the coin-operated Marlboro self-timed practice race course. Visitors should check with Guest Services for the daily hours of operation.

Accommodations

Hotels

Throughout this review, the reader has been told that Taos is different from other ski resorts. Its four main lodges are the primary reason for this difference. Their emphasis on guests' forming a close-knit unit is unique in America.

The St. Bernard situated at the foot of the #1 lift is owned and managed by Jean Mayer, one of Ernie Blake's oldest acquaintances. The exterior of these accommodations resembles any of the numerous cow barns found on the slopes of Ernie's native Switzerland. The interior, however, is warm and inviting. Walking into the Dog's bar or dining room is like stepping back into a less complicated time when skis were made of hickory and ski clothing was baggy. A testament to St. Bernard's popularity is that it is usually fully booked two years in advance. Only a last minute cancellation will yield a room for the first-time guest.

The Hondo Lodge was the first accommodation facility built at Taos Ski Valley. Located only a few steps from the St. Bernard and built in 1955, the Hondo has a grotto-like quality about it. It is a very comfortable establishment where the warm, yellow glow of candles and soft, diffused light emanating from stained glass windows soften the Swiss decor and immediately set skiers at ease.

The largest lodge, the Thunderbird, is situated on the banks of the Rio Hondo and is only a short walk from the lifts. This modern, well-maintained hotel is owned and operated by Tom and Elisabeth Brownell, who take a personal pride in knowing their guests and responding to their needs. The Thunderbird consists of three separate chalets constructed in the Swiss style typical of the entire valley. The main lodge building consists of twenty-four rooms, a dining hall, a recreation room, ski tuning room, sauna, hot tub, and the Twining Tavern. The two other chalets, which have larger rooms than the Thunderbird, are within steps of the main complex.

The rooms in the Lodge are small and somewhat utilitarian when compared to accommodations at other major resorts such as the Lodge in Sun Valley or the Sonnenalp in Vail. However, all lodging accommodations at Taos are relatively small. What sets the Thunderbird apart is its cleanliness and adherence to the original design concept. All rooms have humidifiers and are well insulated against outside noise. Their decor is developed through the use of knotty pine, stucco, and Laura Ashley prints. Each room is different, but always complementary to the whole. The bathrooms are misnamed since they do not contain bath tubs; instead, they have showers with copious quantities of hot water.

There are neither televisions nor telephones in the rooms. Children are served in the dining room before adults, and after dinner many of the guests' children head for the recreation room which contains a large screen TV, VCR, games, and books. Should guests' skis need attention, there is a well-stocked ski tune-up room with a bench and vise. Unlike many tune-up rooms, this one is spotlessly maintained, with only a hint of hot wax in the air.

Whereas most resorts have a hot tub and perhaps a sauna, the Thunderbird has a "bath department." The department consists of separate men's and women's locker rooms. The indoor hot tub room is abundantly decorated with ferns and other tropical plants. Adjacent to the tub is the massage room where a resident masseuse is on call to administer to guests' assorted aches and pains. Each locker room has its own sauna and attendant. During après-ski, cocktail service is available.

The large Twining Tavern features a dance floor. Each year the Thunderbird hosts its famous Jazz Festival which is described in the *Activities* section of this review. The dining room and tavern are gathering spots for guests who engage in congenial conversation, usually centering around the day's ski activities. Meals are served family-style, and the tables accommodate six to eight persons. The tables' large size promotes guests' interaction. Many visitors will share ski classes and quickly become acquainted with one another. The gathering of guests during and after dinner is common to all the lodges. Many of the lodges also host mountainside picnics during the ski season, weather permitting. The picnic luncheon served by the Thunderbird could grace the pages of *Gourmet*. Its picnics typically include fresh flowers, table cloths, and silver service. Wine, beer, soft drinks, and freshly baked goods accompany the kitchen's creations, which are always excellent.

Seven day Ski Week Packages at the Thunderbird during the 1988-1989 season are $930 per person based on double occupancy. Chalet rates are $1,005 per person per week. These prices stipulate check-in at 3:00 P.M. Saturday and check-out at noon the following Saturday. Included in the rates are seven nights accommodations, twenty-one full meals, six days use of all lifts, free NASTAR race as well as all the amenities of the Lodge. Upon checking in, skiers will notice that their room key is attached to a frisbee. Only very determined guests will attempt to ski with it in their pocket! Guests are advised to leave $60 per person upon check-out, rather than tipping individually. Tips are evenly divided among the staff.

Located next to the beginner's hill, the Edelweiss Lodge is another Swiss/Austrian establishment whose watchword may well be attention to every guest's needs. Its small, intimate lobby is accented by a large rock fireplace. The faint scent of burning wood is inviting to guests who choose to sit in one of the comfortable chairs, enjoy a libation, and relax before contemplating the evening's activities.

Rooms in the Edelweiss are small but well-appointed. Most rooms have views of the mountain, and there are neither televisions nor telephones in them.

The hot tub area, located indoors on the second floor, has a balcony where guests frequently romp in the snow while alternately enjoying the tub's steaming water. This is a very unusual hot tub room. Complemented with ferns and tropical shrubs, it has a very large tree growing through the floor and out the ceiling. A sauna is also available.

Edelweiss's La Croissanterie is a fine restaurant specializing in French and Austrian pastries. Situated directly on the slopes and decorated with antique skis and ski memorabilia, La Croissanterie offers a perfect setting for the mid-day meal.

Hotel Edelweiss rates during the 1988-1989 season for a hotel room on the Ski Week Package for two adults are $990 - $1,130 per person. These rates include breakfast at the La Croissanterie and dinner at the St. Bernard as well as all lift tickets, free NASTAR clinic, and race.

Condominiums

For those guests who do not want to stay in one of the lodges, or for those who want to ski Taos but cannot book accommodations in a lodge, there are several condominiums to choose from. The Kändähar Condominiums are situated high on a hill overlooking the Strawberry Hill beginner ski slope and base facility. Climbing to the uppermost units from the base parking lot requires energy and determination as there are no fewer than 122 steps. Most guests only make this trek once! The easy way to arrive at the Kändähar is to ski down Raspberry Hill or across Strawberry Hill. If walking to the base area or other accommodations, it is easier to walk diagonally across the lower portion of Strawberry Hill than to walk all the way down the steps and then across the bottom of Strawberry Hill.

The Kändähar is built so beautifully into its environment that its buildings appear to be cantilevered out over the Ski Valley. All units have balconies off their main living areas, as well as rear balconies accessible through the kitchen's Dutch door. The rear balcony is used for convenient firewood storage, which also helps keep the units clean. Walking along the rear balconies is similar to walking in an ice cave. Due to of the steepness of the hill on which the buildings are located, tarpaulins have been strung from the roof's eves to the floor of the balconies. These tarps prevent snow from filling up the balconies and also help keep the firewood dry. After enough snow has accumulated, the tarpaulins are removed, thereby creating the ice tunnels.

The Kändähar two bedroom models have bedrooms along with a full bath on the lower floor. The kitchen, dining, living areas, and another bath are found upstairs. The kitchens are fully equipped and appliances include Jenn-Air ranges, microwaves, disposals, and dishwashers. A counter which serves as an extra dining area separates the living area from the kitchen. All units have color cable TV and, unlike the lodges, have telephones.

Decor is typical of the Southwest with emphasis on Indian art and culture. The fireplaces are stucco with an arched opening, a style also common to the area.

During the 1988-1989 season, rentals are available as either hotel rooms, studios, one bedroom or two bedroom condos. The nightly rate for a one bedroom unit during regular season is $155 per person. The same unit's double occupancy is $97 per person; triple occupancy is $73 per sperson, and quad occupancy is $60 per person. A 15% tax and gratuity is automatically added to the bill.

Guests staying in Taos's condominiums are encouraged to enroll in the Ski Week Program in order to improve their skills and to meet other guests.

Across the slopes from the Kändähar near the Thunderbird Lodge are the Sierra del Sol Condominiums. Situated on the banks of Lake Fork Creek and overlooking the Carson National Forest, these 18 year-old condos are about 80% refurbished. When guests are booking into the Sierra del Sol, they are advised to only book the refurbished units. Fireplaces are made of free-standing metal on a brick pad. The kitchens are fully equipped with dishwashers, disposals, and all the amenities necessary to prepare daily meals during a guest's stay. Because not all units contain microwave ovens or stereos, if such items are important, guests should specifically request them at the time of booking. None of the units have telephones.

Sierra del Sol condominiums are available as studios, one bedroom, or two bedroom units. The refurbished units are decorated in warm hues including mauve, sea foam, and teal. The 1988-1989 rates vary each month. Typically, however, the February and March rate for a one bedroom unit is $190 per night. Weekly rates, as well as Ski Week Package rates, are also available.

Other accommodations available at the Taos Ski Valley are the Innsbruck Condos, Hide & Seek Apartments, Twining Condominiums, and the St. Bernard condos.

Restaurants

There are no restaurants available for evening dining at Taos Ski Valley other than those serving guests staying in the lodges. Condominium guests are expected to prepare their own meals or to go into the town of Taos for meals. Occasionally, the lodges will have dining space available for a few people. If dining in the various lodges is desired, condominium guests will need to telephone them in advance.

Take-out pizza is available from Dolomite Pizza until 9:00 P.M. every evening.

Fine dining in the town of Taos is available at The Taos Inn, Brett House, Carl's French Quarter, and Taos Lodge.

Activities

Although the emphasis at Taos is on skiing, numerous ski-related or non-ski activities are available. The most notable activity is the annual Jazz Legends at the Thunderbird Lodge each January.

The program of Legends changes each year, depending on artist availability. Thirteen greats who appeared during the 1987-1988 season included Monty Alexander, Herb Ellis, Ray Brown, Milt Hinton, Ross Tompkins, Kenny Davern, Warren Vaché, Ralph Sutton, Gus Johnson, Eric Schneider, Eddie Higgins, Brian Torff, and Butch Miles.

The fee during the 1987-1988 season for these performances was $8 for Thunderbird dinner guests and $10 for bar guests.

The town of Taos is a Southwest cultural center. As such, many cultural and artistic events are staged there monthly. Among them are native Indian dances such as the Deer or Buffalo dance and the Turtle dance. A lecture series offers subjects like "Healing with Crystals," "Hinduism and the Hanuman Temple," "Floral Arrangement," and "Stoneware." There are demonstrations such as papermaking, the lost wax process for bronze, weaving, Old Master painting technique, Navajo saddle blankets, watercolor techniques, sculpting in alabaster, masterworks of Colonial silver, and gold and silver jewelry making.

Theatrical musical entertainment is also available and has featured artists such as Michael Martin Murphey, John McEuen, Josh White and Tom Chapin.

Visitors will enjoy Taos's shops and art galleries, some of the Southwest's finest. Movies are shown at the Taos Plaza Theatre. Other activities include hot mineral baths at the Ojo Caliente Mineral Springs and sleigh rides at the Taos Indian Horse Ranch. Lastly, fine museums such as the Kit Carson Home and Museum, Martinez Hacienda, Blumenscheim Home, Millicent Rogers Museum can be found at Taos.

Services

A full complement of sporting goods stores, apparel shops, pharmacies, grocery stores, liquor stores, furniture, bath, and specialty shops is within the immediate Taos area. In addition, there are antique shops, massage services, art galleries, bakeries, beauty salons, book stores, florists, movies, theatre, banks, churches, dry cleaning, optical clinics, and baby-sitting services.

TELLURIDE SKI RESORT, INC.

P.O. Box 307
Telluride, Colorado 81435

(800) 525-3455 Central Reservations
(303) 728-4424 Information
(303) 728-3614 Snow Report

Transportation

Telluride may be reached on clear days by flying directly to the Telluride Regional Airport, located three miles from the slopes. This is the highest airport in the United States served by regularly scheduled airlines. The skier visiting Telluride should book tickets directly to the Telluride Airport but should understand that he might land in Montrose, 64 miles from Telluride, because Telluride Airport is strictly limited to operating in totally clear weather. Montrose is a sheltered valley which almost always is available, and complimentary bus service is provided by the airlines on which passage is booked.

Service to Telluride or alternatively to Montrose is provided daily from Denver via Continental Airlines. Mesa Airlines offers service from Denver, Phoenix, Albuquerque, Grand Junction, Durango, Montrose, and Cortez. United Express, operated by Aspen Airways, provides service only to Montrose. All air service is via small aircraft. Continental uses planes specially designed for short runways and high altitudes.

Daily bus service from Montrose is available, but reservations should be booked at least one week in advance. One-way fare during the 1987-88 season was $5.00. Bus service from other regional airports such as Cortez, Grand Junction, and Durango is also available. Pricing information is available from Telluride Central Reservations or Telluride Transit at (303) 728-4105.

All major car rental agencies are available at Telluride's regional airports including Avis, Budget, Hertz, National, and Thrifty. Once in Telluride, a car is more of a hindrance than a convenience. Transportation within the town of Telluride is amply provided by Telluride Transit which runs every twelve minutes throughout the town and every fifty minutes to the Meadows Day Lodge.

Mountain Statistics

By anyone's definition, Telluride Mountain is awesome! Located in the Uncompahgre National Forest deep in the San Juan Mountains, its ski trails offer terrain for skiers of every skill level. The view from the top is unequalled anywhere in the United States. The town of Telluride is nestled at the base of Ajax Peak, with its back against the most breathtaking box canyon imaginable. The majority of the trees surrounding the town and lining its trails are lodgepole, but unlike those at resorts closer to Denver these trees are towering. Perhaps the size of the trees is due to the heavy annual precipitation received in this region.

Telluride Mountain has 3,155 vertical feet (962 meters). Its base is located at 8735 feet (2,663 meters) and its summit is at 11,890 feet (3625 meters). The skiable terrain comprises 735 acres (297 ha) and is serviced by:

1 Detachable Quad Chairlift
6 Double Chairlifts
2 Triple Chairlifts
1 Poma Lift

The longest beginner run is Telluride Trail, situated in the Gorrono Basin and serviced by the world's longest detachable quad chair lift—2.85 miles (4.58 km) long. The longest intermediate run is See Forever, and the longest expert run is The Plunge.

Due to the diversity of terrain at Telluride, its mountain management has decided to deviate from the usual method of identifying trails by using circles, squares, and diamonds to denote a slope's difficulty. Telluride has expanded upon these graphics and has added double circles, double squares, and double diamonds in order to assist skiers in carefully choosing trails suited to their ability.

In total, there are forty-five trails of which 24% are considered beginner, 50% are intermediate, and 26% are expert. These figures do not tell all, however. Of the 26% comprising the terrain defined as expert, a healthy percentage is beyond the typical 40-year old expert's ability. Several runs are nothing more than avalanche chutes (such as Electra), and skiing them not only requires skill, but stamina and endurance as well. Even some of the intermediate trails can be considered only marginally intermediate. What is expert at Vail, Copper, and Aspen is frequently considered intermediate at Telluride. For example, one of the few intermediate runs down the face of Telluride Mountain is Coonskin. This is a double blue square which, under all but the best conditions, skis like an expert trail. It has large bumps and is relatively steep.

During the 1987-88 season, Telluride invested over $150 thousand in a winch cat to groom certain areas of the front face. This equipment allows grooming of some areas of The Plunge and The Spiral Stairs, thereby effectively rendering them double blue intermediate. This is great news for most intermediate skiers, because it will open up an entirely new area of the mountain for them.

A great deal has been written and said about the difficulty of Telluride's expert runs. They do deserve their reputation for making Telluride a tough mountain. What sets it apart from other areas' expert terrain is the unforgiving nature of its runs. Whereas most expert runs at other resorts contain areas within the trails that are intermediate, none exist on the front face of Telluride. Once a skier starts down, the trail is expert from top to bottom. Skiing the front face demands strong conditioning. If skiers are in shape though, they are rewarded with some of the best skiing available anywhere in the world.

The total skiable acres divided by the maximum number of skiers transported per hour on Telluride Mountain is .066. This is substantially lower than at other major ski resorts, and it assures skiers that the slopes will never be terribly crowded nor will the lift lines be long.

Telluride's annual snowfall is 300 inches (762 cm). Its monthly average snowfall is:

Nov.	20"	(51 cm)
Dec.	53"	(135 cm)
Jan.	50"	(127 cm)
Feb.	37"	(94 cm)
Mar.	66"	(168 cm)

The town of Telluride is totally dominated by its mountains. First-time visitors to Telluride may well suck in their breath and ask themselves, "What have I gotten myself into?" The view of the skiable terrain from town can only be compared to the view of terrain at Taos, New Mexico. One's field of vision is totally occupied by the highly vertical and legendary front face. Beginners and intermediates should take comfort in the knowledge that somewhere up there is easier skiing. Access to the gentler slopes can best be reached by taking one of the two chair lifts bordering on downtown. These chairs are high and provide spectacular views for photography or gripping the chair, depending upon how well one handles heights. On a typical day, the snow under the lifts may be pock-marked with the charcoal grey stain of an exploded mortar from the previous evening. Due to the steepness of the front face, constant attention is paid to the snowpack by the highly qualified ski patrol.

The ride up the mountain ends at See Forever, where the backside is exposed and a vast network of intermediate and beginner slopes opens up. The abundant snowfall, complemented by snowmaking as needed, assures quality conditions every day. Ice is something that never seems to be a problem in Telluride due to its exceptionally consistent natural snowfall and the meticulous grooming performed each day and night. In fact, some of the finest beginner terrain in the country can be found at Telluride. For those who do not like moguls, long runs such as See Forever, Sundance, and Cabin Trail are over two miles each and are as smooth as silk. For the typical expert there are challenging trails such as The Plunge, The Spiral Stairs, Zulu Queen, Kant Mak-M, Dynamo, and Apex Glades. As the saying goes, there is something for everyone at Telluride.

Records of average daily temperature during the season are not maintained by this resort.

Helicopter Skiing

Helicopter skiing at Telluride should be on most skiers' agenda. Offered through Helitrax whose office is located in the lobby of the New Sheridan Hotel, day trips of 10,000 (3,048 meters) vertical feet are completed in four runs. The cost for this service is a relatively modest $275 per person. Helitrax has been operating under a U.S. Forest Service permit for six years, and it has an unblemished safety record. Prior to departure, every client is instructed in helicopter safety, avalanche hazards, back-country travel, and the correct way to use a safety beacon.

Lest readers think they may not possess the ability to helicopter ski, Helitrax's records of previous clients indicate that 70% of the helicopter skiers have skied for 10 years and that 50% are between 30 and 40 years old, with a full 20% over 40!

Seventy percent of the terrain skied with Helitrax is in bowls above the tree line. The remaining runs are through the trees. Skiing commences atop towering 13,000 (3,962 meters) peaks, while the majestic peaks of Colorado, New Mexico, and far-away Utah are spread out in front of the skier!

Lift Ticket Prices *(1988-89)*

$ 32	Adult Daily
$162	6 Days Out of 7
$140	5 Days Out of 7
$116	4 Days Out of 7
$ 90	3 Days Out of 7
$ 16	Child (5 Through 12)
Free	Senior Citizen (70 and up)
Free	Toddlers (Through 4)

Lower lift rates come with certain packages and are available by booking lodging through Central Reservations.

Hours of Operation

9:00 A.M. to 4:00 P.M. daily
Mid-November through Mid-April

Lift Ticket Purchase Locations

Lift ticket purchase locations are conveniently located at the Oak Street and the Coonskin base lifts. There is also a purchase location at the base of Telluride Mountain Village, known as the Meadows Base Facility.

There is virtually never any waiting for ticket purchases. On those rare occasions when a line does exist such as the period between Christmas and New Year's, it is minimal.

Crowd Control

There are no crowds at Telluride.

Ski School

Whether skiers are just learning to ski or sharpening skills, they will find that Telluride's ski school is unique. It is directed by Annie Vareille-Savath who believes that skiers should not only be grouped by their specific level of ability, but also by their learning styles. Therefore, Ms. Vareille-Savath divides her classes first by skill level and then further by learning style. The learning styles identified include those skiers who are intimidated by speed, those who "want to look good," and those who want to go fast. Each group thus identified is taught the proper techniques on slopes that will challenge their ability while developing their style. By bracketing their classes in this manner, the ski school believes it can improve on the traditional learning curve of its students and increase their skill levels more quickly than with traditional methods.

The ski school meets in various locations depending on the classes selected. All five to twelve-year old children's classes meet at the Meadows Base Facility, unless the children already know how to parallel ski. In the latter case, they should meet at the base of the Coonskin Lift. Access to the Meadows is via either the Oak Street or Coonskin Lift to the top of the front face and then by skiing down to the Meadows via See Forever, which is rated easy intermediate. In addition, a shuttle bus that circulates throughout the entire town every twelve minutes transports skiers to the Meadows Base Facility.

Adult classes usually meet at the Coonskin Base Facility in town.

- $ 44   First-Time Skier, Snowboarder or Telemarker
- $ 22   2 Hour Clinic
- $ 33   3 Two Hour Clinics (with multi-day lift ticket)
- $115   3 Day Ski Week (includes lift ticket)
- $175   5 Day Ski Week (includes lift ticket)

Telluride offers a wide variety of special classes for all levels of ability, as well as private lessons by the hour, half day, or full day. Among the special classes offered are:
Snowboarding
NASTAR Clinic
Skill Building Workshops

Steep and Deep

Equipment Rental

Six ski rental companies with a total of ten locations are represented at Telluride. Telluride Ski Resort Rentals is conveniently located at the base of all mountain lifts. Its 1988-89 rates for a complete rental (skis, poles, boots, bindings) vary from $12 per day to $25 per day for a high-performance package.

Camels Garden Sports is located at the Coonskin Base. Rental rates run from $10 per day for K2 skis, poles, and Salomon or Nordica boots to $24 per day for RD, K2 or Pre skis, poles, and Salomon or Nordica boots. Cross-country skis are also available.

Olympic Sports boasts the largest selection of rental skis. Located in the heart of downtown Telluride on Colorado Ave., Olympic Sports' rates begin at $12 per day for packages consisting of either Rossignol or Dynastar skis and Nordica boots to $25 per day for K2, Dynastar, Olin, Rossignol, Pre, or Lang skis and either Nordica or Salomon boots.

Paragon Ski and Sport is conveniently located by the Oak Street Lift and has packages ranging from $10 to $15 per day. Additionally, it will allow skiers to demo Atomic, Elan, Völkl, and Lange for $20 per day.

In addition to the above shops, there are two other sporting good stores located in Telluride. These are Summit Sports on Oak Street and Telluride Sports on Colorado Avenue.

Breakage insurance or damage waivers are required at most ski rental establishments. Olympic also rents ski clothing, should the non-skier decide to give it a try.

Ski Tuning and Repair

All the ski rental establishments mentioned above will provide tuning and repairs. The rates for these services during the 1987-88 season were:
- $ 5 Hot Wax
- $25 Flat Filing
- $ 7.50 (Pair) Edges Sharpened
- $25 Complete Tune-up
- $15 Bindings Adjusted
- $20+ P-tex

Mountain Restaurants

As with most of the resorts featured, the food service and quality of the restaurants at Telluride is excellent. The crown jewel of the mountain restaurants is the Cactus Cafe. Located in the La Chamonix condominiums at the base of the #3 and #4 lifts, the Cactus Cafe features dishes from the Southwest. The restaurant is tastefully decorated using bright colors such as dark green Mexican tiles, whitewashed pine tables and chairs. Terra-cotta accessories and plants add ambience to this well-lighted and comfortable restaurant. Full bar service is available during lunch, dinner, and après ski. Try the veggi chili for a different warm-up during cold weather.

Situated one lift ride uphill from the Cactus is the Gorrono Restaurant. This is a collection of old weather-beaten buildings that provide the setting for one of the country's best mountain restaurants.

Although the meals are served cafeteria-style, the quality of the food and the selection of items offered are equal to those of any sit-down restaurant. Full bar service is available. On fair weather days, the large deck is converted into several mini-food emporiums. One corner will have a service of hot, spicy shrimp and shish kebabs; in the other a full Bar-B-Que featuring hot dogs, hamburgers, spare ribs, cole slaw, beer and wine will be found. Sitting on the deck soaking up the sun's rays, watching others ski while enjoying the taped sounds of Paul Simon can soothe the soul and prepare one for an afternoon of mogul bashing!

Because it is difficult to ski from the Gorrono Basin area of the mountain to the front face, Telluride has located a small beer and pizza restaurant at the top of the #9 Lift. It is featured on the cover of this book. Although a minimal selection is available, the quality of the pizza is very good.

At the base of the Coonskin Lift is a quality Mexican restaurant appropriately called the Faceplant Café. The Faceplant serves a full breakfast as well as lunch. There is nothing fancy about this restaurant, and the food is adequate. Its main claim to fame is the après-ski activity which features a laser light show and loud music. For those who need more excitement than they can get on the mountain, the Faceplant is the in-place after 4:00 P.M.

One other minimal mountain restaurant is located at the Meadows Base. The Meadows Base, where beginning skiers congregate, has basic amenities. The Prospector Restaurant has limited selections, and many of its offerings are pre-packaged fare. For those skiers who want their lunch to form a part of the total ski experience, this restaurant is not recommended.

Day Care

Telluride has two day care centers available for its guests. One center is located on the second floor in Columbia Place at the Mountain Village. The other center is located at the Meadows Base. Both facilities are clean and well maintained. Staff members are conscientious and appear to truly love children. The Mountain Village facility can accomodate a maximum of fifteen children up to and including three year olds. The Meadows facility takes children from two to five years old. Parents are advised to provide diapers and the child's meals. Snacks such as crackers are provided by the nursery. The operating hours are from 8:00 A.M. till 4:00 P.M., and reservations are suggested.

Medical Facilities

Medical facilities at Telluride are of an emergency nature only. Should hospitalization be necessary, the seriously ill or injured skiers are transported to Montrose's hospital. Transport can be via either ambulance or helicopter, depending on the severity of the problem and weather conditions.

Cross-Country Skiing

Telluride has two tracks for cross-country: 10 km. and 20 km. Most of the Nordic skiing takes place on high mesa ground with beautiful Alpine views.

The Nordic Center is located close to the Meadows Base and can be reached by shuttle bus or by private car. Telluride will exchange a downhill lift ticket for a Nordic ticket, and rental of suitable equipment is available for a modest fee. The 1987-88 rates for equipment were $10 per day.

Various instructional packages are available starting at $22 for half day (1987-88).

Special Events

A NASTAR course operates daily from 1:00 P.M. to 3:00 P.M. on Misty Maiden.

On New Year's Eve a torchlight parade will be staged. Other events include NCSA Collegiate Ski Week, Telemark GS Race, Annual Governor's Cup, Powder Magazine/Telluride Ski Resort "Best Skier in the Rockies" race, and the Annual Telluride Classic Race.

Accommodations

One of the finest condominium complexes at Telluride is the River Watch Condominiums. These are very expensive, well-appointed units which even the most discriminating guest would be pleased with. From the moment guests enter the terra-cotta entry, they are impressed with both the accommodations and appointments. All units have heated garages with automatic door openers and furnished patios overlooking the San Miguel River as it winds its way through dense pines.

These two and three bedroom condos are professionally decorated using natural colors such as beige and brown. Wool berber carpeting, creative lighting, whirlpools, and steam showers produce an air of affluence. The TV and VCR are concealed in beautiful custom-crafted cherry cabinets that are built into one side of the moss rock fireplaces. The large, exposed, naturally-finished pine roof trusses add a dramatic focal point to the main rooms. The kitchen is totally furnished with all the appliances a guest could require, including a Scottsman ice maker, disposal, bar sink, gas convection oven, microwave, coffee maker, blender and much more.

The master bedroom overlooks the slopes. The massive king-size bed has a white comforter, and the bed itself was hewn from logs that would be overpowering in a smaller room. All units have central humidity controls, and some units even have eight person hot tubs on their patios. During the 1987-88 season these units rented for up to $900 per night.

Only slightly less opulent than the River Watch condominiums are the Telemark Condominiums located in the Mountain Village. Here again, the Southwest influence dominates. Bleached oak cabinets, sea green carpets, mauve, and other complementary colors are exquisitely used. The Telemark overlooks Gorrono Basin and visitors can relax in their condos while watching skiers return home in the afternoon, or they can soak in the hot tub while enjoying their favorite libations. The cathedral ceiling is accented by large bleached beams that support the roof over the living and dining areas. The dining table comfortably seats six and should enjoy great use, because the kitchen is a gourmet cook's delight.

Appliances include a Jenn-Air range, a convection and a radiant oven, microwave, garbage disposal and much, much more. All fixturing in these units is of the finest quality brass, kept at its shiniest by a conscientious maintenance crew.

Entry to the bedrooms is by a spiral staircase located adjacent to the tile and stucco fireplace. There are double sinks in all the bedrooms. Custom laminated cabinets in the baths attest to the developer's attention to detail.

During the 1987-88 ski season, these condos rented for $400 per night. The Telemark Condominiums are not located in the town of Telluride, and the prospective guest should be aware that there is little night life in the Mountain Village after the lifts close. The only restaurant within walking distance is the Cactus Cafe.

The Etta Place II condominiums are conveniently located near the Coonskin Lift. Named after Butch Cassidy's girlfriend, the Etta Place condos are within walking distance of all the town's restaurants, shops, and entertainment spots. Each unit in Etta Place contains its own private hot tub situated in the master bathroom; access to the tub is either from the bedroom or from the living room. Guests staying here will want to be certain to turn the tub off at night because its operation is quite noisy. These condominiums are very nice and are well maintained. From the moment guests enter the grey and white tile entry, they are aware of being in exceptional accommodations. Etta Place's kitchens contain all the essentials necessary to prepare family meals during a vacation. In addition to all the expected appliances, there are washer and dryers in each unit.

The dominant colors used in Etta Place are mauve, grey, and white. There is an outdoor heated swimming pool for guest use between the two buildings that comprise the complex. Sitting in the pool or in the hot tub and watching the snow fall on Woozley's Way is a great way to relax after a hard day of skiing and a wonderful prelude to an evening on the town.

Close to the Oak Street Lift and only two blocks from downtown Telluride are the Manitou River Houses. This project is available either as hotel rooms or as two bedroom condominiums. The project is eight years old and is nicely maintained. One of its central features has to be its hand-crafted outdoor hot tub, situated in a wooden shelter with a lattice roof. The shadows in this area created by the full moon and reflections from the snow laden slopes can create quite a romantic moment. This is a small condominium project with only ten condos. Priced well within the means of most people, the Manitou River Houses might well be one of the better housing bargains in Telluride.

The Riverside Condominiums are, as one would expect, along the San Miguel River. Medium priced and well maintained, these units include gas fireplaces, complete kitchens with Jenn-Air ranges and ice makers, steam showers and a dining area that seats six comfortably.

First time visitors to Telluride should use caution in selecting their hotel or condominium. Many of the older condos have very poor acoustics, are poorly lighted, and are not well maintained. Some accommodations do not even have private baths or toilets.

Restaurants

While all the resorts reviewed have great restaurants, Telluride seems to have more than its fair share. Of the outstanding eateries, Silverglade is the absolute best. Located in a basement on Colorado Ave., the Silverglade is furnished in a chrome and neon decor best described as California style. Its menu is also California inspired and includes grilled fish over mesquite wood and Cajun specialties. An excellent wine cellar with an exceptionally large selection of California varietals will impress even the most jaded guest. The desserts fashioned by the pastry chef include such items as baked apples with raisins and walnuts in a creme caramel sauce and a yogurt-custard strawberry and kiwi tart.

Julian's in the New Sheridan Hotel is almost equal to The Silverglade. Those readers who have visited Aspen's Hotel Jerome will find Julian's comparable. The Victorian ambience of Julian's befits the period in which the hotel was built. The murals and statuary remind guests that they are in an Italian restaurant. The aroma of garlic wafts across the room as diners await the opportunity to order dinner. Service is friendly, and the choice of entrées is abundant. Fresh seafood is a daily menu item as are the lamb chops in Marsala sauce; the delicious chicken breast on spinach is ladden with spicy Italian sausage.

For some reason that escapes this author, breakfast is a major event at Telluride. For those readers who are big breakfast aficionados, there is no better place than Leimgrubers von Telluride on Pacific Ave. This restaurant is as German as the name suggests. It is one of the few places on or off the slopes where one will find a waiting line. The line begins to form about half an hour before Leimgrubers opens in the morning. This is due to the limited seating, also largely responsible for the ambience of the restaurant. The waitresses are large, amply endowed ladies who have a great sense of humor. The menu matches their exuberance. One should try the Belgian waffles with fresh strawberries or the freshly brewed coffee and omelet. One last word about Leimgrubers; if it snowed the evening before, arrive early and watch the waitresses shovel snow from the roof before opening the restaurant for breakfast.

During the 1987-88 season, a new restaurant was opened that is worthy of comment. Located in an old ice house, the La Marmotte Restaurant Francais deserves skiers' attention. Its old brick walls have been scrubbed clean, and its ceiling has been painted dark blue. A single wood-burning stove occupies a central location in the restaurant and offers a warm glow to chilly evenings. Each table at La Marmotte is graced with a single rose, and the walls and various shelves are decorated with strings of garlic cloves and wicker baskets bursting with mountain greenery.

As outstanding as La Marmotte's physical facility is, it is second to the food prepared there. Attention to detail is immediately apparent when the bread and butter arrive at the table: a solitary rose petal adds color to the butter service. The escargot, overflowing with delicious garlic, is served hot in its own indented pottery dish. The chunky tomato and mushroom soup is tasty and unusual because it is not a purée. Each evening the owners, Bertrand and Noelle Lepel-Cointet, offer special soups, appetizers, and entrées such as homemade pasta with smoked salmon, capers, shallots and cream sauce, chunky fish soup, duck confit and grilled breast, braised leg of lamb with apple curry sauce.

La Marmotte is a small restaurant, seating only about fifty diners. Table settings are authentically French, and the early evening view of the sun setting on Ajax Peak is worth the visit alone. The bar is small and not convenient for casual cocktails. Reservations are a must because tables tend to fill up early. Dining is expensive; expect to spend $40 to $50 per person, including wine.

Other fine eateries abound in Telluride, and there is not enough space in this chapter to mention them all. However, a few worth mentioning include the Floradora Saloon (ask about the time someone tried to rob the bank next door by tunneling under it from the Floradora), Sofios (the margaritas will provide stamina to ski The Plunge), The Senate Bar & Restaurant (excellent international dishes and Victorian ambience in a former bordello).

Activities

In addition to unparalleled skiing, Telluride offers its visitors sleigh rides along the San Miguel River.

Nightly movies are featured at the Nugget Theatre as well as occasional concerts and live shows. At the Masonic Hall, a multi-image slide presentation of local flower and fauna is featured daily during the season.

Snowmobiling and sightseeing trips by Jeep or by air are also available.

The Telluride Athletic Club, located just outside of town on the road to Telluride's airport, offers visitors aerobics classes, handball/racquetball courts, gymnasium, free weights,and Biocycles. Complete locker room facilities are available.

Ice-skating at the town rink is open to the public on a scheduled basis. The rink also offers skating and hockey lessons. Skate rentals are available at Olympic Sports at 101 W. Colorado.

San Juan Balloon Adventures offer daybreak hot air balloon trips of one hour duration and a champagne toast with the crew. Telephone (303) 728-4904 for information and reservations.

Services

A full complement of sporting goods stores, apparel shops, pharmacies, grocery stores, liquor stores, furniture, bath, and specialty shops is within the immediate town. In addition there are antique shops, acupressure services, art galleries, bakeries, beauty salons, book stores, florists, flotation tanks, massage, and tanning studios.

VAIL ASSOCIATES, INC.

P.O. Box 7
Vail, CO. 81658

(800) 525-2257 Reservations
(303) 476-5601 Information
(303) 476-4888 Snow Report

Transportation

Vail and Beaver Creek are extremely easy destination points to reach. Whereas so many major ski resorts test the skier's ability to endure fickle weather and unreliable air service, Vail is only a short 100 miles west of Denver. The resort is reached via I-70, a four lane road scrupulously maintained by the Department of Highways. Crossing the Continental Divide is usually easy regardless of weather conditions because the Eisenhower Memorial Tunnel eliminates driving through the worst high altitude weather. The only potentially difficult portion of the drive is over Vail Pass, but it is also well maintained and rarely impassable.

Once in Vail, it is not necessary to have an automobile because everything is convenient, and free shuttle service is provided. It may be of interest, therefore, to consider flying non-stop into the Avon STOLport via Continental's specially designed mountain planes. Continental flies eight daily flights into Avon, located approximately 10 miles west of Vail. For flight information and current rates, telephone (800) 525-0280.

If skiers neither want to rent a car in Denver nor fly into the mountains, they can reserve space on a seventeen passenger van from Resort Express and travel in comfort while someone else does the driving. The 1987-88 rates were $31 to Vail and $33 to Beaver Creek. Resort Express may be reached by calling (800) 334-7433; if you are booking reservations on Continental, the airline's reservationists will be pleased to reserve ground transportation for you. It is important to note that return reservations must be confirmed at least 48 hours prior to departure. This is especially important during peak periods such as Christmas and Spring Break.

Skiers who wish to drive from Denver will find the following major car rental agencies represented at Denver's Stapleton Airport:
Avis
Budget
Dollar
Hertz
National
Other car rental agencies are located outside of the airport property and offer free airport pickup and drop-off, among them:
Alamo
Enterprise
AI
Thrifty

All rental agencies provide free maps to their clients. Due to possible road restrictions which may require chains or snow tires, the traveler to Vail or Beaver Creek is advised to always rent a car that is *Skierized*, i.e. equipped with snow tires and ski racks. For a slightly higher price, many rental agencies can also provide four-wheel drive vehicles. Travelers wishing to reserve these vehicles are advised to do so far in advance because the demand for them is great.

Although there is more than enough skiable terrain and activities to keep anyone busy in Vail, the added mobility of an automobile makes it easy to take a one-day side trip to either Copper Mountain, Breckenridge, or Keystone, all located approximately 30 to 40 minutes east of Vail.

Mountain Statistics

Vail Mountain is one of the greatest ski mountains in North America, and it is fitting that one of America's finest resorts is established at its base. By anyone's definition, Vail Mountain is BIG, consisting of 12,500 acres (5,059 ha) of which 3,787 acres (1,533 ha) are developed trails. Vail is the largest single ski mountain in America. Unlike most resorts, Vail distinguishes between total number of skiable acres and developed trails, because its famous back bowls are so vast and totally skiable. The developed trails total 102 runs, the longest being Riva Ridge at three miles (4.82 km).

Located in the White River National Forest, Vail has a base elevation of 8,150 feet (2,485 meters) and rises to 11,250 feet (3,430 meters) at its summit. This equates to a 3,100 foot (945 meters) vertical drop.

This abundant terrain is serviced by the following lift equipment:

1 Gondola
1 High-Speed Enclosed Quadruple Chairlift
5 High-Speed Detachable Chairlifts
1 Fixed-Grip Chairlift
3 Triple Chairlifts
9 Double Chairlifts
2 Surface Lifts

Vail's uphill lift capacity is 35,020 skiers per hour. The total skiable acres (developed) divided by the number of skiers transported per hour on Vail Mountain is .108. This compares favorably with .087 for Steamboat and .077 at Snowmass, but is higher than Jackson Hole's .280. This rating firmly places Vail near the center of crowd accommodation; although lift lines will occur, they will not occur often nor will they be of unbearable duration.

Vail with its excellent mix of terrain offers challenge and excitement to skiers of all ability levels. The front face of the mountain, on which all of Vail centers, consists of 32% beginner trails, 36% intermediate trails, and 32% expert trails. The backside of the mountain presently consists of four bowls, three of which are classified from advanced intermediate to expert depending on snow conditions. The third bowl, Game Creek, is definitely intermediate and definitely not intimidating. It is reached by skiing down a catwalk from the top of the LionsHead Gondola or from the top of the Hunky Dory Lift.

Expert skiers enjoy skiing to the Game Creek Express Lift at the bottom of Game Creek Bowl by going off the side of the catwalk on runs such as Ouzo, Faro, and Deuces Wild. However, by following the catwalk to its terminus, easy, open skiing is available for intermediate skiers. Showboat has a double fall line, meaning it not only goes down, but also (in this case) goes down right to left. This is a good area to ski when weather is cold and windy because the bowl protects skiers from the worst elements. The trails are short, though, and most people become bored with them after several hours.

The other two back bowls, Sun Down and Sun Up, are much larger than Game Creek Bowl. Their runs are classified as expert, but in truth, a strong intermediate skier can handle them if conditions are ideal. These trails are long and bumpy and have double and triple fall lines. When it is snowing hard or if the light is flat, skiing can be difficult in the bowls even for experts. The good news, however, is that Vail enjoys sunshine 75% of the time during ski season. Due to the size of the mountain's bowls, powder can almost always be found somewhere, but the frequently skied tracks become packed shortly after a snowfall.

The front face of Vail Mountain may be roughly divided into three sections:

Golden Peak
Vail Village
LionsHead

Golden Peak is the eastern-most area of Vail, and it is entirely beginner to intermediate terrain. Of all the areas at Vail, this is the least impressive. It is gentle and virtually treeless. Some have been known to call it dull. Many of Vail's ski classes are held in this area.

The center of the mountain is unusual in that most of the beginner to intermediate skiing is on the upper portion, while the lower portion is expert. Returning in the evening, beginner and intermediate skiers should stick to Gitalong Road, easy but safe. More accomplished skiers should reserve enough strength to handle the very demanding Giant Steps, International, and Adios. These runs are so steep that until recently they were frequently closed. However, the recent acquisition of a winch cat has enabled Vail Associates to maintain these runs and keep them open most of the ski season.

The LionsHead area is primarily intermediate skiing. Many skiers who enjoying the upper portion of Mid-Vail take Eagle's Nest Ridge to return home in the evening. This is a run that begins at the top of Vail's #3 and 7 lifts. By taking Eagle's Nest Ridge, one can easily trek to the top of the LionsHead Gondola and take any number of intermediate trails to the LionsHead base. If it is cold or windy, Minturn Mile can be very uncomfortable because it is totally open to the elements. However, once off the ridge, the skier is sheltered.

Some of the finest skiing at Vail is located in the Northeast Bowl. Although it is actually a bowl, the perception is that of a face, and one is not necessarily aware of skiing in a bowl, unlike at Sun Down or Sun Up. These runs are primarily intermediate with some expert trails arranged along the ridges that form the bowl. Extremely difficult double black diamond runs are found directly under the top of the # 11 Lift (Northwoods Express) and off the east side of Prima. Unless the skier is very accomplished and fit, these runs should not be attempted. Unless you are an expert skier, avoid South Rim, North Rim, Prima Cornice, and Pronto.

The other double black diamond runs, Blue Ox, Rogers Run, Highline, and Prima, though difficult, are not dangerous. These runs are distinguished by their unending mogul fields. Bump skiers love these runs.
In order to leave Northeast Bowl in the evening, take chairlift #6 located at the base of this bowl up the backside of Golden Peak and ski into Vail Village via Follow Me. During the summer of 1988, Vail developed another ski route from the base of #6 which will allow skiers to ski directly to Golden Peak Village, eliminating the necessity to ride up chairlift #6.

Due to the mountain's size and its natural terrain, Vail does not have a great deal of congestion on many runs at the end of the day. No matter where one exits from the mountain, there is free shuttle service to transport skiers to other points in the village.

Vail Mountain receives an annual snowfall of about 300-350 inches (762 cm-889 cm). Its average monthly snowfall is:

Nov.	60"	(153 cm)
Dec.	62"	(157 cm)
Jan.	62"	(157 cm)
Feb.	54"	(136 cm)
Mar.	65"	(166 cm)
Apl.	34"	(86 cm)

Vail's snowmaking capabilities are substantial, though small in relation to the vastness of the mountain itself. Vail can cover 320 acres (130 ha) of trails with man-made snow.

The average daily temperatures at the summit during ski season are:

	High	Low	High	Low
Nov.	28°	9°	-2°C	-12°C
Dec.	21°	5°	-6°C	-15°C
Jan.	20°	4°	-6°C	-16°C
Feb.	23°	5°	-5°C	-15°C
Mar.	28°	9°	-2°C	-12°C
Apr.	35°	13°	2°C	-10°C

New at Vail for the 1988-1989 season will be high-speed quad chairlift service in the China Bowl area and on the face of LionsHead. In terms of skiable terrain, this addition will increase existing lift capacity by nearly 5,000 skiers per hour and, no doubt, will eliminate the long lift lines previously found at the bases of Sun Up and Sun Down Bowls, as well as at LionsHead.

Lift Ticket Prices (1987-1988)

$ 32 Adult Full Day
$ 64 2 Day Consecutive
$ 96 3 Day Consecutive
$124 4 Day Consecutive
$155 5 Day Consecutive
$180 6 Day Consecutive
$ 22 ages 64-69

Lift tickets for children 12 years old and younger are reduced.

Hours of Operation

8:30 A.M. to 3:30 P.M. daily

Lift Ticket Purchase Locations

Purchasing lift tickets at Vail is simple. Ticket counters are conveniently located near all four uphill lift systems. There is a counter at the base of Golden Peak, at the base of LionsHead, at the base of the new Vista Bahn Express located in Vail Village, and at Cascade Village, a new location west of LionsHead.

In order to expedite lift ticket transactions, Vail has initiated a program of automatic tellers dealing in cash or credit card machine transactions. The machines are fast and easy to operate. Just insert Visa, Master Card, or American Express into a slot, indicate the type and quantity of tickets desired, and in seconds the lift tickets are dispensed.

Crowd Control

A mega resort, Vail is the largest single ski mountain in the United States. There are bound to be crowds most of the time. However, Vail's new, high-speed quad lifts transport skiers uphill faster than those at any other ski area in the world. The terrain at Vail is large enough to accommodate the additional skiers this system unloads. Excessive lift lines are, therefore, limited to the base areas from approximately 9:00 A.M. to 10:30 A.M. and from noon until around 1:30 P.M. The lifts from the Mid-Vail restaurants are generally very crowded immediately after lunch. The crowds that always formed at the LionsHead Gondola should be eliminated or greatly reduced with the addition of the new Born-Free Express detachable quad.

Skiers can avoid delays in the morning by skipping the Vista Bahn and the LionsHead Gondola and instead taking one of the double chairlifts or LionsHead Express located nearby.

The only way to elude the lines at Mid-Vail is not to stop and eat there during the traditional lunch period. Eat earlier or later to avoid the crowds. An alternative to eating at Mid-Vail is to eat at one of the many restaurants at the base or at LionsHead.

Ski School

Vail's ski school is among the best in the country. It is also the largest in the world with over 650 instructors, who are credited with assisting in the creation and development of teaching methods employed by the Professional Ski Instructors of America. Ski schools are located conveniently at the base of Golden Peak, the Vail Village area, LionsHead, Eagles Nest (at the top of the LionsHead Gondola), Mid-Vail, and at the top of the #14 lift in the Northeast Bowl.

Ski classes are divided into nine separate groups according to ability, from beginner through advanced. In addition, there are specialty classes for style, racing, bumps, and powder. Vail also offers what is termed a "super" class. In order to qualify, one must be at a Level 8 or 9. Skiing is with only "light" instruction on terrain especially chosen by the instructor, but usually off the beaten track. A "SyberVision" workshop which deals with the emotional and relaxational aspects of skiing is offered. The classes are deliberately kept small in order to maximize learning opportunities.

Ski programs may also be custom designed to meet individual needs. These can be on an individual or small private group basis. The 1987-1988 prices started at $60. Bookings for special classes or private lessons must be made 24 hours in advance.

The 1987-88 ski season prices for lessons were as follows:
Adult
$ 35 1 Day
$ 90 3 Day
$171 3 Day with lift ticket
$ 30 Beginner, Half Day
$ 35 Never-Ever (Lift and Lesson, Half Day
$ 60 1 Hour Private
$ 80 1 Hour Private, 2 Persons

$115 Half Day Private, 1 Person
$250 All Day Private, 1 Person
$ 35 Race Class, Style Clinic, Bump/Powder
$ 65 SyberVision

Children

3½ to 6 Years Old
$43 All Day
$25 Half Day
6½ to 12 Years Old
$32 1 Day

Additional classes are also offered for very young children. Parents should consult with the ski instructors in order to place their children in the proper lessons.

Vail Associates has made every effort imaginable to ensure that young children have a good time learning to ski at its resort. Vail Mountain has been honeycombed with small theme parks which children can visit throughout the day. These include a "lost" silver mine, Dragon's Breath Mine, Monsterous Mounds, and many other play areas designated for children only. The youngsters are even provided with their own trail map detailing the locations of the parks. Throughout each week, Disney's Sport Goofy visits the ski schools. There is even a weekly schedule of special Sport Goofy events, including Breakfast with Sport Goofy, Sport Goofy Challenge, and Kid's Night Out.

For children too young to ski, Vail features the Small World Play School located in the Children's Center at the base of Golden Peak. This facility accommodates children from two months through six years. The cost for the program varies from $35 to $40 per day (1987-88). Diapers and special food should be provided by parents, and reservations are strongly advised. Prepayment of one day's fee is required to reserve a place.

Equipment Rental

During the 1987-1988 ski season, there were twenty-four ski rental shops in twenty-nine separate locations throughout Vail. Although the rates for equipment varied, following is a representative accounting of charges and equipment selections:

Christy Sports offered three types of rental packages. The basic package consisted of Pre 1100 skis, Scott poles, Saloman 337 bindings, and Saloman SX-51 or SX-61 boots and was priced at $10 per day. For an extra $5, this package could be upgraded to a Sport Package that included Pre Electra skis in lieu of the Pre 1100's.

Still another upgrade into what Christy refers to as its Performance Package included Rossignol 4S skis or Quantum skis and ST-81 Salomon boots. The Performance Package during 1987-88 rented for $22 per day.

Breeze Ski Rentals, like Christy's, offered three rental packages. The basic package was called the Recreational Package and included SX-31 Salomon boots, Scott poles, K2 XT skis and rented for $11.10 per day. However, the rates for all packages offered by Breeze could be reduced if they were ordered at least 24 hours in advance. Thus, the Recreational Package if ordered on the previous day could be rented for $10.

The Performance Package utilized the same poles and boots but the ski was up-graded to Pre 1200's. The advance reservation price for this package during the 1987-1988 season was $14. For an additional $4 Breeze would upgrade the boot to Nordica.

Breeze's other ski package choice was its Demo Package in which any brand of skis sold by them was available for rental at $16 per day.

As with all rental establishments, the renter is required to post a cash or credit card deposit with Breeze. Upon return of the equipment, the deposit is returned, or if a credit card imprint has been made, the copy is destroyed.

Ski Tuning and Repair

Vail has a large selection of companies and locations for ski repair. All rental establishments also repair skis, and, in addition, there are companies which only sell new skis and repair older ones. Almost without exception, any of the shops does a competent job of repairing or waxing skis. However, there are a few shops that have state-of-the-art ski tuning equipment. All things being equal, skiers should consider having their equipment tuned or repaired where this up-to-date equipment is utilized.

Performance Sports, located in the LionsHead area, is one of the firms in Vail that has Montana Crystal Glide ski tuning equipment. Performance marks up its normal tuning fees by $10 for the service, but this writer believes the extra charge is worthwhile when a complete tune-up is needed. Rates for tune-up services are competitive, and there will probably not be more than a dollar or two difference among shops. Unless a complete tune-up is required, skiers should leave their skis at the most convenient shop. Typical rates are:

$ 5   Hot Wax
$15   Flat File
$20   Complete Tune (belt sander)
$ 5   Bindings Adjusted
$15+ P-tex

Gorsuch Ltd., Vail Select, and Ski Valet all have Tezzani stone grinding equipment which is similar and equivalent to the Montana equipment.

For a complete explanation of the benefits of state-of-the-art ski tuning, refer to the *Ski Tuning and Repair* section of the review of *Killington* in this book.

Mountain Restaurants

Seven mountain restaurants are located on Vail's slopes. In addition, over one hundred restaurants are located within Vail Village. Most of these restaurants are accessible from the base of the mountain and should not be overlooked when it is time to stop for lunch.

Of the actual mountain restaurants, the best is located above the cafeteria at the terminus of the LionsHead Gondola at Eagle's Nest. The Stube restaurant specializes in German cuisine but offers a savory selection of American dishes as well. Dining at The Stube is an elegant experience, complete with white table linens and silver service. The views from its windows can be breathtaking on clear days when one can see almost the entire Gore Range.

Located on the first level of the Eagle's Nest is the Eagle's Nest cafeteria. The food served here is typical mountain fare, unremarkable but filling. During good weather, the staff will arrange an outdoor Bar-B-Que featuring hamburgers, hot dogs, and ribs.

The newly renovated restaurant at Mid-Vail offers two levels of cafeteria-style dining. This mountain restaurant is the most crowded because it is at the top of the Vista Bahn lift and at the base of the Hunky Dory and Mountain Top Express lifts. The views from this restaurant are exceptional. On warm, clear days, the staff will prepare an outdoor Bar-B-Que similar to the one at LionsHead. The outside service usually opens by the end of January, and it is very pleasant to while away a few moments sitting outside and enjoying the sun's warming rays, while quenching your thirst with a hot or cold beverage.

Located east and below the Mid-Vail cafeterias is the Cook Shack. Recently renovated, the Cook Shack features a Southwest menu. The ambiance is informal and the service is attentive. Reservations are suggested and are an absolute must during peak vacation periods. Telephone 476-6050.

The Wildwood Shelter is situated at the top of the Hunky Dory Lift and Game Creek Express. This restaurant is usually less crowded than either the Eagle's Nest at LionsHead or Mid-Vail. However, its selection of menu items is also more limited. The best item to order here is the pizza, which is quite tasty.

Located on the eastern-most side of the mountain at the top of the Sourdough Lift is the Far East Bowl Shelter. This small, quaint facility is the least crowded mountain restaurant. Although the usual cafeteria items are offered, the green chili, which includes red and green peppers with large chunks of beef, is superb.

If truly high-quality luncheons are desired, you should consider one of the restaurants in town. The trip back up the mountain after lunch is quite easy, thanks to the new Vista Bahn lift or the LionsHead Gondola.

Day Care

Day care facilities are located at the base of Golden Peak, Vail's eastern-most mountain and the site of most beginner lessons. Free transportation to Golden Peak is available via Vail's bus system, which has convenient stops throughout the village. Vail's Children's Center accepts children from two months to six years of age. Parents are advised to make reservations for their children at the same time they book their accommodations because space is limited.

Those parents who would like their youngsters to receive both ski instruction and nursery attention should enroll them in the Nursery Ski Program, open to children aged two and a half through six. Not only do the children receive full day care, but they also receive a daily hour of instruction. Book reservations by calling (303) 476-5601.

Medical Facilities

Medical facilities at Vail are without peer when compared to other ski resorts throughout the United States. Vail has a complete hospital, fully staffed 24 hours a day. Conveniently located on Meadow Drive midway between LionsHead and downtown Vail, the clinic has the capacity to care for critically ill patients and to perform surgery should it be necessary. In addition, there are numerous specialists in residence.

Cross-Country Skiing

Three types of cross-country skiing are available at Vail: track, back-country, and telemark.

Track skiing is available on prepared trails over the Vail Golf Course. The golf course meanders throughout Vail Valley, just east of Golden Peak.

Back-country skiing is demanding because the skier traverses mostly flat terrain in specially selected areas of Vail.

Telemark skiing combines skills necessary to ski downhill with equipment that is similar to that used in skiing the flat track of the golf course. Rental equipment is available from Vail Mountaineering, located in the LionsHead Mall. Telephone (303) 476-4223.

Cross country instruction is available through the Vail/Beaver Creek Ski School. Classes meet at the base of Golden Peak at 10:00 A.M. and 12:00 P.M. daily. During the 1987-1988 season, lessons were $20.

The McCoy Park Track System is located atop the #12 Lift at Vail's other resort, Beaver Creek, about ten miles west of Vail proper. McCoy Park consists of 30 km. of machine groomed tracks of which 20% is advanced beginner, 60% is intermediate, and 20% is advanced. Cost for use of the tracks during the 1987-1988 season was $11 for adults and $6 children. Half day rates were $8 for adults and $4 for children. The park's hours were from 9:00 A.M. through 3:00 P.M. daily.

Special Events

Because Vail is so large and attracts so many people, special events are always scheduled. During the 1988-89 season, however, there will be even more activity than usual because Vail will host the 1989 World Alpine Ski Championships. This event will be held between Jan. 29 and Feb. 12, 1989 and will include:

Women's Combined Slalom
Men's Combined Slalom
Women' Combined Downhill
Men's Combined Downhill
Men's Downhill
Women's Downhill
Women's Slalom
Men's Super Giant Slalom
Women's Super Giant Slalom
Men's Giant Slalom
Women's Giant Slalom
Men's Slalom

NASTAR and Marlboro practice race course self-timers operate daily and are located on Hunky Dory.

Other special events typically include one or several of the following:

North American Pro Tour
Dos Equis Pro Mogul Tour

Grand Marnier Chef's Race
American Ski Classic

During the 1988-89 season, Vail will host the biennial World Alpine Ski Championships. This will only be the second time these championships have ever been held in the United States. Opening ceremonies will take place on January 29, with daily events occuring through February 12. Vail is expecting 600 athletes from 50 countries and between 1,500 and 1,600 press and television reporters. Events will be televised to approximately 200 to 300 million viewers around the world.

For the first time in the over 60 years of such events, a new downhill race is a scheduled event. Tested during the previous two seasons, the Centennial Men's Downhill course will include a channel, scooped out of the side of the hill. This bobsled-like portion of the race must be negotiated by the skiers. It will be 450 feet long, 30 feet high, and the sides will be banked 45°. Entrance into the channel will be 60 feet wide, but the channel will narrow to only 20 feet at its terminus.

In order to accommodate the large audiences expected, Vail will construct a 3,000 seat stadium and will install a DiamondVision high-resolution television screen which will enable seated guests to view the race course's entire length. Admission tickets to each race will be sold at the ticket windows, beginning at $5 for on-course standing room and going to $30 for finish-area stadium seating. Finish-area seating should be purchased at the time accommodations are booked, as it is anticipated to be a sell-out event. Discounts will be available for multi-event purchases. This is predicted to be The Ski Event of the year!

Accommodations

With the exception of Aspen and Heavenly, there is no other American ski resort with a greater preponderance of quality accommodations. It is impossible to say which accommodations are best, but the list will definitely include the Lodge at Vail, Sonnenalp, Christiania, Doubletree Hotel Vail, Marriott's Mark Resort, and the Westin Hotel.

The original hotel in Vail, The Lodge at Vail, is on the slopes and in the middle of the village's activity. Recently remodeled, The Lodge is run as a condominium hotel. From its impressive porte cochere to its large moss rock fireplace, the lodge ranks among the top resort hotels in the world. All guest rooms or condominiums have cherry paneling and feature marble baths. The view from the rooms is either of the mountain itself or of the picturesque village. A few accommodations contain fully equipped kitchens, fireplaces, and balconies. The decor is Swiss/Austrian-style with warm fabric prints and brass fixtures.

By far, the most impressive feature of The Lodge is the amenities it offers guests. Not only is there concierge service, but a valet greets all returning skiers and takes their skis to night storage. The valet also arranges for ski waxing or tuning and is responsive to any other guest needs. The Lodge has a swimming pool and Jacuzzi on the premises.

After skiing, go to The Lodge and relax in Mickey's Bar. While enjoying a favorite beverage, be entertained by Mickey who plays the piano each evening. Later enjoy dinner in the Lodge's informal Arlberg Cafe or splurge on a fine meal at the Wildflower Inn restaurant, one of Vail's finest eating establishments.

Rates during the 1987-1988 season ranged from $190 per night for a hotel room to $900 per night for a three bedroom condominium.

Marriott's Mark Resort is considerably less formal than either The Lodge or the Sonnenalp. It has 350 rooms and frequently caters to the convention trade. Located near the Gondola at LionsHead, the Marriott offers both hotel rooms and suites. Many of the suites have balconies, fireplaces, and fully-equipped kitchens.

The motel-style rooms are not too dissimilar from other Marriott hotels throughout the United States. Furnished with queen-sized beds and traditional furniture upholstered in printed fabrics, guests know in advance what amenities to expect.

Typical of Vail's accommodations but with a fine location, the Sitzmark Lodge exemplifies lodging which encourages people to return year after year.

The Sitzmark, located on the Gore Creek only a few steps from Vail's finest retail shops, has only 35 rooms, each complete with color TV, HBO, and refrigerator. All rooms have views either of the mountain or of the creek. The rooms, accented in darker shades of brown and tan, are traditionally furnished with commercial hotel furniture. Daily maid service is provided, as is guest laundry service and underground parking. Complimentary breakfast is served daily in the lobby, and guests are advised to take full advantage of the resort's outdoor swimming pool, sauna, and steam room.

1987-1988 rates were from a low of $72 per night to a high of $165 per night for a DeLuxe room with fireplace.

Europeans and Latins tend to favor the Sonnenalp, a truly world class hotel with all the expected amenities. Its hotel rooms remind one of a Bavarian lodge high in the German Alps. Tastefully furnished with Bavarian furniture that to the untrained eye looks like country French, the grey wool upholstery with orange piping complements the wood's natural patina.

The Sonnenalp consists of three buildings with heated outdoor pools, a health spa complete with tanning beds, exercise machines, Jacuzzi, and a beauty salon for the exclusive use of its guests. There are two excellent restaurants and the Bully III Pub. Try to finish a Spaten Beer while visiting the pub; it's a full pint and is imported from Munich. Add a slice of lime for additional flavor.

A hotel room in the Sonnenalp, based on the European plan, ranged from $135 to $190 per night during the 1987-1988 ski season. DeLuxe rooms and suites were priced considerably higher.

Restaurants

With well over 100 restaurants in Vail, it is impossible to do all of them justice. However, a few stand out and should be reviewed since they are of such high quality.

The Wildflower Inn located in the Lodge at Vail is an old world style restaurant. It is circular in design and overlooks Vail Mountain. Its tiled entry is lined with custom-built cherry wine storage cabinets. Tables in the light and airy dining room are set with fine linens and beautiful china. Large clusters of fresh-cut flowers provide spectacular displays on tables, cabinet shelves, and even hang from baskets suspended from the ceiling. The expert architectural use of low steps, which creates a terraced effect, lends character to the room. The dominant color is white, and the contrast of the floral arrangements is stunning.

The Continental menu is equal to the ambience of the room. A variety of creative items is presented along with daily specials, and the service is excellent. Due to the Wildflower's popularity, guests are advised to book dinner reservations during peak seasons two to four months in advance.

Another excellent dining choice has to be La Tour. Owned by Marie-Claire and Walter Moritz, La Tour is truly a family affair: Walter is the chef and Marie-Claire is the hostess. Because this restaurant is so popular, it is advisable to book reservations several days in advance (or longer) during peak holiday periods such as Christmas.

La Tour has a French menu and features several selections of veal, poultry, game, beef, lamb, and seafood in addition to its daily specials. Walter's creations are served in an intimate dining room furnished in the Swiss/Austrian style so prevalent in Vail. Located at 121 East Meadow Dr., La Tour is in the center of Vail's activity.

Another fine Vail restaurant is The Left Bank, which has excellent Continental and nouvelle cuisine. The Left Bank is located on Gore Creek Dr., the Rodeo Drive of Vail. Before or after dinner, it is always fun to take a short walk and look in the shops along this very exclusive street.

For lighter fare, try Sweet Basil located midway between downtown and LionsHead. A tea room which specializes in California cuisine, Sweet Basil is a great place to relax after skiing.

Other moderately priced and casual dining establishments include the Uptown Grill, Blu's Restaurant, Gasthof Gramshammer's, Bart & Yeti's, Purcell's, The Chart House, LionsHead Bar & Grill, D.J. McCadam's, and Cyrano's.

Visitors should be aware that many Vail restaurants are closed on Monday and that several do not take American Express credit cards.

Activities

One of Vail's most popular activities is shopping. Other than Aspen, there is not another resort with the extensive shopping selections of Vail. Most of the fine shops are situated along Gore Creek Dr. and include Gucci, Fila, Ralph Lauren, Helga of Vail, Cartier, Benetton, and Crabtree & Evelyn. Numerous art galleries are found throughout Vail, and visitors are always impressed by the sculptures placed among the malls and walkways.

For the non-skier or for the person who just wants to take a day off from the slopes, there are numerous activities running the gamut from active to passive. Ice skating is available daily at the indoor John A. Dobson Arena. Snowmobile tours are conducted through the White River National Forest. Free transportation is available to the snowmobile site. The staff will also provide a guide, if one is desired, as well as a warm suit and boots. Because weather conditions change rapidly in the mountains, be sure to take along warm mittens, goggles, and sunglasses. If you have never driven a snowmobile, it can be an exhilarating experience. Snowmobiles are as easy to operate as a lawnmower, so do not hesitate to try them on the basis of a misguided idea that they are difficult to operate.

Unique activities include snowcat-drawn sleigh rides to Beano's Cabin in Beaver Creek, located 10 miles west of Vail. This is not only an enjoyable ride, but the meal and service at this private club are peerless. What a truly great way to spend the evening!

Briefly, other available activities include:

Heli-Skiing
Sleigh Rides
Snowcat Tours
Wildlife Tours
Hot-Air Ballooning

Racquetball
Swimming
Snowshoeing
Vail Library
Ski Museum

Surprisingly, there are not a great many spas or health clubs in Vail. However, the Marriott's Mark Resort does have limited facilities which can be used for a small fee. Also, the Town of Vail Recreation Department has a weight room at the Red Sandstone Elementary School. Telphone (303) 476-2040 to find out when the city's weight room is available.

The most expansive health facilities are located in the Westin Hotel at the Cascade Club. Comprising over 70,000 square feet, the Cascade Club is available to all Vail visitors for a nominal $10 daily fee. This club features six racquetball courts, four indoor tennis courts, full Nautilus, aerobics, gymnasium, swimming, and a sports medicine center.

Located under the parking garage at LionsHead is the Vail Teen Center. The Teen Center is a two story building with ping pong and pool tables on the second floor, while the main floor is divided into several unique restaurants. There is a snack shop with video games and an ice cream parlor with fousball. The music is loud, and the Center is open for children and young adults aged six to nineteen.

Movies are shown daily at the Crossroads Cinema. Ski movies, such as those by Warren Miller, are also featured at special times.

Services

A full complement of sporting goods stores, apparel stores, pharmacies, grocery stores, liquor stores, furniture, bath, and specialty stores is within the immediate town. In addition there are antique stores, acupressure services, art galleries, bakeries, beauty salons, book stores, florists, flotations tanks, massage, and tanning studios.

Table 1

The total number of skiable acres divided by the maximum uphill lift capacity yields an indicator of potential maximum crowding at a resort's mountain. Following is a list of featured resorts ranked from the most crowded to the least crowded. The reader should consider other factors, such as limits on lift ticket sales (Taos) or quantity of beds (Sun Valley) which may limit the actual number of skiers before interpreting the figures as more than simple guidelines.

Resorts

Killington	.027
Copper Mountain	.043
Aspen Highlands	.050
Keystone (combined Keystone Mountain, Arapaho Basin, and North Peak)	.050
Sun Valley	.053
Taos	.057
Aspen Mountain	.058
Crested Butte	.061
Breckenridge	.065
Telluride	.066
Snowmass	.077
Steamboat	.087
Vail	.108
Park City	.117
Squaw Valley	.210
Snowbird	.215
Jackson Hole	.280

Index

Adager 113
Adios 193
Aerie Restaurant, The 118
Ajax 14
Ajax Peak 181
Al's run 172
Albuquerque International Airport 169
Alexander's Bar and Grill 139
Alpenhof Dining Room 78
Alpenhof, The 77
Alpine Meadows 137
Alta 101, 102
Alta View Hospital 117
Ambush Cabin 67
American Teaching System 31, 39, 60, 103, 114, 137, 148
Amfac Resorts 165
Anderson's 113
Andy's Encore 48
Angle Station 100
Annual Cowboy Downhill 152
Antler Motel 77
Apex Glades 183
Apple Strudel 29
Après Vous 70
Arapaho National Forest 87
Arapahoe Basin 38, 82-85, 87
Arby's 89
Argentine 88
Arlberg Cafe 200
Arrowhead 146
Artichoke, The 65
Ashcroft Ski Touring Center 20, 128
Asia 25

Aspen 13–26, 112, 182, 200
Aspen Club Condominiums 24
Aspen Club, The 24, 127
Aspen Golf Course 127
Aspen Highlands 27–33, 14, 15, 58, 100, 121, 123, 126, 135
Aspen Mountain 14, 28, 100, 121, 123, 126
Aspen Resort Association 19
Aspen Skiing Company 125
Aspen Sports 125
Aspen Sprouts 19
Aspen Valley Hospital 20
Aspens Athletic Club, The 79
Assay Hill 122
ATM 31
ATS 31, 103, 114, 137, 148
Averell's 162
Avon STOLport 191
Axtel Building 63

B.K. Corral, The 151
B.O.E.C 39
Back Behind Saloon Restaurant 95
Bakery Cafe, The 66
Bald Mountain 158
Baldy 157
Bar One 142
Barkley's 54
Bart & Yeti's 202
Bashor Race Area 149
Bear 91
Bear Claw 122

Bear Mountain 92
Bear Paw 14
Beaver Creek 191
Beaver Run Resort 43
Belle of the Roaring Fork
Belly Button Babies 52
Belly Button Bakery 52
Best Western 153, 166
Big Burn 29, 122
Big Burn, The 122
Big Emma 112, 113, 171
Black Eagle 58
Blackjack 113
Blind Outdoor Leisure Development 125
Blu's 202
Blue Ox 193
Blue Spruce, The 54,
Blueslip Bowl 101
Bob Adam's STOLport 145
BOLD 125
Bonanza 36
Bonnie's 18
Boogie's 25
Boreas 36
Bottoms Up 123
Brand Building 23
Brandywine, The 155
Breckenridge 35-45, 49, 51, 54, 58, 103, 192
Breckenridge Athletic Club 45
Breckenridge Cafeteria 19
Breckenridge Hilton 43
Breckenridge Medical Center 42
Breckenridge Nordic Ski Center 42
Breckenridge Outdoor Education 43
Breeze Ski Rentals 51, 104, 115, 196
Bridge End Complex 52
Bridger Teton National Forest 70
Brighton 101, 102
Brush Creek Road 128
Bubba's 62
Burgess Creek 146
Butte and Company 62
Butte Busters 61
Buttermilk Mountain 14, 28, 121, 123
Buttetopia Nursery and Day Care 62

Cabin Chute 48

Cabin Trail 183
Cactus Cafe 185
Café Creole 66
Café Suzanne's 19
Café Thunderhead 151
Camels Garden Sports 185
Campground 122
Cantina, The 25
Carson City 134
Carson National Forest 174, 178
Cascade 92
Cascade Club 203
Cascade Village 194
Cascades Lodge 97
Casey's Caboose 98
Cashier 36
Casper Bowl 75
Castle Creek 128
CeCe's 126, 127
Cedars Condominiums, The 44
Centennial 36, 37
Centennial Men's Downhill 200
Center, The 50-53
Central Plaza 117
Cesspool 58
Chamonix 129
Charity's 54, 89
Chart House, The 202
Chateaux d'Mont 88
Cheyenne Bowl 71, 77
Chez Grandmère 130
Chickadee Ski School 115
Children's Center 87, 96, 114, 116, 196
Chip's run 112
Christiania 200
Christin's Silver 158
Christmas Bowl 159
Christmas Ridge 159
Christy Sports 51, 196
Chute One 146
Cimarron 36, 37
Cinnamon Hut, The 139
Cipriani's 155
Cirque Traverse 113
Cisero's 108
Cliff Lodge Rental Shop 116
Cliff Lodge, The 114, 117, 118

Cliff Restaurant 117
Cliffhouse, The 18
Clock Tower Sports 149
Cloud 9 Restaurant 31, 32
Clubhouse, The 54
Cody Bowl 77
Cole Sport, Ltd. 104
College 161
Colorado Superchair 36, 39
Columbia Place 186
Columbine 36
Company Store 138
Contest 36
Cook Shack 198
Copper Mountain 47–55, 36, 103, 135, 182
Copper Mountain Inn 53
Copper Mountain Racquet and Athletic Club 54
Copper Penny 97
Copper Rentals 51
Corbet's Couloir 70, 77
Cornball Special 120
Corsair 37
Country Club Villas 129
Coyote 62
Coyote Grill 18
Creekside Restaurant 143
Creole 101
Crested Butte 57–67, 122
Crested Butte Athletic Club 67
Crested Butte Lodge 64
Crested Butte Nordic Center 63
Crested Butte Ski Rental 61
Crowtrack 146
Crystal 36
Crystal Glide 150
Crystal Glide 197
Crystal Glide Finish 95
Crystal Palace, The 26
Crystal Springs Inn 77
Cyrano's 202

D.J. McCadam's 202
Dago Cut Road 17
Dairy Queen 54
Decatur 88
Deer Valley 101, 102
Denver's Stapleton Airport 145
Descente Star Test 39
Deuces Wild 192
Dietrick's Bar & Bistro 78

Dillon 51, 54
Dog, The 174
Dollar Cabin 161
Dollar Mountain 157, 158
Dolomite Pizza 178
Dos Amigos 155
Doubletree Hotel Vail 200
Duke's Run 36
Dynamo 183

Eagle's Nest cafeteria 198
Eagle's Nest Lounge 119
Eagle's Nest Ridge 193
Eagle's Rest 71
Eagles Nest 195
Easiest Way Down 100
Easter Bowl 159
Edelweiss Lodge 177
Edgewater 88
Ego 148
Eisenhower Memorial Tunnel 13, 27, 121, 145, 191
Electra 182
Elk Camp 122, 123, 126
Elkhorn Lodge 166
Elkhorn Resort 161, 165
Emigrant Peak 135
Etta Place II 188
Extreme Limits 58

Face of Bell 14
Faceplant Café 186
Fanny Hill 122
Far East 48
Far East Bowl Shelter 198
Farley's 89
Faro 192
Fatty's 45
First Time 101
Fishhook Yurt 164
Flora Dora 29
Floradora Saloon 189
Flying Dutchman 88
Follow Me 193
Forget-Me-Not 36
Forklift 116, 119
Four O'Clock 36
Four Points 146
Franklin Dump 17
Freewater Saloon 86
Frisco 51
Front Face 58

Frosty's 36

Gad Chutes 113
Galena Lodge 164
Game Creek Bowl 192
Garden Room 89
Gassy Thompson 86
Gasthof Gramshammer's 202
Gene Taylor's Sports 125
Geronimo 82
Giant Steps 193
Gitalong Road 193
GLM 31, 103, 160
Go Devil 82, 83
Go for the Gold 72
Gold Coast 139
Golden Barrel 31
Golden Cliff 118
Golden Horn 29, 31
Golden Horn, The 25
Golden Peak 193
Gondola Square 149
Goodbye Girl 36
Gorrono Basin 182, 187
Gorrono Restaurant 185
Gorsuch, Ltd. 51, 197
Gracie's Cabin 128
Graduated Length Method 31, 103, 16
Grand Prix 29
Grand Teton National Park 76
Grande Butte Hotel 60, 64
Granite Chief 135
Granite Chief Service Center 138
Green Mountain III 98
Greens at Copper Creek, The 53
Gretchen's Gold 158
Gros Ventre 71
Guido's Lounge 77
Gulf Coast Restaurant 65
Gunnison 57
Gunnison National Forest 67
Gwynn's 62, 126, 127

Hanging Valley Glades 123
Hanging Valley Wall 123
Hard Slab 58
Harper's Ferry East 113
Hazie's 150
Heavenly Daze 148
Heavenly Valley 137, 200
Helitrax 183

Hemingway's 98
Herman's World of Sporting Goods 104
Hide & Seek Apartments 178
High Alpine 122, 123, 126
High Anxiety 36
High Camp 139
High Camp Delicatessen and Bar 139
High Life 58
High Noon 146, 148
High Ridge 97
Highline 48, 193
Hite's 130
Hobacks 70
Holy Cross Hospital 175
Holy Family Health and Emergency Center 105
Home Day Care 175
Homestead 16
Homestead/Lodgepole 88
Homestead Resort 106
Homewood 137
Hondo Lodge 176
Honeysuckle 171
Honeysuckle/Rubezahl 171
Horseshoe 36
Horseshoe Springs 58
Hostel 77
Hotel Jerome 22, 188
Hotel Lenado 21
Hunan Restaurant 108
Hunky Dory 198
Hunziker Bowl 171

Ice Garden 26
Independence Square Hotel 22
Inferno, The 154
Inn at Jackson Hole 77
Innsbruck Condos 178
Innsbruck Inn 23
Interconnect 101
International 59, 193
Iron Blosam, The 118
Iron Man Competition 77
Irwin Lodge 63

Jackson Airport 69
Jackson Hole 69–80, 100, 112, 159, 170, 192

Jackson Hole Kinderschule 75
Jackson Hole Racquet Club Resort 69, 77
Jacob's Corner 22
Jazz Legends 176, 179
Jeremy Ranch Cross Country Ski Area 106
Jimmy's 142
Juggernaut 92
Julian's 188
Junior Elite 173
Junior Ranch 52
Jupiter Bowl 101
Jupiter Jones Powder Cats 155

K.I.D.S. Hotel 105
Kachina Peak 171
Kändähar Condominiums 173, 177
Kant Mak-M 183
Kastle Ski Rental Shop 74
Kentucky Fried Chicken 54
Ketchum 158
Key Condo 88
Keystone 81–90, 15, 36, 38, 49, 54, 103, 112, 122, 192
Keystone Gulch 88
Keystone Mountain 82, 83
Keystone Mountain Plaza 85, 86
Kid's Night Out 196
Kiddie Corral 149, 152
Kids Ski FreeTM 148
Killington 91–98, 48
Killington Health Club 98
Killington Peak 91
Killington Village 97
Kinderhut Children's Center 41
Kinderkafig 173
Kirkwood 137
Kitzbühel Collection, The 167
Konditorei 166
Krabloonik 126, 127
KT-22 135
KT Gully 123

L'Apogee 155
La Croissanterie 177
La Marmotte Restaurant Francais 189
La Tour 202
Lake Fork Creek 178
Lakeside 88

Lancaster Lodge 88
Larami Bowl 71
Last Dollar 14
Last Hoot 83
Last Lift Bar 86
Le Bosquet 66
Le Chamois 143
Learn to Ski Better Week 173
Left Bank, The 202
Leimgrubers 188
Lenawee 88
Limelite Lodge 23
LionsHead 193
LionsHead Bar & Grill 202
LionsHead Express 195
Little Cottonwood Canyon 111
Little Easter Bowl 159
Little Feet 19
Little Johnny 36
Little Nell 17
Lodge at Vail 200
Lodge Club, The 119
Lodge Dining Room 166
Lodge, The 88
Lodgepole 123
Loges Peak 30, 135
Longhorn 171
Lookout Bowl 159
Lookout Restaurant 162
Loverly 53
Lower Powderhorn 122
Lowerstein 31

Mach 1 36
Mach One 58
Magnifico 17
Mall 88
Mangy Moose Saloon 76, 79
Manitou River Houses 188
Mardi Gras in February 128
Maroon Creek 127
Marriott's Mark Resort 200, 201, 203
Max Park 124
Maxie's 175
Mayday Bowl 159

McCoy Park Track System 199
McDonald's 54, 89

Meadows 184
Meadows at Eagleridge, The 154
Merry-Go-Round 32
Mi Casa 45
Mickey's Bar 200
Mid Gad restaurant 116
Mid-Mountain Lodge 105
Mid-Vail 195
Million Dollar Highway 58
Minturn Mile 193
Miss Billie's Kids Campus 105
Moment of Truth 29
Montana Crystal Glide 126
Montana Ski Service 95
Montezuma 88
Moritz Community Hospital 163
Mother Lode, The 25
Mountain Experience Program 115
Mountain Haus 39
Mountain Inn 97
Mountain Meadows 96
Mountain Plaza Hotel 53
Mountain Run, The 135, 137
Mountain Top 96
Mountain Village 186, 187
Mozart 82
Mt. Rose 137
Mustang 37

Naked Lady 123
National Elk Refuge 79
National Ski Jump Championships 153
Navigator, The 54, 89
New Sheridan Hotel 183, 188
Nez Perce 78
Nor'eastern 92
Nordic Center at Warm Springs Ranch, The 164
North Face 58
North Face Hut 161
North Face of Peak 9 36
North Peak 82-84
North Rim 193
Northeast Bowl 193, 195
Northeast Passage 92
Northstar 36, 137
Norwegian Log Condominiums 153
Norwegian School of Nature 106

Nugget 29

Oasis, The 139
Old Park City 101
Olympic Bowl 29
Olympic Glades 29
Olympic Hotel 105
Olympic House 142
Olympic Plaza 142
Olympic Sports 185
Olympic Village Inn 141
Outer Limits 92
Ouzo 192
Over the Hill Gang 155
OVI 141
Owl Creek Trail 127

Packsaddle bowl 87
Pallavicini 123
Panache 167
Panda Garden 155
Paradise 58
Paradise Restaurant 62
Paragon Ski and Sport 185
Park Avenue 29, 31
Park City 99–109, 111
Parkway 77
Parkway Medical Clinic 42
ParkWest 101, 102
Parlor Car, The 25
Pay Day 101
Payday 100
Peak 9 Restaurant 41
Peek-a-Boo Day Care Center 174
Peel 59
Peerless 36
Performance Sports 197
Perry's Prowl 14
Peter Duchin Room 165
Peter's Restaurant 167
Philipe's 107
Phoenix Restaurant 174
Phoenix Steps 58
Pika 36
Pine Creek Cook House 20
Pines 88
Pioneer Sports 40
Pizza Hut 54, 89
Plaza 88
Plaza, The 54, 89
Plaza Woodcreek Condominiums 65

Pogonips 95
Pokolodi 129
Polo Bar 45
Potato Patch Kids 163
Pour La France 18
Powder Pandas, The 19
Powderhorn 171, 175
Precision Tuning 86
Prima 193
Prima Cornice 193
Pronto 193
Prospector Restaurant, The 186
Prospector Square 105
Ptarmigan 36
Ptarmigan Inn 153
Purcell's 202
Pyramid Park 29

Quicksilver 88
Quicksilver SuperChair 39
Quit'n Time 101

Rabbit Ears Pass 145, 152
Race and Events Center, The 19
Rackets 54
Rafter's Cafeteria 60
Ragnar's 151
Ram, The 166
Rams Head Mountain 91
Ranch, The 54, 89, 166
Rawhide 77
Red Onion 29
Regulator Johnson 112, 113
Regulator Traverse 112
Rendevous Bowl 71
Rendezvous 78
Rendezvous Mountain 70, 77
Rendezvous Saddle 146, 151
Rendezvous Saddle Restaurant 151
Reno Cannon International 133
Resort Center 103
Resort Center Meeting Place 103
Resort Express 191
Ridge, The 146
Rio Grande Trail 127
Riva Ridge 192
River Run 158
River Run Plaza 85, 86
River Watch Condominiums 187
Rock Island 123
Rogers Run 193

Rope drop 147
Rossignol Ski Touring Center, The 76
Roundabout 48
Roundhouse 162
Routt Memorial Hospital 152
Routt National Forest 146
Rubezahl 172
Ruthie's Restaurant 18
Ruthie's Run 17
Rutland Airport 91
Rutland Medical Center 96

St. Bernard condos 178
St. Bernard Hotel 45, 174, 176
St. John Hospital 76
Saints John 88
Salt Lake International Airport 1, 99
Sam's Knob 122, 124, 126, 127
San Juan Mountains 181
San Miguel River 188
Sangre de Cristo Range 169
Sardy Field 27, 13, 121
Sardy House 22
Sawmill 38
Sawtooth 48
Sawtooth National Forest 162
Scarlett's Run 29
School Inn 107
Schoolmarm 82
Schuss Transportation 35
Searchlight 136
Seattle Ridge 161
See Forever 182-184
Senate Bar & Restaurant, The 189
Senior Ranch 52
Sestriere 158
Shadows 146
Shaft 100
Shalako 171
Sheraton Village Hotel 149, 153

Sherburne 94
Shirley Lake 135
Short Snort 14
Shoulder of Bell 14
Siberia Express 135

Sierra del Sol Condominiums 178
Siggi's Bowl 158, 159
Silver Bullet Gondola 146
Silver Fox 113
Silver King 107
Silver King Mining Company 105
Silver Queen 25
Silver Queen, The 107
Silver Queen, The 22
Silverglade 188
Silverthorne 51, 54
Silvertree 129
Sitzmark Lodge 201
6-K Motel 77
Ski Area Central 60
Ski Haus International 150
Ski Hill Condominiums 44
Ski Incline 137
Ski Service Center 18, 126
Ski the Summit 38, 49
Ski Time Square 149, 155
Ski Tip Lodge 87, 89
Ski Valet 197
Ski Watch 44
Skids Club 156
Skye Peak 91
Sleeping Giant 150
Sleeping Indian 78
Slogar, The 65
Slot 58
Small World Play School 196
Snake River Health Services 87
Snake River Saloon, The 54, 89
Snow Bowl 18
Snow Cubs, The 19, 127
Snow Hut, The 105
Snow King Ski Resort 73
Snowbird 111–120, 100-102, 159, 170
Snowbunnies 127
Snowbunnies Program 125
Snowbunnies Ski School 42
Snowdon Mountain 91
Snowmass 121–131, 15, 29, 112, 192
Snowmass Club, The 128
Snowmass Club Touring Center 128
Snowmass Lodging Company 130
Snowmass Mountain 122
Snowmass Resort Association 19
Snowpuppies 32

Snowpuppies Ski School 19
Snowshed 92
Snug 161
Soda Spring 88
Soda Spring II 88
Sofios 189
Sojourner Inn 77
Soliloquy 48
Solitude 101, 102
Solitude Station 50, 51
Sonnenalp 176, 200, 201
Soupçon 66
South Peak 146, 151
South Rim 193
Southern Comfort 158
Southern Cross 36
Spaghetti Slope Restaurant 66
Spar Gulch 17
Spaulding Bowl 48
Spellbound Bowl 58
Spencer's 44
Spitfire 37
Sport Goofy 196
Sport Kaelin 18, 125, 126
Sport Stalker, The 115, 116, 149, 150
Spring Dipper 82
Spruce 16
Spruce Face
Spruce Lodges 53
Squaw Peak 142
Squaw Tahoe Resort 142
Squaw Valley 133–143
Squaw Valley Lodge 140
Squaw Valley Mall 138
Squaw Valley Nordic Center 139
Stag Lodge 107
Staircase 58
Stapleton International Airport 35, 13
Starwood 14
Steak Pit 119
Steamboat 145–157, 192
Steamboat Express 153
Steamboat Health & Recreation Company 156
Steamboat Select Inc./Pro Select 150
Steamboat Springs Chamber Resort Association 148

Steaming Jack's 155
Steeplechase 29
Stein Erickson Lodge 107
Stein Eriksen's 125
Stoker Bar, The 151
Storm Peak 146
Stowe 28
Strawberry Hill 177
Stube, The 197
Sturetevants of Sun Valley 161
Subaru U.S. Alpine Championships 53
Sugar Bowl 137
Summit County Medical Center
Summit House 86, 105
Summit Sports 185
Summit Stage
Sun Down 38, 193, 194
Sun Up 193, 194
Sun Valley 159–168, 176
Sun Valley Health Club 167
Sun Valley Lodge 166
Sun Valley Resort 14, 165
Sun Valley Resort Nordic Center 164
Sun Valley Trekking Company 164
Sundance 102, 183
Sundeck, The 18
Sunrise 92
Sunrise Mountain 91
Sunset Ski Repair 126
Sunshine Peak 146
SuperChairTM 14
Swatch Freestyle World
Sweet Basil 202

T-Lazy-7 Ranch 26
Tahoe City 134
Tahoe Queen 143
Tailwinds Aviation 26
Taos 169–179, 182
Taos Municipal Airport 169
Taos Ski Valley Rental 173, 174
Tazzari G.L. 95, 197
Teens' Ski Week, The 125
Teewinot Condominiums 78
Telemark Condominiums 187
Telemark Returns 43
Telluride 181–190, 122
Telluride Athletic Club, The 189
Telluride Regional Airport 181

Telluride Ski Resort Rentals 185
Telluride Sports 185
Telluride Trail 182
Ten Little Indians Snow School 138
Tennis Townhouses 88
Tensleep/Gros Ventre 78
Teocali 58
Terry Sports 150
Teton Village 1, 70, 77, 79
The Cirque 113
The Glades 58
The Lodge at Snowbird 118
The Plunge 182
The Slot 122
The Spiral Stairs 182, 183
The Wall 30, 58
Thunderbird Lodge 176
Thunderbowl 29, 31
Thunderhead 146
Thunderhead Lodge and Condominiums 155
Thunderhead Peak 146, 150
Thunderhead Restaurant 149
Tiger 36
Timber Ridge 78
Timberline 92
Timbermill Restaurant 125, 127
Tiny Tots Playschool 163
Tom's Thumb 16
Too Much 48
Tourelotte Park 18
Tourist Trap 123
Tower Restaurant 130
Tower Ten Road 17
Traverse 146
Treasury 58, 59
Treble Cliff 50
Triple Treat 48
Truckee 134
Truckee Hospital 139
Truckee Medical Group 139
Trudy's Discovery House 175
Tuso's 54
Twining Condominiums 178
Twining Tavern 176
Twister Warming House 62
Tyrolean Lodge 166

Ullr Fest 42

Ullrhof 126
Uncompahgre National Forest 181
Unicorn Balloon Company 26
Union Bowl 48
Union Creek 50
Union Creek Base 52
United States Film Festival 106
Upper Greyhawk 158
Upper Jerome Bowl 31
Upper Lehman 36
Upper Peel 59
Uptown Grill 202
Ute City Banque, The 25
Ute Indians 122
Ute Nordic Center 20

Vagabond 148
Vail 191–203, 171, 182
Vail Associates 123, 193
Vail/Beaver Creek Ski School 199
Vail Children's Center 198
Vail Golf Course 199
Village At Breckenridge, The
Village Center 77
Village Center Ski Rentals 150
Village Mall 124, 125
Village Square , The 51
Vista Bahn Express 194
Vistahaus 41
Vistahaus Restaurant 39

Warm Springs 159
Warm Springs Day Care 163
Warm Springs Property Management 166
Warners' Storm Hut 150
Wasatch Mountain State Park Golf Course 106
Wasatch Powderbird Guides 120
Wasatch State Park Golf Course 120
White Crown 36
White Pine Touring 106
White River National Forest 14, 28, 122, 192
Weber's 44, 54, 89
Wendy's 54, 89
Western Motel 77
Westin Hotel 200, 203
Whale's Tail 45
Wildwood Hotel 129

Wildwood Shelter 198
Willows 88
Wind River Condominiums 77
Winter Carnival, The 153
Wintersköl 21, 128
WinterSteiger 104, 162
Whitefeather 171, 172
Whitefeather Whistlestop 174
Why Not 146
Widowmaker 48
Wilbere Race Course 117
Wild Irishman 88
Wildcat 122
Wildflower Inn 200, 201
WJW 146
Wobbly Barn Steakhouse, The 98
Woman's Way Ski Seminars 138
Wooden Nickel 66
Wooden Nickel, The 97
Woodrun Place 130
Woodrun V 130
Woods at Copper Creek, The 53
Woody Creek 127
World Alpine Ski Championships 199
Wort Hotel 77

Yampa Valley 150
Yampa Valley Regional Airport 145
Yarrow Hotel, The 106
Yellow Bird Program 173
Yellowstone National Park 69, 76
Zaugg Dump 14
Zugspitze 122
Zulu Queen 183

ORDER FORM

Order now your 1989-90 copy of *The Greatest Ski Resorts in North America* at the pre-publication price of only $10.95 plus $4.00 postage and handling. Texas residents please add 8% sales tax.

    YES. Please send me _____ copy(ies). Enclosed find my check or money order in the amount of $_____.

Ship Book(s) to:

Name_____

Address_____

City_____ State_____ Zip_____

Order by Phone: 214/733-4530

        MAKE CHECKS PAYABLE TO: GUIDEBOOK PUBLISHING CO.

Mail to: GuideBook Publishing Co., 7306 McKamy Blvd., Dallas, Texas 75248

ORDER FORM

Order now your 1989-90 copy of *The Greatest Ski Resorts in North America* at the pre-publication price of only $10.95 plus $4.00 postage and handling. Texas residents please add 8% sales tax.

    YES. Please send me _____ copy(ies). Enclosed find my check or money order in the amount of $_____.

Ship Book(s) to:

Name_____

Address_____

City_____ State_____ Zip_____

Order by Phone: 214/733-4530

        MAKE CHECKS PAYABLE TO: GUIDEBOOK PUBLISHING CO.

Mail to: GuideBook Publishing Co., 7306 McKamy Blvd., Dallas, Texas 75248

ORDER FORM

Order now your 1989-90 copy of *The Greatest Ski Resorts in North America* at the pre-publication price of only $10.95 plus $4.00 postage and handling. Texas residents please add 8% sales tax.

_____ YES. Please send me _____ copy(ies). Enclosed find my check or money order in the amount of $_____.

Ship Book(s) to:

Name_____

Address_____

City_____ State_____ Zip_____

Order by Phone: 214/733-4530

MAKE CHECKS PAYABLE TO: GUIDEBOOK PUBLISHING CO.

Mail to: GuideBook Publishing Co., 7306 McKamy Blvd., Dallas, Texas 75248

ORDER FORM

Order now your 1989-90 copy of *The Greatest Ski Resorts in North America* at the pre-publication price of only $10.95 plus $4.00 postage and handling. Texas residents please add 8% sales tax.

_____ YES. Please send me _____ copy(ies). Enclosed find my check or money order in the amount of $_____.

Ship Book(s) to:

Name_____

Address_____

City_____ State_____ Zip_____

Order by Phone: 214/733-4530

MAKE CHECKS PAYABLE TO: GUIDEBOOK PUBLISHING CO.

Mail to: GuideBook Publishing Co., 7306 McKamy Blvd., Dallas, Texas 75248